LEARNING TO READ:

Basic Research and Its Implications

LEARNING TO READ:

Basic Research and Its Implications

Edited by

Laurence Rieben
University of Geneva, Switzerland

Charles A. Perfetti
Learning Research and Development Center
University of Pittsburgh

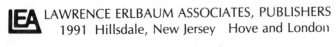 LAWRENCE ERLBAUM ASSOCIATES, PUBLISHERS
1991 Hillsdale, New Jersey Hove and London

Lawrence Erlbaum Associates, Inc. Publishers
365 Broadway
Hillsdale, New Jersey 07642

Library of Congress Cataloging–in–Publication Data

Learning to read : basic research and its implications / edited by
  Laurence Rieben, Charles A. Perfetti.
      p.   cm.
  Includes bibliographical references and index.
  ISBN 0–8058–0564–8
  1. Reading—Research. 2. Reading readiness 3. Reading,
Psychology of. I. Rieben, Laurence. II. Perfetti, Charles A.
LB1050.6.L43—1991
372.4'072—dc20
                                                    90–43493
                                                        CIP

Printed in the United States of America
10 9 8 7 6 5 4 3 2

CONTENTS

PART III. PHONOLOGICAL ABILITIES

PART IV. READING SKILL AND READING PROBLEMS

INTRODUCTION

How children learn to read, and especially how children are taught to read, are problems of sustained scientific interest and enduring pedagogical controversy. The scientific problems are clear and engaging to anyone who has thought about them. How does a young child come to make sense out of squiggles on a page? Is learning to read largely an extension of the already acquired language abilities to print? If so, what comprises this extension? A new code? If not, what is the nature of the new learning? The questions multiply.

Fortunately, there has been considerable research progress in addressing some of these questions over the years. Although one can argue that we still lack a credible theory of the acquisition of reading that is both specific in detail and developmentally sensitive to the long-range nature of the acquisition process, much has been learned about the basic processes that occur as part of learning to read. One of the most important things to have been learned is that learning to read requires mastering the system by which print encodes the language (i.e., the orthography). This mastery, in turn, requires the child to attain understanding of how the spoken language works. If the child is learning to read an alphabetic orthography, then this mastery specifically requires that the child come to appreciate, at some level, that the speech stream contains units that correspond to the orthographic units.

There is much more that has been learned about reading acquisition, but the preceding reflects some of the most important aspects of learning to read. It turns out that some of this, so obvious to most researchers in this area, has escaped notice in some important places, including some of the training grounds for teachers of reading. Controversies continue, long after the debate has been settled empirically, about whether children ought to be taught to decode, whether phonological awareness is significant, etc. Many teachers of reading continue to be trained in the spirit of whole word and, its offspring, whole language. Such approaches are fine to the extent that they allow the principles of decoding, especially the alphabetic principle, to be acquired by the child. But in some of their purest versions, these pedagogical approaches ignore much of what has been learned in research on reading.

All of which finally brings us to why we have compiled a book on learning to read. The idea for the book sprang from what was for one of us

(C.A.P.) a disappointing revelation and for the other (L.R.) a long-standing source of concern. This was the total adherence to the whole-word and "psycholinguistic guessing game" approaches to reading instruction in French-speaking Europe (especially France and Switzerland), accompanied by lack of awareness of the research on beginning reading that supports alternative approaches. So we gathered a group of people from here and there—mainly the United States, but also Canada, Australia, Switzerland, France, and Belgium—and asked them to write short chapters explaining their newest and/or important research on how children learn to read. Our hope was that the chapters would contain theoretically and empirically compelling material in a form that might be appreciated both by researchers themselves and by people who might want to know what this body of research implies for the practice of reading instruction. The first result of the authors' efforts is the French-language book published by Delachaux et Niestle of Neuchatel and Paris in the winter of 1989; *L'Apprenti lecteur: Recherches empiriques et implications pedagogiques.*

Our decision to attempt an English-language book based on these chapters was prompted by the fact that the authors had produced, in most part, original texts not previously available in English. Moreover, in those few cases where similar material had been published, the chapters added distinctly to what we see as a unique collection: A set of relatively concise (by edited volume standards) treatments of central issues in learning to read by some of the researchers who have helped shape the issues and inform the debates about learning to. In addition, the collection would include some work by some European researchers whose work is less well known in the United States. We are very grateful to the publishers Delachaux and Niestle for permitting us to publish an English-language book based on chapters prepared for their publication. We are also grateful to Lawrence Erlbaum for agreeing to this unique arrangement.

The 14 chapters are organized into four parts that reflect our goal of presenting views of beginning reading that are fairly narrow in their scope—all deal with central issues in the early acquisition of reading—but varied in their emphases. Thus, we have conceptual and theoretical analyses of learning to read, and these are in Part I. The second part includes research that speaks directly to the very beginning process of learning to read. The third part reports and discusses research specifically on phonological abilities. The final section contains chapters that discuss research on children who have problems in learning to read.

Part I, Principles and Theories, comprises three chapters and provides general theoretical shape to the issues of beginning reading. Liberman and Shankweiler, in the first chapter, provide a clear and strongly argued account of the fundamental role played by phonological factors in beginning reading. Their chapter is especially appropriate as a first chapter, because so much of the work by the authors of other chapters has built on the groundbreaking work of these authors. In the second chapter, Keith Stanovich notes the progress made in research on reading. He observes that the debate concerning "top-down" and "bottom-up" approaches to word identification has been settled empirically, and the need in understanding reading acquisition is now at a more specific level, including especially the detailed analysis of word learning and the study of precursors of phonological sensitivity. In Chapter 3, Perfetti presents a theory of reading acquisition that emphasizes the child's development of quality lexical representations. Important in his account are the distinction between "computational" and "reflective" knowledge and the dimensions of quality—specificity and redundancy—that representations acquire as a result of successful experiences with words. In this account, phonological awareness and word reading develop together.

The four chapters of Part II are concerned with the very beginning steps of learning to read. In Chapter 4, Gough and Juel provide their account of how a child first comes to recognize words by a process of "selective association" before moving on to the "cipher" stage of recognition. Their "simple" account of reading makes interesting predictions about children's reading and spelling performance in the early stages. Chapter 5, by Linnea Ehri, continues the same theme, but reflects a slightly different, or perhaps more detailed, account of the early learning process. Ehri's research has focused on how young readers learn to use the graphemic cues that words contain. Her theory, supported by experiments, provides a large role to the phonemic values of letter names in the child's transition to true reading. In Chapter 6, Brian Byrne reports some experiments carried out with preschool children prior to any reading experience. The intriguing results of these experiments cast serious doubt on the assumption that children will learn the phonemic correspondences important for true reading simply by learning to recognize words "holistically." Byrne's additional training experiments lead to the conclusion that direct instruction on both phonemic segmentation and on letter–phoneme correspondences are necessary for the child to use the alphabetic principle in reading. The final chapter on very early reading, by Rieben, Meyer, and Perregaux, reports a classroom study that exploits an interesting first-grade learning activity, in which a classroom, as a whole, creates a story that is written for classroom display by the teacher. The key observations for Rieben et al. occur as each child writes his or her own version of the story by going to the classroom display to search for the needed words. The result is an analysis of individual differences in word-search strategies, differences reflecting the child's developing knowledge of graphemic–phonemic correspondences with already available semantic and contextual strategies.

Part III contains four chapters that focus more specifically on phonological abilities, beginning with a chapter by William Tunmer that reviews the issues surrounding phonological awareness and literacy development and summarizes some recent research by the author. Tunmer also considers the source of deficits in phonological awareness, relating it to general cognitive developmental lag for some (but not all) children. In Chapter 9, Virginia Mann reports longitudinal research that, with use of cross-lag correlations, supports a causal role for phonological abilities in learning to read. Phonological abilities, Mann concludes, are not mere by-products of reading ability but causal antecedents to reading acquisition. In Chapter 10, Alegria and Morais present an analysis of the relationship between segmental analysis and learning to read. They conclude that this relationship is highly interactive in that it is only through reading in an alphabetic orthography that discovery of speech segments is encouraged. They are in agreement with Mann and others in concluding a causal role for phonemic knowledge in the acquisition of skill, but they emphasize the differences among orthographies and methods of teaching in the degree to which phonemic knowledge is acquired in the reading environment. Rebecca Treiman, in Chapter 11, brings an additional level to the analysis of speech as it relates to reading. She argues, based on considerable research, that the onset and rhyme of syllables provide natural units in speech and also serve as speech-based units for learning to read. Treiman suggests that instruction that begins at this level might be more effective than instruction that begins with the phoneme level.

Part IV includes three chapters that address reading disability as a problem of learning to read. Fred Morrison, in Chapter 12, provides a developmental framework in which both successful and unsuccessful learning can be considered. This framework places reading acquisition in three phases from Grades 1 through 6. The framework, Morrison points out, can provide an interpretive system for the analysis of specific reading disorders. Liliane Sprenger- Charolles, like Morrison, emphasizes the value of a developmental framework in studying reading problems. In Chapter 13, she reports a study of word-identification strategies, comparing children with reading problems and skilled readers. Her procedure allows her to observe the children's use of semantic context compared with their use of lexical forms. She concludes that the poor readers lack sufficient lexical and grapheme–phoneme knowledge, instead developing rather inflexible context-driven strategies for word identification. In the final chapter, Vellutino and Scanlon report a study comparing three different methods of teaching word identification to skilled and less-skilled readers of different ages. The interesting results included the finding that a combination of "phonics" and "meaning-based" approaches was more successful than either one alone. Vellutino and Scanlon conclude that the child's approach to word identification will be significantly influenced by the method of instruction, and that "disabled readers" are the ones least likely to overcome the shortcomings of instructional methods. Theirs is an especially appropriate conclusion to a collection that aims to make contact between the progress made in research on beginning reading and the problems of instructional practice that continue to be more difficult to address.

It is clear that the research in beginning reading has made much progress in recent years. It is also clear that there is much important research not included in this collection, and a glance at the reference lists indicate some of it. We think that it is at least representative of the kind of careful analytic work that is beginning to characterize the field. We are sure that some of this work will influence the kinds of research questions that get asked next, and we hope that it will make at least a small difference in the way in which instructional issues get formalized.

Charles A. Perfetti, Pittsburgh
Laurence Rieben, Geneva

ACKNOWLEDGMENTS

We wish to acknowledge the support we received while working on this book. During 1988, work on the book began while one of us (C.P.) was a fellow at the Netherlands Institute for Advance Studies in the Social Sciences and Humanities, Wassenaar. The support of the NIAS and its director Dirk van de Kaa for international scholarship is appreciated. The work continued at our respective home institutions, the University of Geneva and the Learning Research and Development Center of the University of Pittsburgh, and we are grateful for their support. We especially thank Suzanne Schnur, who helped with early stages of editorial work, and Mara Georgi, who contributed invaluable editorial efforts to the final preparation of the manuscript.

It is impossible to imagine the work on beginning reading represented in this book without the example of Isabelle Liberman. She, perhaps more than any other individual, is responsible for insisting that learning how to read depends on the learner's knowledge of language and speech. Her clear vision of the essence of learning how to read and her insights on reading disabilities and the teaching of reading provide models without equal.

Isabelle Liberman died on July 19, 1990. This book is dedicated to her memory.

Principles and Theories

1

Phonology and Beginning Reading : A Tutorial

Isabelle Y. Liberman
Donald Shankweiler
University of Connecticut, and Haskins Laboratories

INTRODUCTION

Our research and that of many others in the field for the past 15 years has persuaded us that most problems in learning to read and write stem from deficits in language-related skills, not from deficiencies in the visual or auditory systems. Moreover, we have come to believe we can pinpoint more specifically where in language the difficulties might most reasonably be found. Early in our research (Liberman, 1971, 1973) we were motivated to begin by looking at the phonology: Because an alphabetic orthography represents the phonology, that seemed the right place to start. The results of research have, we think, justified that assumption.

In the beginning, we concentrated most of our attention on deficiencies in awareness of the phonology, that is, on metalinguistic abilities. We review those findings briefly here. Later, we came to consider that metalinguistic deficits may be only the symptoms of a more general underlying deficiency in the phonological domain. Research in verbal short-term memory provided some of the earliest evidence in this connection. Recently, corroborative evidence has come from other sources—for example, experiments in speech perception, speech production, and naming, and the reading of congenitally deaf subjects. We highlight the salient evidence in all these areas, as space permits. We then look into the implications for educational practice.

But first, we wish to comment on the terminology that we all use, often rather loosely. In our view, we cannot discuss the problems of phonology and reading disability reasonably unless we are clear about exactly how we are using certain terms.

SOME CLARIFICATION OF TERMINOLOGY

"Letter-to-Sound Correspondences": A Misnomer

It is common practice for investigators to remark on the relatively poor match between the orthography and the "sounds" of English, and to blame reading difficulties on the consequent difficulty of learning "letter-to-sound correspondences." Leaving aside the question of whether there is indeed a poor match (an interesting question, but a topic for another paper), we suggest that it might clarify our thinking about what is required in the reading task if we used the term *phonemes* in this connection rather than *sounds*. The correspondences under consideration, after all, are not really correspondences with "sounds," but with the phonology of the language, a very different matter, and a distinction of great practical importance. The distinction has practical importance for at least two reasons. First, it underscores the point that the problem is more than one of simply getting the child to learn to associate a visual shape and a sound—even mentally retarded children can be taught quite easily to do that (House, Hanley, & Magid, 1980). Instead, the problem is getting the child to understand how the visual shapes relate to the phonology of the word. There are compelling reasons why that is hard to do, as we see later. The second reason the distinction has practical importance is that it shifts the reading problem away from shape and sound or the sensory modalities and returns it to the phonology and the language modality, where the difficulty so often is found.

The Phonology: Abstract Categories, Not Sounds

But what exactly is the phonology? The phonology is the system of representation that all members of the human race use for producing and storing an indefinitely large number of words by means of a few dozen abstract, meaningless elements, the phonemes. These phonemic elements are, of course, normally conveyed by sound but are not themselves sounds. Instead, they are abstract categories of language.

Perhaps the best way to clarify what the phonology is all about is to imagine what language would be like if there were no phonology. In that case, each word in the language would have to be represented by a separate signal—for example, a sound—that differed holistically from the signals for all other words. The obvious consequence would be that the number of words could be no larger than the number of holistically different signals a person can efficiently produce and perceive. Of course, we don't know precisely what that number is, but surely it must be small, especially in the case of speech, by comparison with the hundreds of thousands of words that a language commonly comprises.

What a phonology does for us, then, is to provide the basis for constructing a large and ever expandable set of words out of only two or three dozen abstract signal elements. These abstract signal elements, the phonemes, are not themselves sounds. They are represented by sounds, but only after complex transformations.

Words: Basically Phonological Structures

So, in dealing with words, whether written or spoken, we are dealing basically with phonological structures. Whatever else words may be, they are always phonological structures. If we have perceived or produced a word, whether in speech or in reading, we have in fact engaged a phonological structure. If we have misperceived or misproduced a word, we have in fact engaged the wrong phonological structure.

But why, then, should reading words be difficult in an alphabetic orthography, considering that the alphabetic transcription represents, even if only approximately, the phonological structure that the reader must grasp?

PHONOLOGICAL PROCESSING IN LISTENING AND READING

Listening to Speech

To understand the problem one faces when required to read a word, we must first consider how the word is perceived when it is spoken. As we have said, the word is formed by a phonological structure, so when the word is perceived, it is that structure that is accessed. But the speaker of the word did not produce the phonological units one at a time, each in its turn—that is to say, the speaker did not spell the word. Instead, in producing the syllable "ba," for example, the speaker assigned the consonant we know as "B" to the lips, and the vowel we know as "A" to a shaping of the tongue, and then produced the two elements at pretty much the same time. Note that in normal speech, then, we do not say "buh-ah," or "B," "A," but "ba."

The advantageous result of such coarticulation of speech sounds is that speech can proceed at a satisfactory pace—at a pace indeed at which it can be understood (Liberman, Cooper, Shankweiler, & Studdert-Kennedy, 1967). Can you imagine trying to understand speech if it were spelled out to you letter by painful letter? So coarticulation is certainly advantageous for the perception of speech. But a further result of coarticulation, and a much less advantageous one for the would-be reader, is that there is, inevitably, no neat correspondence between the underlying phonological structure and the sound that comes to the ears. Thus, though the word "bag," for example, has three phonological units, and, correspondingly, three letters in print, it has only one pulse of sound: The three elements of the underlying phonological structure—the three phonemes—have been thoroughly overlapped and merged into that one sound—"bag."

The first question that needs to be answered, then, is how do *listeners* recover the discrete units of the phonological structure from that seamless sound and thereby manage to make contact with the exact word as it must be stored in their heads? The short, and, for our purposes here, sufficient answer is that in listening to speech, the phonological segments are recovered from the sound by processes that are deeply built into that aspect of our biology that makes us capable of language. Therefore, in listening we are no more aware of the processes by which we arrive at the word than we are aware of how we perform other deeply biological processes, as for example the way we compute the location of a sound from the difference in time at which it arrives at the two ears.

A Difference Between Listening and Reading

Reading is different from listening in that it is, in some significant ways, a secondary, less natural use of language—part discovery, part invention. It follows, then, that even though its processes must make contact with those of the natural and primary language system, special skills will be required if the proper contact is to be made. The point of that contact is the word, which is, of course, represented in the print by a transcription of the phonological structure. But that transcription will make sense to beginning readers only if they understand that the transcription has the same number and sequence of units as the spoken word.

Beginners can understand, and properly take advantage of, the fact that the printed word *bag* has three letters, only if they are aware that the spoken word "bag," with which they are already quite familiar, is divisible into three segments. They will probably not know that spontaneously, because, as we have said, there is only one segment of sound, not three, and because the processes of speech perception that recover the phonological structure are automatic and quite unconscious. Moreover, it may be somewhat difficult to teach them what they need to know because, given the overlap of phonological information, the merging by coarticulation that characterizes the spoken word, there is no way to produce many of the consonant segments in isolation. The teacher can try, as is commonly done in the so-called phonics method, to "sound out" our word "bag," but the learner must still make a formidable leap from that to the spoken word. Fortunately, the phonics method need not, of course, be limited to the "sounding out" approach; it can be expanded to include many other techniques to achieve the intended goal (see Liberman, Shankweiler, Camp, Blachman, & Werfelman, 1980).

In any case, the phonics approach is, in our view, vastly preferable to a currently popular procedure, dubbed by its creators the "psycholinguistic guessing game" (Goodman, 1976). In this widely used procedure and its off-shoot, the so-called "whole language" method, the students are encouraged to bother as little as possible with the phonological structure as it is represented by the graphemes. Instead, they are encouraged to use their "natural language processes" (which apparently do not include phonological processes!) to reach the meaning as quickly as possible. This goal is to be achieved by guessing from a few known words in the message and the context. We have more to say about that later.

But even with the much preferable phonics method of instruction,it can be hard to get some children to become aware of the underlying phonological structure of the spoken word and, accordingly, to see why it makes sense to represent the monosyllable "bag" with three letters.

AWARENESS OF PHONOLOGICAL STRUCTURE

Development of Phonological Awareness

Given all that we have said, we might well expect young children to have difficulty in becoming aware of the phonological structure and, in fact, they do. Some 15 years ago we began to examine developmental trends in phonological awareness by testing the ability of young children to segment words into their constituent elements (Liberman, Shankweiler, Fischer, & Carter, 1974). We found that normal preschool children performed rather poorly. We learned further that of the two types of sublexical units—the syllables and the phonemes—the phoneme, which happens to be the unit of our alphabetic writing system, presented the greater difficulty by far.

It was clear from these results that awareness of phoneme segments, the basic units of the alphabetic orthography, is initially harder to achieve than awareness of syllable segments and develops later, if at all. More relevant to our present purposes, it was also apparent that a large number of children have not attained either level of understanding of linguistic structure, syllable or phoneme, even at the end of a full year in school. They are the ones we need to worry about, we believe, because they are the ones who are deficient in the linguistic awareness that may provide entry into the alphabetic system. There is much evidence now that awareness of linguistic structure—an awareness that so many young children lack—may be important for the acquisition of reading and spelling.

Awareness of Phonological Structure and Literacy

Much evidence is now available to suggest that metalinguistic awareness of the phonological constituents of words is germane to the acquisition of alphabetic literacy. This evidence comes from studies that have shown that this awareness is predictive of reading success in young children. In English, there are, to name a few, studies by Blachman (1983), Bradley and Bryant (1983), Fox and Routh (1980), Goldstein (1976), Helfgott (1976), and Treiman and Baron (1981). Their findings have been supported by studies in Swedish by Lundberg and associates (1980) and Magnusson and Naucler (1987), in Spanish by de Manrique and Gramigna (1984), in French by Bertelson's laboratory in Belgium (Alegria, Pignot, & Morais, 1982), and recently in Italian by Cossu and associates (Cossu, Shankweiler, Liberman, Tola, & Katz, 1988).

Effect of Training in Awareness

Not only is there abundant research showing that phonological awareness is predictive of future literacy, there is now growing evidence that training in awareness may actually help the novice to learn to read and write. It is of special interest, then, to find recent training studies showing that phonological awareness can be trained even in preschool (Content, Morais, Alegria, & Bertelson, 1982; Olofsson & Lundberg, 1983; Vellutino, 1985). Early evidence for the effect of such training comes from the landmark study of Bradley and Bryant (1983). In the first of a pair of experiments, they found high correlations between preschoolers' phonological awareness as measured by rhyming tasks and the children's reading and spelling scores several years later. In the second experiment, they found that the children with initially low levels of phonological awareness who were subsequently trained in phonological categorization were superior to a semantically trained group on standardized tests of reading and spelling. Those trained with grapheme correspondences in addition to the phonological training were even more successful.

We see then that phonological awareness can be trained in very young children, and that this training can have beneficial effects on the children's future progress in learning to read and spell. There is now a broad data base relating reading disabilities to deficiencies in the awareness of the phonology, including studies of people of a wide range of ages, of many language communities, and a full range of cultural and economic backgrounds from inner city and rural poor to suburban affluent.

Most of this research has concentrated on deficiencies in metalinguistic awareness. Lately, as we intimated earlier, evidence of various kinds has led us to consider seriously the possibility that the problems of the disabled reader may not be limited to metalinguistic deficits but may reflect a more general deficiency in the phonological domain.

OTHER DEFICIENCIES IN THE PHONOLOGICAL DOMAIN

Evidence from Short-Term Memory and Language Comprehension

Because short-term memory depends on the ability to gain access to phonological structure and to use it to hold linguistic information (Conrad, 1964; Liberman, Mattingly, & Turvey, 1972), we might expect people who have these phonological deficiencies to show various limitations on verbal short-term memory tasks. This expectation is amply borne out. The research literature contains many reports that young children who are poor readers are deficient at holding verbal materials in short-term memory. Typically they retain fewer items from a set of fixed size than age-matched good readers (see Liberman & Shankweiler, 1985; Wagner & Torgesen, 1987). We must underscore that the problem seems to be a material-specific one, not an all-embracing memory impairment. Memory difficulties arise where the items to be retained are words or nameable objects. When the test materials do not lend themselves to verbal encoding (as in memory for nonsense shapes or unfamiliar faces), the results of memory testing do not find poor readers at a disadvantage (Katz, Shankweiler, & Liberman, 1981; Liberman, Mann, Shankweiler, & Werfelman, 1982). Moreover, memory differences between good and poor readers may also depend on other demands of the task—tasks that require subjects to retain unstructured items may be less differentiating than tasks that require both processing and storage of incoming material (Daneman & Carpenter, 1980; Perfetti & Goldman, 1976).

A verbal short-term memory deficit could be expected to have repercussions on comprehension of language. This expectation is based on the important role that verbal short-term memory plays in continuous processing of discourse or text. For example, in sentence parsing, the grouping of phonological segments into higher level phrasal structures requires phased control of the phonological information within the language apparatus. We could readily expect that children with reading disability would sometimes comprehend sentences poorly because of their difficulties in setting up and retaining phonological structures. The poor reader's bottleneck in lower level processing and its consequences for comprehension was described by Perfetti and Lesgold (1979). The difficulty, though especially severe in reading, where the problem of decoding from print may create an additional processing load, should also affect spoken language processing, especially if the sentence material contains remote dependencies or structural ambiguities (Shankweiler & Crain, 1986). Several reports in the literature indicate that disabled readers do have problems in comprehending such sentences, in spoken form as well as in reading (Byrne, 1981; Mann, Shankweiler, & Smith, 1984; Stein, Cairns, & Zurif, 1984). More recent findings indicate that the poor readers fail not because they lag behind their good reading peers in comprehension of grammar as such, but because short-term memory is overloaded.

By changing the task in various ways to reduce the demands on memory while testing the same grammatical structures, it has been shown that poor readers can succeed as well as good readers in comprehending complex grammatical structures (Crain, Shankweiler, Macaruso, & Bar-Shalom, 1990; Smith, Macaruso, Shankweiler, & Crain, 1989). A memory impairment, stemming from a weakness in phonological processing, can masquerade as a grammatical or semantic deficit.

Evidence from Speech Perception

A general deficiency in the phonological domain is suggested also by some preliminary research into the speech perception of poor readers that was carried out by Brady and associates at Haskins Laboratories (Brady, Shankweiler, & Mann, 1983). In their experiments, poor readers apparently needed a higher quality of signal than the good readers for error-free performance in perception of speech but not of nonspeech environmental sounds. Though the differences were not robust, the results suggest that the perceptual deficit of the poor readers may be related not to auditory perception in general, as is often thought, but rather to the apprehension of the phonological structure of speech.

Evidence from Speech Production and Naming

Support for the notion that poor readers may have underlying deficits in phonological processing comes also from a study of speech production, specifically, the errors of junior high school students (Catts, 1986). The critical finding was that the reading-disabled students made significantly more errors than matched normals on three different tasks in which their speech production was stressed. It was concluded that their difficulties in speech production may be an extension of deficits in the phonological realm.

A similar conclusion was reached in regard to the naming problems of poor readers in a study (Katz, 1986) that examined the performances of second graders on the Boston Naming Test (Kaplan, Goodglass, & Weintraub, 1976). As might be expected, the poor readers named more words incorrectly, but their errors were not arbitrary. Whether their faulty responses were nonwords ("glov" for glove) or real words ("tornado" for volcano), the errors appeared to relate to the phonological aspect of the words, not their meanings.

The phonological source of the naming errors was subsequently verified in two ways: First, when quizzed about the characteristics of the incorrectly named item, the poor readers were often able to describe it accurately (e.g., they described a volcano, not a tornado). And second, given the name of the item, they could select it correctly from a group of pictured objects. Thus they demonstrated that they had the meaning of the item in their lexicon, properly attached to the appropriate phonological structure, though they did not produce it correctly.

Distorted production of the word for an item that had been correctly identified could stem either from deficient specification of the phonological structure in the lexicon, or from deficient retrieval and processing of the stored phonological information. In either case, the source of the difficulty relates to the phonological structure of the words and not to their meanings.

Evidence from the Congenitally Deaf

Finally, let us turn to the evidence from research on the congenitally deaf. The phonological structure of language is, of course, normally conveyed to us, after certain complex transformations, by the sounds of speech. Knowing that phonological awareness can be difficult even for many would-be readers who can hear normally, we would expect that the learner who has trouble hearing the sounds of speech would be even more affected. And indeed we know that the hearing impaired of all ages tend to read far below grade expectations. But there are some congenitally, profoundly, deaf individuals who can read well, even up to college level. How are they different? Vicki Hanson and her associates at Haskins Laboraories asked that question in a series of experiments (Hanson, 1982; Hanson & Fowler, 1987; Hanson, Liberman, & Shankweiler, 1984). What they found was that the successful deaf readers were not limited to reading English words as if they were logographs; that is, they were not, as one might assume, dependent on a limited store of words learned as visual designs by paired associate memory. The results showed that unlike their poor reading peers among the deaf, these subjects, despite profound hearing loss since birth, were able to utilize abstract phonological information both in reading and in short-term memory.

In reading, the good readers among the deaf displayed their phonological sensitivity by responding differentially to rhyming and nonrhyming pairs of words (save/wave vs. have/cave) and by being able to name the real word equivalents of nonwords (flame for f-l-a-i-m; tall for t-a-u-l). In a short-term memory experiment, the successful deaf readers were more affected by phonetically confusing words than by those that were orthographically confusing or whose signs were formationally confusing. These results certainly suggest that successful deaf readers are using phonological processing, a conclusion also reached by Conrad on a different population of deaf readers (Conrad, 1979).

THE LINGUISTIC MODALITY IN SPEECH AND READING

We are not surprised to find that the successful deaf reader uses phonological processing in reading and in short-term memory, for we take it as given that in understanding language whether it is written or spoken, one gets to the meaning by dealing in distinctively linguistic ways with the units of the language. To comprehend language, both the reader and the listener must carry out some kind of linguistic processing, however automatic it may be. The reader is not going to get to the meaning directly from the optical forms of the orthography any more than the listener can get to the meaning directly from the auditory patterns of the acoustic signal. The processes by which we extract meaning from language are different in important ways from those by which we extract meaning from nonverbal visual or auditory stimuli. What needs to be made clear is that words are distinguished from all other meaningful signals by the fact that all words, and only words, have phonological structure and, moreover, that the basic phonological units that form the structure of words, the phonemes, are neither visual nor auditory. Instead, they are, to varying degrees, abstractly linguistic.

Whether language comes in through the ear or through the eye, it is necessarily transformed into a different mode, one that relates to the structures of language. Thus, the perception of speech is only peripherally auditory; it involves, in addition, specific processes in the language mode, both phonological and syntactic, that are different from the perception of nonspeech sounds like automobile horns or church bells (A. M. Liberman, 1982; Liberman & Studdert-Kennedy, 1978).

As for the reading of print, that is also only peripherally sensory. Printed words are, of course, in the first instance, apprehended visually. But the letters of the orthography are not simply optical displays to be apprehended like a Mondrian painting. They represent the units of language and have been crafted to fit its phonology. And because they do, normal readers can invoke their normal and natural language processes to apprehend the message that the orthography conveys. Conversely, a would-be reader, with deficits in such language processing abilities, might well have difficulties.

Here we can probably use some further clarification. The "whole language" proponents in reading instruction apparently assume that our normal and natural language processes are limited to semantics, syntax, and pragmatics. They seem not to consider that before one can get to the meaning or the syntax of a sentence, one must first get to its constituent words. And to get to the words, whether one is a beginning or a skilled reader, one must understand the alphabetic principle, that is, how the alphabetic orthography maps on to the phonological structure of the words.

When we say that even the skilled reader must follow the alphabetic principle to get to the message, we do not mean that skilled readers, like many struggling beginners, must "sound out" words letter by letter. It is true that research is beginning to show that training in the phonological constituents of words is an efficient way to introduce the beginner to the reading process (Bradley & Bryant, 1983; Vellutino & Scanlon, 1987). But as we have noted elsewhere (Liberman, Liberman, Mattingly, & Shankweiler, 1980; Liberman, Shankweiler, Liberman, Fowler, & Fischer, 1977), neither the beginner nor any other reader, no matter how skilled, can recover words from print on a letter-by-letter basis. Instead, every reader must group the letters to put together just those strings of consonants and vowels that are, in the normal process of speech production, collapsed, merged, coarticulated into a single, pronounceable unit. There is no simple rule by which a reader can do this. The pronounceable unit may comprise almost any number of letters from one to nine, or at the level of prosody, even more. We believe that acquiring the ability to combine the letters of a new word into the appropriate pronounceable units, efficiently and automatically, is an aspect of reading skill that, as much as any other, separates the fluent reader from the beginner who does not understand what an alphabetic orthography is all about.

IMPLICATIONS FOR INSTRUCTION

Unfortunately, many teachers are being trained to teach reading without themselves ever learning how an alphabetic orthography represents the language, why it is important for beginners to understand how the internal structure of words relates to the orthography, or why it is hard for children to understand this.

In fact, our teachers are all too often being provided with an instructional procedure that directs them specifically not to trouble the child with details of how the orthography works. The procedure encourages beginners to memorize the appearance of words as visual patterns by whatever means they can muster and to use the known words as a basis for guessing the rest of the message from picture cues and context.

Fortunately, many children—the lucky 75% or so who learn to read whatever the method—pick up the alphabetic principle on their own; that is, they simply begin to discover for themselves the commonalities between similarly spoken and written words. When tested in kindergarten, these children turn out to be the ones with strengths in the phonological domain. Unfortunately, for the many children with phonological deficiencies who do not understand that the spoken word has segments, and who have not discovered on their own that there is a correspondence between those segments and the segments of the printed word, the current vogue for the so-called (and from our point of view, misnamed) "whole language," "psycholinguistic guessing game," or "language experience" approaches are likely to be disastrous. Children taught this way are likely to join the ranks of the millions of functional illiterates in our country who stumble along, guessing at the printed message from their little store of memorized words, unable to decipher a new word they have never seen before.

We think we should at the very least insist that prospective teachers understand the need to provide for individual differences in the phonological abilities that are required for reading in an alphabetic system. Moreover, until phonological instruction has been fully integrated into the method of reading instruction, we should be wary of explanations that attribute reading failure to nonlanguage factors like differences in the visual or auditory learning styles of the children (see Liberman, 1985, for further discussion) or the motivational or cultural shortcomings of their families (see Blachman, 1987; Read & Ruyter, 1985, for relevant research).

ACKNOWLEDGMENTS

Parts of this chapter were adapted from "Phonology and the problems of learning to read and write," *Remedial and Special Education*, 1985, *6*, 8–17. Preparation of the chapter was aided by grants from the National Institutes of Health to Haskins Laboratories (NIH-NICHD-HD-01994) and to Yale University/Haskins Laboratories (NIH-21888-O1A1). We are grateful to Alvin M. Liberman for valuable criticisms.

REFERENCES

Alegria, J., Pignot, E., & Morais, J. (1982). Phonetic analysis of speech and memory codes in beginning readers. *Memory and Cognition, 10,* 451–456.

Blachman, B. (1983). Are we assessing the linguistic factors critical in early reading? *Annals of Dyslexia, 33,* 91–109.

Blachman, B. (1987). An alternative classroom reading program for learning disabled and other low-achieving children. In W. Ellis (Ed.). *Intimacy with language: A forgotten basic in teacher education.* Baltimore: The Orton Dyslexia Society.

Bradley, L., & Bryant, P. E. (1983). Categorizing sounds and learning to read—a casual connection. *Nature, 301,* 419–421.

Brady, S. A., Shankweiler, D., & Mann, V. A. (1983). Speech perception and memory coding in relation to reading ability. *Journal of Experimental Child Psychology, 35,* 345–367.

Byrne, B. (1981). Deficient syntactic control in poor readers: Is a weak phonetic memory code responsibile? *Applied Psycholinguistics, 2, 201–212.*

Catts, H. W. (1986). Speech production/phonological deficits in reading disorders children. *Journal of Learning Disabilities, 19(8),* 504–508.

Conrad, R. (1964). Acoustic confusions in immediate memory. *British Journal of Psychology, 55,* 75–84.

Conrad, R. (1979). *The deaf child.* London: Harper & Row.

Content, A., Morais, J., Alegria, J., & Bertelson, P. (1982). Accelerating the development of phonetic segmentation skills in kindergartners. *Cahiers de Psychologie Cognitive, 2,* 259–269.

Cossu, G., Shankweiler, D., Liberman, I. Y., Tola, G., & Katz, L. (1988). Awareness of phonological segments and reading ability in Italian children. *Applied Psycholinguistics, 9,* 1–16.

Crain, S., Shankweiler, D., Marcaruso, P., & Bar-Sholom, E. (1990). Working memory and sentence comprehension: Investigations of children with reading disorder. In G. Vallar & T. Shallice (Eds.), *Neuropsychological impairments of short-term memory.* Cambridge: Cambridge University Press.

Daneman, M., & Carpenter, P. A. (1980). Individual differences in working memory and reading. *Journal of Verbal Learning and Verbal Behavior, 19,* 450–466.

Elkonin, D. B. (1973). U. S. S. R. In J. Downing (Ed.), *Comparative reading.* New York: MacMillan.

Engelmann, S. (1969). *Preventing failure in the primary grades.* Chicago: Science Research Associates.

Fox, B., & Routh, D. K. (1980). Phonetic analysis and severe reading disability in children. *Journal of Psycholinguistic Research, 9,* 115–119.

Goldstein, D. M. (1976). Cognitive-linguistic functioning and learning to read in preschoolers. *Journal of Experimental Psychology, 68,* 680–688.

Goodman, K. S. (1976). Reading: A psycholinguistic guessing game. In H. Singer & R. B. Ruddell (Eds.), *Theoretical models and processes of reading.* Newark, DE: International Reading Association.

Hanson, V. L. (1982). Short-term recall by deaf signers of American Sign Language: Implications of encoding strategy for order recall. *Journal of Experimental Psychology: Learning, Memory, and Cognition, 8,* 572–583.

Hanson, V. L., & Fowler, C. A. (1987). Phonological coding in word reading: Evidence from hearing and deaf readers. *Memory and Cognition, 15(3),* 199–207.

Hanson V. L., Liberman, I. Y., & Shankweiler, D. (1984). Linguistic coding by deaf children in relation to beginning reading success. *Journal of Experimental Child Psychology, 37,* 393–398.

Helfgott, J. (1976). Phoneme segmentation and blending skills of kindergarten children: Implications for beginning reading acquisition. *Contemporary Educational Psychology, 1,* 157–169.

House, B. J., Hanley, M. J., & Magid, D. F. (1980). Logographic reading by TMR adults. *American Journal of Mental Deficiency, 85,* 161–170.

Kaplan, E., Goodglass, H., & Weintraub, S. (1976). *The Boston Naming Test* (experimental edition). Boston: Veterans Hospital.

Katz, R. B. (1986). Phonological deficiencies in children with reading disability: Evidence from an object-naming task. *Cognition, 22*, 225–257.

Katz, R. B., Shankweiler, D., & Liberman, I. Y. (1981). Memory for item order and phonetic recoding in the beginning reader. *Journal of Experimental Child Psychology, 32*, 474–484.

Liberman, A. M. (1982). On finding that speech is special. *American Psychologist, 37(1)*, 148–167.

Liberman, A. M., Cooper, F. S., Shankweiler, D. P., & Studdert-Kennedy, M. (1967). Perception of the speech code. *Psychological Review, 74*, 431–461.

Liberman, A. M., Mattingly, I. G., & Turvey, M. (1972). Language codes and memory codes. In A. W. Melton & E. Martin (Eds.), *Coding processes and human memory*. Washington, DC: V. H. Winston and Sons.

Liberman. A. M., & Studdert-Kennedy, M. (1978). Phonetic perception. In Held, R., Leibowitz, H., & H-L. Teuber (Eds.), *Handbook of sensory physiology, Vol. VIII, Perception* (pp. 143–178). Heidelberg: Springer–Verlag.

Liberman, I. Y. (1971). Basic research in speech and lateralization of language: Some implications for reading disability. *Bulletin of the Orton Society, 21*, 71–87.

Liberman, I. Y. (1973). Segmentation of the spoken word and reading acquisition. *Bulletin of the Orton Society, 23*, 65–77.

Liberman, I. Y. (1985). Should so-called modality preferences determine the nature of instruction for children with learning disabilities? In F. H. Duffy & N. Geschwind (Eds.), *Dyslexia: A neuroscientific approach to clinical evaluation*. Boston: Little, Brown.

Liberman, I. Y., Liberman, A. M., Mattingly, I. G., & Shankweiler, D. (1980). Orthography and the beginning reader. In J. F. Kavanagh & R. L. Venezky (Eds.), *Orthography, reading, and dyslexia*. Baltimore: University Park Press.

Liberman, I. Y., Mann, V., Shankweiler, D., & Werfelman, M. (1982). Children's memory for recurring linguistic and nonlinguistic material in relation to reading ability. *Cortex, 18*, 367–375.

Liberman, I. Y., & Shankweiler, D. (1979). Speech, the alphabet and teaching to read. In L. B. Resnik & P. A. Weaver (Eds.), *Theory and practice of early reading*. Hillsdale, NJ: Lawrence Erlbaum Associates.

Liberman, I. Y., & Shankweiler, D. (1985). Phonology and the problems of learning to read and write. *Remedial and Special Education, 6*, 8–17.

Liberman, I. Y., Shankweiler, D., Camp, L., Blachman B., & Werfelman, M. (1980). Steps toward literacy. In P. Levinson & C. Sloan (Eds.), *Auditory processing and language: Clinical and research perspectives*. New York: Grune & Stratton.

Liberman, I. Y., Shankweiler, D., Fischer, F. W., & Carter, B. (1974). Explicit syllable and phoneme segmentation in the young child. *Journal of Experimental Child Psychology, 18*, 201–212.

Liberman, I. Y., Shankweiler, D., Liberman, A. M., Fowler, C., & Fischer, F. W. (1977). Phonetic segmentation and recoding in the beginning reader. In A. S. Reber & D. Scarborough (Eds.), *Toward a psychology of reading: The proceedings of the CUNY Conference*. Hillsdale, NJ: Lawrence Erlbaum Associates.

Lundberg, I., Olofsson, A., & Wall, S. (1980). Reading and spelling skills in the first school years, predicted from phonemic awareness skills in kindergarten. *Scandinavian Journal of Psychology, 21*, 159–173.

Magnusson, E., & Naucler, K. (1987). Language disordered and normally speaking children's development of spoken and written language: Preliminary results from a longitudinal study. *Reports from Uppsala University, Linguistics Department, 16*, 35–63.

Mann, V. A., Shankweiler, D., & Smith, S. T. (1984). The association between comprehension of spoken sentences and early reading ability: The role of phonetic representation. *Journal of Child Language, 11*, 627–643.

deManrique, A. M. B., & Gramigna, S. (1984). La segmentacion fonologica y silabica en ninos de preescolar y primer grado. *Lectura y Vida, 5*, 4–13.

Olofsson, A., & Lundberg, I. (1983). Can phonemic awareness be trained in kindergarten? *Scandinavian Journal of Psychology, 24*, 35–44.

Perfetti, C. A., & Goldman, S. R. (1976). Discourse memory and reading comprehension skill. *Journal of Verbal Learning and Verbal Behavior, 14*, 33–42.

Perfetti, C. A., & Lesgold, A. M. (1979). Coding and comprehension in skilled reading and implications for reading instruction. In L. B. Resnick & P. A. Weaver (Eds.), *Theory and practice of early reading* (Vol. 1).

Read, C., & Ruyter, L. (1985). Reading and spelling skills in adults of low literacy. *Reading and Special Education, 6*, 43–52.

Shankweiler, D., Liberman, I. Y., Mark, L. S., Fowler, C. A., & Fischer, F. W. (1979). The speech code and learning to read. *Journal of Experimental Psychology: Human Learning and Memory, 5*, 531–545.

Shankweiler, D., & Crain, S. (1986). Language mechanisms and reading disorder: A modular approach. *Cognition, 24*, 139–168.

Slingerland, B. H. (1971). *A multisensory approach to language arts for specific language disability children: A guide for primary teachers.* Cambridge, MA: Educators Publishing Service.

Smith, S. T., Macaruso, P., Shankweiler, D., & Crain, S. (1989). Syntactic comprehension in young poor readers. *Applied Psycholinguistics, 10*, 429–454.

Stein, C. L., Cairns, H. S., & Zurif, E. B. (1984). Sentence comprehension limitations related to syntactic deficits in reading disabled children. *Applied Psycholinguistics, 5*, 305–322.

Treiman, R. A., & Baron, J. (1981). Segmental analysis ability: Development and relation to reading ability. In G. E. MacKinnon & T. G. Walker (Eds.), *Reading research: Advances in theory and practice (3).* New York: Academic Press.

Vellutino, F. R. (1985). Phonological coding: Phoneme segmentation and code acquisition in poor and normal readers. In J. Kavanagh & D. Gray (Eds.), *Biobehavioral measures of dyslexia.* Parkton, MD: York Press.

Vellutino F. R., & Scanlon, D. (1987). Phonological coding and phonological awareness and reading ability: Evidence from a longitudinal and experimental study. *Merrill-Palmer Quarterly, 33/3*, 321–363.

Wagner, R. K., & Torgesen, J. K. (1987). The nature of phonological processing in the acquisition of reading skills. *Psychological Bulletin, 101*, 192–212.

2 Changing Models of Reading and Reading Acquisition

Keith E. Stanovich
Oakland University

INTRODUCTION

Just 20 years ago writings about word recognition in textbooks and in curriculum materials were nine parts speculation to one part information. There were so few established facts about word recognition that many authors simply started out with a theoretical view on the nature of reading and then developed the implications of their theory for word recognition. Thus, it is not surprising that the reading literature came to contain much theoretical speculation masquerading as established scientific fact. However, far more is known now, and many of the issues that just two decades ago were in the realm of speculation have been empirically resolved and are the subject of a broad-based scientific consensus. Parts of that consensus are discussed here.

The Importance of Word Recognition Skill

There is now overwhelming evidence that problems at the word recognition level of processing are a critical factor in most cases of dyslexia; that word recognition efficiency accounts for a large proportion of the variance in reading ability in the early elementary grades; and that even among adults word recognition efficiency accounts for a sizeable amount of variance in reading ability (Bertelson, 1986; Gough & Tunmer, 1986; Morrison, 1984, 1987; Perfetti, 1985; Vellutino, 1979).

As the evidence linking word recognition skill to reading ability became more and more overwhelming, the debate about how to conceptualize word recognition in reading shifted from questioning the linkage itself to a dispute about what psychological mechanisms were responsible for the superior word recognition skill of the better reader. This dispute evolved into the famous top-down versus bottom-up debate in reading theory. The debate boiled down to the question of whether the superior word recognition efficiency was due to skill at bottom-up processes of spelling-to-sound decoding and direct visual recognition or whether it was due to superior top-down processes of expectancy generation and contextual prediction. Evidence is now strongly on the side of the former view. Poorer readers are markedly inferior at the bottom-up skills of word recognition but appear to be relatively competent at using top-down processes to facilitate decoding. Several reviews and summaries of the large literature on this issue have been published (see Gough, 1983; Perfetti, 1985; Stanovich, 1980, 1984, 1986, 1988). The consensus in this research area has recently been bolstered by developments in two additional areas: the study of eye movements and advances in computer simulation and artificial intelligence.

What Eye Movement Studies Reveal About Word Recognition

Research is consistent in indicating that the vast majority of content words in text receive a direct visual fixation (Balota, Pollatsek, & Rayner, 1985; Ehrlich & Rayner, 1981; Just & Carpenter, 1980, 1987; Perfetti, 1985). Short function words and highly predictable words are more likely to be skipped, but even the majority of these are fixated. In short, the sampling of visual information in reading, as indicated by fixation points, is relatively dense. Readers do not engage in the wholesale skipping of words that is sometimes implied in presentations of top-down models.

The study of the processing of visual information within a fixation has indicated that the visual array is rather completely processed during each fixation. It appears that visual features are not minimally sampled in order to confirm "hypotheses" but instead are rather exhaustively processed, even when the word is highly predictable (Balota et al., 1985; Ehrlich & Rayner, 1981; McConkie & Zola, 1981; Zola, 1984). An important study by Rayner and Bertera (1979) demonstrated that efficient reading is dependent on a detailed sampling of the visual information in the text. Using the contingent display possibilities afforded by modern computer technology, they had subjects read text while a computer masked one letter in their foveal vision on each fixation. The loss of this *single letter* reduced reading speed by 50%. Clearly, efficient reading depended on the visual information contained in each of the individual letters that were within foveal vision.

In summary, research indicates that (a) sampling of the text during reading, as indicated by fixation points, is relatively dense; (b) visual feature extraction during a fixation is relatively complete. These research findings indicate that the implication of some of the early top-down models of reading, that the visual information in text is almost of secondary importance (e.g., "it is clear that the better reader barely looks at the individual words on the page." Smith, 1973, p.190), is quite patently false. Nevertheless, a critical point emphasized in the early top-down writings—that efficient reading occurs when the reader expends processing capacity on higher level comprehension processes rather than on word recognition—is shared by bottom-up models and appears to be a valid insight. We now know, however, *how* this occurs: via efficient decoding processes rather than by using context to speed word recognition. Where the top-down models went wrong was in their tendency to conflate the use of the visual features in the text with the cognitive resources necessary to process those features. It is not that the good reader relies less on visual information, but that the visual analysis mechanisms of the good reader use less capacity. Good readers are efficient processors in every sense: They completely sample the visual array *and* use fewer resources to do so.

Reading and Models in Cognitive Science

Models of word recognition in reading have always been heavily influenced by theoretical developments within the interrelated fields of cognitive science. For example, early models of word recognition were heavily influenced by the analysis-by-synthesis models of speech perception and by the highly interactive computer models that were popular in artificial intelligence work. For example, Rumelhart's (1977) interactive model has had considerable influence on reading theory. Drawing on work in artificial intelligence during the preceding 10 years (the Hearsay speech recognition system, for example), his model emphasized top-down influences and hypothesis testing at every level of the processing hierarchy, including the lexical and letter levels.

The problem for reading theory—and especially for top-down theories that rested their case primarily on the then-current consensus in AI research—is that the worm has turned. The current vogue is not top-down, hypothesis-testing models, but parallel-architecture connectionist models (McClelland & Rumelhart, 1986; Rumelhart & McClelland, 1986; Schneider, 1987; Tanenhaus, Dell, & Carlson, 1988) that have a heavy bottom-up emphasis. There are no explicit "hypotheses" in such models at all. Learning and recognition do not occur via hypothesis testing but by the updating of connection strengths in the network and by a settling of activation after a stimulus has been presented. Solutions to problems emerge from patterns of activation generated by incoming information and previously established connections; they are not expressed as "hypotheses" put forth by an executive processor. One such model, NETtalk (Sejnowski & Rosenberg, 1986, 1987), learns to read by being exposed to pairings of letter strings and phoneme strings. The simulation contains no spelling-to sound "rules," makes no use of contextual information beyond learned letter constraints within a seven-space window, and has no executive processors that make hypotheses or generate expectancies. The network learns simply by readjusting connections between units after being exposed to input.

A similar example occurs in the psychology of perception. Some of the first top-down models of the reading process (e.g., Smith, 1971) were influenced by developments in what has been termed the *New Look* in perceptual research, a theoretical framework that emphasized the influence of context and expectancies on perception. However, the current vogue in the study of perception is completely antithetical to the New Look framework. The popular concept is now modularity (Fodor, 1983, 1985; Seidenberg, 1985; Tanenhaus, Dell, & Carlson, 1988; Tanenhaus & Lucas, 1987)—the idea that basic perceptual processes are "informationally encapsulated": that they are not driven by higher level hypotheses and real-world knowledge.

Both of these examples indicate that current models in artificial intelligence and cognitive science provide no sustenance at all for top-down models of word recognition in reading. Nevertheless, the purpose of highlighting these examples is not to argue for one class of model over another. Considering them does serve as a caution, however, that theories of reading should probably always rest more on empirical facts about the process of reading than on the latest theoretical fashion in cognitive psychology and artificial intelligence.

Phonological Sensitivity and Early Reading Acquisition

One exciting outcome of research in reading during the last 20 years is that researchers have isolated a process that is a major determinant of the early acquisition of reading skill and one of the keys to the prevention of reading disability. Whereas there are many correlates of the ease of initial reading acquisition, a large number of studies have demonstrated that phonological abilities stand out as the most potent specific predictor (Juel, Griffith, & Gough, 1986; Liberman, 1982; Share, Jorm, Maclean, & Matthews, 1984; Stanovich, in preparation; Stanovich, Cunningham, & Cramer, 1984; Tunmer & Nesdale, 1985; Wagner & Torgesen, 1987). Additional research has supported the existence of a causal link running from phonological abilities to reading skill (Bradley & Bryant, 1983, 1985; Fox & Routh, 1984; Lundberg, 1987; Maclean, Bryant, & Bradley, 1987; Olofsson & Lundberg,

1985; Perfetti, Beck, Bell, & Hughes, 1987; Torneus, 1984; Treiman & Baron, 1983; Vellutino & Scanlon, 1987).

Research on phonological processing has recently moved from merely documenting the causal connection with reading and has begun to address more specific questions. For example, researchers are currently linking experiences prior to school entry—such as experience with nursery rhymes—to the development of phonological sensitivity (e.g., Maclean, Bryant, & Bradley, 1987) and are speculating on how to model phonological process training on what is known about syllable structure (Treiman, 1988).

Researchers are largely agreed on why phonological abilities are so important in the early stages of reading. To enable the powerful self-teaching mechanism inherent in an alphabetic orthography (Gough & Hillinger, 1980; Jorm & Share, 1983), the child must learn the general principle that spelling corresponds to sound and then must learn sufficient examples of spelling-to-sound correspondences to support efficient decoding. To utilize the alphabetic principle, the child must adopt an analytic attitude toward both written words and the spoken words they represent; that is, the child must discover and exploit the fact that the mapping takes place at the level of letters and phonemes. Segmenting visual words into letter units is well within the perceptual capabilities of every nonimpaired school-age child, but the development of the tendency to exhaustively process all of the visual detail in words (particularly the sequence of interior letters) may be difficult for some children (Frith, 1985; Gough & Hillinger, 1980). However, an even greater source of individual differences resides in the sounds to which the letters map. Segmenting speech at the level of phonemes is notoriously difficult for young children (Bruce, 1964; Calfee, Chapman, & Venezky, 1972; Lewkowitz, 1980; Liberman, Shankweiler, Fischer, & Carter, 1974). Phonological sensitivity tasks relate to reading acquisition because they predict the ease or difficulty with which a child will learn to segment spoken words at levels below the syllable.

In a seminal and provocative paper, Gough and Hillinger (1980) asserted that we should consider learning to read to be an "unnatural act." This characterization followed from their two-stage model of the earliest stages of reading acquisition. Gough and Hillinger posited that the first stage was one of paired-associate learning utilizing minimal cues; that is, children initially begin to associate spoken words with particularly salient cues in the visual array. For example, "dog" might be associated with the initial letter, "hole in the middle," or "tail at the end"; in short, visual distinctiveness is a key factor at this stage. Gough and Hillinger hypothesized that this paired-associate procedures works well for the first few items but quickly breaks down because of the difficulty in finding a unique distinctive visual cue for each new word encountered. The paired-associate procedure based on distinctive visual cues is not generative (i.e., it is of no help in recognizing unfamiliar words), becomes more difficult as the number of items to be learned increases, and inevitably must be discarded. Normal progress in reading dictates that the child make the transition to the next stage of acquisition, that characterized by fully analytic processing—where words are fully segmented, both visually and phonologically. Unlike the first stage, where the child acquires words naturally and often spontaneously, the fully analytic stage (what Gough and Hillinger term the cipher stage) is not natural and almost always requires intervention by an outsider (teacher, parent, sibling) who gives cues to support analytic processing and/or presents words in ways that foster such processing. Thus, a basic discontinuity in word acquisition is proposed.

Subsequent research has tended to support Gough and Hillinger's (1980) conceptualization. Byrne (1988) has presented evidence indicating that fully analytic processing of words is not the natural processing set of preliterate 4-year-old children. He demonstrated that learning to discriminate FAT from BAT did not enable the children to discriminate FUN from BUN with greater than chance accuracy. Their performance illustrates what would be expected from a child who had not passed beyond Gough and Hillinger's (1980) paired-associate stage.

Young preliterate children often spontaneously learn to name words on television, advertisements, cereal boxes, and billboards. This particular phenomenon has frequently spawned characterizations of reading diametrically opposed to that of Gough and Hillinger (1980), characterizations that view learning to read as a "natural" act, directly analogous to learning spoken language. (To consider other evidence, we put aside the obvious objection that many children require extensive adult intervention in order to acquire reading skills and that some children fail in the acquisition process despite herculean efforts on the part of teachers and parents—a situation vastly unlike that of spoken language.) However, the results of a study by Masonheimer, Drum, and Ehri, (1984) indicate that this type of word learning is like that of Gough and Hillinger's paired-associate stage, and that later stages of beginning reading are not continuous extensions of this type of spontaneous word learning.

Masonheimer et al. studied 3- to 5-year-old children who were environmental print "experts": those who, based on a preliminary survey, could identify at least 8 of the 10 most commonly known environmental labels (McDonald's, K Mart, Crayola Crayons, The Incredible Hulk, Pepsi, etc.) Most of these children ($N = 96$) had virtually no ability to read words outside of the set of labels that they knew. Because a few children ($N = 6$) read all the test words, the distribution of reading ability was markedly bimodal and "was not distributed continuously as one might expect if it were true that the accumulation of environmental print experience leads children into word reading" (Masonheimer et al., 1984, p. 268). The 96 prereaders were completely unable to report anything wrong with labels that had letter alterations (e.g., Xepsi). In addition, the ability to read the labels dropped dramatically when the logos were removed, indicating that the children were "reading the environment" rather than the print. However, Masonheimer et al. are careful to point out that their conclusions refer directly only to the information-processing characteristics of two adjacent stages in early reading acquisition, and to one particular experiential variable: knowledge of the labels of common environmental signs. Their results should not be read as arguing against the general efficacy of prereading experiences.

Gough, Juel, and Griffith (in preparation) report several intriguing tests of the nature of the paired-associate learning-by-selective-cues stage in early reading acquisition. They had a group of 5-year-olds learn sets of words written on flashcards to a criterion of two successive correct trials. One of the flashcards was deliberately marred by a thumbprint on the corner. During the test phase, when the children were shown the thumbprinted word on a clean card, less than half could identify the word. Almost all of them, however, produced the word when shown a thumbprinted card with no word on it. As an additional test, children were shown a thumbprinted card containing a word other than the one that accompanied it during training. Almost all children named the word that accompanied the thumbprint during training, rather than the word that was presently on the card.

The results of Gough et al. (in preparation) clearly converge nicely with those of Byrne (1988) and Masonheimer et al. (1984) and are consistent with the idea that learning fully analytic spelling-to-sound correspondences is an "unnatural" act for young children. Results from an important classroom study also support this conclusion. Seymour and Elder (1986) studied a class of new entrants into a Scottish primary school where the emphasis was on the development of a "sight vocabulary" via whole-word methods, and no phonics training occurred during the first two terms. An examination of their subsequently developed word recognition skills indicated that they were not productive: The children could not recognize unfamiliar words that they had not been taught. Unlike the case of children who have developed some spelling-to-sound decoding skills (see Gough et al., in preparation), the error responses of these children were drawn only from the set of words that they had been taught. The characteristics of their discrimination performance were similar to those that would be expected from Gough and Hillinger's selective cue learning. Bertelson (1986) has argued that the most important implication of the results of Seymour and Elder (1986) is "that there is no continuity between early logographic reading and the direct orthographic reading of the skilled adult, where typically all the available orthographic evidence is taken into account" (p.19).

Controversies About Decoding and the Regularity of English

How does the recent research on word recognition and early reading acquisition that is previously described relate to some of the oldest controversies in reading instruction? First, there is obviously no contradiction between the conclusions in Chall's classic work (1967; and update, 1983) and the basic research outlined here. Word recognition is a critical component of the reading process; individual differences in this component account for substantial variance at all levels of reading; to become fluent, all readers must have stored in memory spelling–sound correspondences that can function as efficient recognition mechanisms. However phonics advocates must resist the temptation to uncritically view the results of research like that outlined earlier as providing justification for their particular methods of instruction. For example, it could well be the case that language experience or whole-language approaches might provide the child with the optimum amount of exposure for the induction of spelling–sound correspondences (although research does seem to indicate that the explicit teaching of specific letter–sound correspondences does facilitate reading acquisition; Anderson, Hiebert, Scott, & Wilkinson, 1985; Chall, 1983; Share & Jorm, 1987; Williams, 1985). Similarly, the conclusion that all readers must acquire functional spelling-to-sound knowledge is not the same as saying that all children must learn phonics rules. The child needs to associate orthographic with phonological patterns in memory, but this need not be done by the learning of rules. Somewhat of an existence proof for this point is contained in the previously mentioned work of Sejnowski and Rosenberg (1986, 1987). They have designed a connectionist computer model that learns to read English words after being exposed to a large number of pairings of letter strings and phoneme strings. This parallel model contains no "rules" at all but simply learns by updating—based on new input—the strengths of connections between elements.

Likewise, however, opponents of phonics as an instructional method have also on occasion jumped too hastily from basic research models of reading and theoretical work in other disciplines to instructional conclusions. One example, the overgeneralization of the early top-down cognitive models, was discussed previously. Another example that recurs in the writings of those hostile to phonics is a tendency to overemphasize the irregularity of the spelling–sound correspondences in English. It is a common ploy in such writings to litter the text with examples of correspondences that are ambigu-

2. CHANGING MODELS OF READING   **27**

ous in reading (e.g., *ea* can be pronounced as in *teach, bread, great,* or *create*) or spelling (e.g., /f/ can be written as in *frog, phone, tough, stuff,* etc.). Although it is true that English is one of the most irregular of the alphabetic orthographies, it is misleading to imply that the regularities that are present are not sufficient to support a substantial role in reading acquisition for spelling–sound correspondences.

First, it is important to distinguish the use of spelling–sound correspondences in reading from the use of sound–spelling correspondences for spelling (Berndt, Reggia, & Mitchum, 1987; Haas, 1970; Henderson, 1982). The distinction is important because the spelling–sound correspondences of English are more regular than the sound–spelling correspondences (Cronnell, 1978; Henderson, 1982; Henderson & Chard, 1980). For example, whereas the phoneme /f/ can map to f, ff, ph, or gh, the letter f regularly maps to /f/, with the exception of the high frequency *of*. Thus, an emphasis on spelling irregularities is somewhat misleading. Most of the consonants of English, like f, have regular reading correspondences (Berndt et al., 1987; Cronnell, 1973; Venezky, 1970). The most notorious irregularities virtually all concern vowels. This fact interacts with the tacit assumption in many critiques that if the correspondences do not yield a unique pronunciation, then they are useless. To the contrary, partially diagnostic cues can indeed be useful. The c-ns-n-nts -r- th- m-st -mp-rt-nt c-mp-n-nts -f w-rds -nd -t -s p-ss-bl- t- r—d w-th—t th-m provided you have some context. Thus, even if a child could only decode the regular consonants, this would be a considerable aid in early reading.

Other critiques ignore the fact that the English orthography is considerably more regular if the positions of letters and/or if units larger than the letter are taken into account. George Bernard Shaw's famous example, that *ghoti* could be pronounced the same as *fish* (gh as in *tough*, o as in *women*, ti as in *nation*), ignores the position-specific constraints of the orthography: gh is never pronounced /f/ when word initial and ti never as /s/ when word final. Furthermore, all analyses of the orthography indicate that there is considerable regularity when groups of letters are considered (Treiman, 1988), particularly when a medical vowel is combined with the following consonant or consonant cluster.

Treiman (in preparation) has imaginatively linked the VC(C) regularity of English orthography with experimental demonstrations of the psychological reality of intrasyllabic speech units (onset and rime—units intermediate between the phoneme and syllable; see Treiman, 1986) for young children. Treiman has found that young children's segmentation skills pass through an intermediate stage where they are much more sensitive to the onset/rime distinction than to the phoneme distinction. She has proposed that at certain points in reading acquisition working with onset/rime (and corresponding C and VC(C) structures) might be optimal because these intrasyllabic units are more generative than syllables but do not require the phonemic segmentation ability that may not be developed in some children until later reading stages where more experience with reading and spelling has been acquired (see Ehri, 1984, 1987; Ehri, Wilce, & Taylor, 1987). The larger point reinforced by Treiman's work is that there may be more ways to exploit the regularities that exist in the English orthography than is commonly recognized (see also, Bryant & Goswami, 1987; Goswami, 1986; Goswami & Bryant, 1988). Treiman's suggestions neatly bypass the biggest problem with the orthography—irregularities at the individual letter level—because they necessitate working with larger units that are considerably more regular.

SUMMARY AND CONCLUSIONS

In summary, research on reading acquisition has recently entered a new era. The top-down versus bottom-up controversy, as it applied to issues surrounding word recognition, has been resolved, at least at a global level. Researchers have turned their attention to microanalyses of word learning, particularly during the very earliest stages of reading acquisition. There is a broad consensus on the importance of phonological sensitivity at this very early stage. Attention has now turned to more specific issues such as identifying the developmental precursors of phonological sensitivity (Maclean et al., 1987) and determining how a child's particular level of phonological sensitivity can be best exploited in reading instruction (Treiman, in preparation). The increasing specificity of the questions being asked are a sure sign of scientific progress. The prognosis for future scientific advance in the area of reading and reading acquisition remains optimistic.

REFERENCES

Anderson, R. C., Hiebert, E. H., Scott, J., & Wilkinson, I. (1985). *Becoming a nation of readers*. Washington, DC: National Institute of Education.

Balota, D., Pollatsek, A., & Rayner, K. (1985). The interaction of contextual constraints and parafoveal visual information in reading. *Cognitive Psychology, 17*, 364–390.

Berndt, R., Reggia, J., & Mitchum, C. (1987). Empirically derived probabilities for grapheme-to-phoneme correspondences in English. *Behavior Research Methods, Instruments, & Computers, 19*, 1–9.

Bertelson, P. (1986). The onset of literacy: Liminal remarks. *Cognition, 24*, 1–30.

Bradley, L., & Bryant, P. E. (1983). Categorizing sounds and learning to read—a causal connection. *Nature, 301*, 419–421.

Bradley, L., & Bryant, P. E. (1985). *Rhyme and reason in reading and spelling*. Ann Arbor: University of Michigan Press.

Bruce, D. (1964). The analysis of word sounds by young children. *British Journal of Educational Psychology, 34*, 158–170.

Bryant, P. E., & Goswami, U. (1987). Beyond grapheme–phoneme correspondence. *Cahiers de Psychologie Cognitive, 7,* 439–443.

Byrne, B. (in preparation). Learning to read the first few items: Evidence of a nonanalytic acquisition procedure in adults and children. In P. Gough, L. Ehri, & R. Treiman (Eds.), *Reading Acquisition.* Hillsdale, NJ: Erlbaum.

Calfee, R. C., Chapman, R., & Venezky, R. (1972). How a child needs to think to learn to read. In L. Gregg (Ed.), *Cognition in learning and memory* (pp. 139–182). New York: Wiley.

Chall, J. S. (1967). *Learning to read: The great debate.* New York: McGraw-Hill.

Chall, J. S. (1983). *Learning to read: The great debate* (updated ed.). New York: McGraw-Hill.

Cronnell, B. (1973). Designing a reading program based on research findings in orthography. *Elementary English, 50,* 27–34.

Cronnell, B. (1978). Phonics for reading vs phonics for spelling. *The Reading Teacher, 31,* 337–340.

Ehri, L. C. (1984). How orthography alters spoken language competencies in children learning to read and spell. In J. Downing & R. Valtin (Eds.), *Language awareness and learning to read* (pp.119–147). New York: Springer-Verlag.

Ehri, L. C. (1987). Learning to read and spell words. *Journal of Reading Behavior, 19,* 5–31.

Ehri, L. C., Wilce, L., & Taylor, B. B. (1987). Children's categorization of short vowels in words and the influence of spellings. *Merrill-Palmer Quarterly, 33,* 393–421.

Ehrlich, S., & Rayner, K. (1981). Contextual effects on word perception and eye movements during reading. *Journal of Verbal Learning and Verbal Behavior, 20,* 641–655.

Fodor, J. (1983). *Modularity of mind.* Cambridge: MIT Press.

Fodor, J. A. (1985). Precis of The Modularity of Mind. *Behavioral and Brain Sciences, 8,* 1–42.

Fox, B., & Routh, D. K. (1984). Phonemic analysis and synthesis as word attack skills: Revisited. *Journal of Educational Psychology, 76,* 1059–1064.

Frith, U. (1985). Beneath the surface of developmental dyslexia. In K. Patterson, J. Marshall, & M. Coltheart (Eds.), *Surface dyslexia* (pp.301–330). London: Lawrence Erlbaum Associates.

Goswami, U. (1986). Children's use of analogy in learning to read: A developmental study. *Journal of Experimental Child Psychology, 42,* 73–83.

Goswami, U., & Bryant, P. B. (in preparation). Rhyme, analogy, and children's reading. In P. Gough, L. Ehri, & R. Treiman (Eds.), *Reading acquisition.* Hillsdale, NJ: Lawrence Erlbaum Associates.

Gough, P. B. (1983). Context, form, and interaction. In K. Rayner (Ed.), *Eye movements in reading* (pp. 203–211). New York: Academic Press.

Gough, P. B., & Hillinger, M. L. (1980). Learning to read: An unnatural act. *Bulletin of the Orton Society, 30,* 171–176.

Gough. P., Juel, C., & Griffith, P. (in preparation). Reading, spelling, and the orthographic cipher. In P. Gough, L. Ehri, & R. Treiman (Eds.), *Reading acquisition.* Hillsdale, NJ: Lawrence Erlbaum.

Gough, P. B., & Tunmer, W. E. (1986). Decoding, reading, and reading disability. *Remedial and Special Education, 7,* 6–10.

Haas, W. (1970). *Phono–graphic translation.* Manchester: Manchester University Press.

Henderson, L. (1982). *Orthography and word recognition in reading.* London: Academic Press.

Henderson, L., & Chard, J. (1980). The reader's implicit knowledge of orthographic structure. In U. Frith (Ed.), *Cognitive processes in spelling* (pp. 85–116). London: Academic Press.

Jorm, A., & Share, D. (1983). Phonological recoding and reading acquisition. *Applied Psycholinguistics, 4,* 103–147.

Juel, C., Griffith, P. L., & Gough, P. B. (1986). Acquisition of literacy: A longitudinal study of children in first and second grade. *Journal of Educational Psychology, 78,* 243–255.

Just, M. A., & Carpenter, P. A. (1980). A theory of reading: From eye fixations to comprehension. *Psychological Review, 4,* 329–354.

Just, M. A., & Carpenter, P. A. (1987). *The psychology of reading and language comprehension.* Boston: Allyn & Bacon.

Lewkowitz, N. (1980). Phonemic awareness training: What to teach and how to teach it. *Journal of Educational Psychology, 72,* 686–700.

Liberman, I. (1982). A language-oriented view of reading and its disabilities. In H. Mykelbust (Ed.), *Progress in learning disabilities* (Vol. 5, pp.81–101). New York: Grune & Stratton.

Liberman, I. Y., Shankweiler, D., Fischer, F., & Carter, B. (1974). Explicit syllable and phoneme segmentation in the young child. *Journal of Experimental Child Psychology, 18*, 201–212.

Lundberg, I. (1987). Are letters necessary for the development of phonemic awareness? *Cahiers de Psychologie Cognitive, 7*, 472–475.

Maclean, M., Bryant, P., & Bradley, L. (1987). Rhymes, nursery rhymes, and reading in early childhood. *Merrill-Palmer Quarterly, 33*, 255–281.

Masonheimer, P. E., Drum, P. A., & Ehri, L. C. (1984). Does environmental print identification lead children into word reading? *Journal of Reading Behavior, 16*, 257–271.

McClelland, J. L., & Rumelhart, D. E. (1986). *Parallel distributed processing: Explorations in the microstructure of cognition* (Vol.2). Cambridge: MIT Press.

McConkie, G. W., & Zola, D. (1981). Language constraints and the functional stimulus in reading. In A. M. Lesgold & C. A. Perfetti (Eds.), *Interactive processes in reading* (pp.155–175). Hillsdale, NJ: Lawrence Erlbaum Associates.

Morrison, F. (1984). Word decoding and rule-learning in normal and disabled readers. *Remedial and Special Education, 5*, 20–27.

Morrison, F. J. (1987). The nature of reading disability: Toward an integrative framework. In S. Ceci (Ed.), *Handbook of cognitive, social, and neuropsychological aspects of learning disabilities* (pp.33–62). Hillsdale, NJ: Lawrence Erlbaum Associates.

Olofsson, A., & Lundberg, I. (1985). Evaluation of long-term effects of phonemic awareness training in kindergarten. *Scandanavian Journal of Psychology, 26*, 21–34.

Perfetti, C. A. (1985). *Reading ability.* New York: Oxford University Press.

Perfetti, C. A., Beck, I., Bell, L., & Hughes, C. (1987). Phonemic knowledge and learning to read are reciprocal: A longitudinal study of first-grade children. *Merrill-Palmer Quarterly, 33*, 283–319.

Rayner, K., & Bertera, J. H. (1979). Reading without a fovea. *Science, 206*, 468–469.

Rumelhart, D. E. (1977). Toward an interactive model of reading. In S. Dornic (Ed.), *Attention and performance* (Vol. 6, pp.573–603). New York: Academic Press.

Rumelhart, D. E., & McClelland, J. L. (1986). *Parallel distributed processing: Explorations in the microstructure of cognition* (Vol. 1). Cambridge: MIT Press.

Schneider, W. (1987). Connectionism: Is it a paradigm shift for psychology? *Behavior Research Methods, Instruments, & Computers, 19*, 73–83.

Seidenberg, M. (1985). The time course of information activation and utilization in visual word recognition. In D. Besner, T. Waller, & G. MacKinnon (Eds.), *Reading research: Advances in theory and practice* (Vol. 5, pp.199–252). New York: Academic Press.

Sejnowski, T. J., & Rosenberg, C. R. (1986). *NETtalk: A parallel network that learns to read aloud.* (Tech. Rep. No. JHU/EECS-86/01). Department of Electrical Engineering and Computer Science, The Johns Hopkins University, Baltimore.

Sejnowski, T. J., & Rosenberg, C. R. (1987). Parallel networks that learn to pronounce English text. *Complex Systems, 1*, 145–168.

Seymour, P. H. K., & Elder, L. (1986). Beginning reading without phonology. *Cognitive Neuropsychology, 3*, 1–36.

Share, D. L., & Jorm, A. F. (1987). Segmental analysis: Co-requisite to reading, vital for self-teaching, requiring phonological memory. *Cahiers de Psychologie Cognitive, 7*, 509–513.

Share, D. L., Jorm, A. F., Maclean, R., & Matthews, R. (1984). Sources of individual differences in reading acquisition. *Journal of Educational Psychology, 76*, 1309–1324.

Smith, F. (1971). *Understanding reading.* New York: Holt, Rinehart, & Winston.

Smith, F. (1973). *Psycholinguistics and reading.* New York Holt, Rinehart, & Winston.

Stanovich, K. E. (1980). Toward an interactive-compensatory model of individual differences in the development of reading fluency. *Reading Research Quarterly, 16*, 32–71.

Stanovich, K. E. (1984). The interactive-compensatory model of reading: A confluence of developmental, experimental, and educational psychology. *Remedial and Special Education, 5*, 11–19.

Stanovich, K. E. (1986). Matthew effects in reading: Some consequences of individual differences in the acquisition of literacy. *Reading Research Quarterly, 21*, 360–407.

Stanovich, K. E. (in preparation). Speculations on the causes and consequences of individual differences in early reading acquisition. In P. Gough, L. Ehri, & R. Treiman (Eds.), *Reading acquisition.* Hillsdale, NJ: Erlbaum.

Stanovich, K. E., Cunningham, A. E., & Cramer, B. (1984). Assessing phonological awareness in kindergarten children: Issues of task comparability. *Journal of Experimental Child Psychology, 38,* 175–190.

Tanenhaus, M. K., Dell, G. S., & Carlson, G. (1988). Context effects in lexical processing: A connectionist approach to modularity. In J. Garfield (Ed.), *Modularity in knowledge representation and natural language understanding.* Cambridge, MA: MIT Press.

Tanenhaus, M. K., & Lucas, M. M. (1987). Context effects in lexical processing. *Cognition, 25,* 213–234.

Torneus, M. (1984). Phonological awareness and reading: A chicken and egg problem? *Journal of Educational Psychology, 70,* 1346–1358.

Treiman, R. (1986). The division between onsets and rimes in English syllables. *Journal of Memory and Language, 25,* 476–491.

Treiman, R. (in preparation). The role of intrasyllabic units in learning to read and spell. In P. Gough, L. Ehri, & R. Treiman (Eds.), *Reading acquisition.* Hillsdale, NJ: Lawrence Erlbaum Associates.

Treiman, R., & Baron, J. (1983). Phonemic-analysis training helps children benefit from spelling-sound rules. *Memory & Cognition, 11,* 382–389.

Tunmer, W. E., & Nesdale, A. R. (1985). Phonemic segmentation skill and beginning reading. *Journal of Educational Psychology, 77,* 417–427.

Vellutino, F. (1979). *Dyslexia: Theory and research.* Cambridge, MA: MIT Press.

Vellutino, F., & Scanlon, D. (1987). Phonological coding, phonological awareness, and reading ability: Evidence from a longitudinal and experimental study. *Merrill-Palmer Quarterly, 33,* 321–363.

Venezky, R. L. (1970). *The structure of English orthography.* The Hague: Mouton.

Wagner, R. K., & Torgesen, J. K. (1987). The nature of phonological processing and its causal role in the acquisition of reading skills. *Psychological Bulletin, 101,* 192–212.

Williams, J. P. (1985). The case for explicit decoding instruction. In J. Osborn, P. Wilson, & R. Anderson (Eds.), *Reading education: Foundations for a literate America* (pp.205–213). Lexington, MA: Heath.

Zola, D. (1984). Redundancy and word perception during reading. *Perception & Psychophysics, 36,* 277–284.

3 Representations and Awareness in the Acquisition of Reading Competence

Charles A. Perfetti
University of Pittsburgh

INTRODUCTION

My aim in this chapter is to present a general theoretical account of how a child comes to acquire competence in reading. This account includes special attention to the role of phonemic knowledge, which has a critical role in the development of reading competence. Its exact role, however, depends on some distinctions that must be made among kinds of phonemic knowledge. If there is a core concept of phonemic knowledge, its relationship with the acquisition of reading competence is one of mutual support, or reciprocity.

In summary form, my argument is as follows: (a) Learning to read does not involve learning rules but is rather a matter of incrementing a store of graphemically accessible words; (b) phonemic knowledge is of two types, one of which, *computational knowledge*, is a critical component of reading words, and the other, *reflective knowledge*, represents an important aid to learning to read; (c) reflective knowledge, or what is typically considered "phonemic awareness," develops in mutual support of reading acquisition. The most explicit manifestations of this reflective knowledge depend on prior reading acquisition, whereas the less explicit manifestations precede and enable acquisition. In what follows, I first describe a general account of reading acquisition and then suggest the role that phonemic awareness plays within this general account.

Reading Expertise

Reading, in the sense of identifying written words, is a process described by what I call the *Restricted-Interactive Model*. This is a hybrid model that combines two important features of the major theories of word identification: The interaction of information sources and restrictions on these interactions. Word identification is interactive, in the strong sense of "interactive," in that multiple sources of information are combined in parallel. "Multiple" means that letter features, letters, phonemes, and word level units are connected in mutual activation networks along the lines described by Rumelhart and McClelland (1981). (One might imagine such networks as distributed as well as parallel, along the line of PDP proposals; e.g., McClelland, 1986. However, these models have some theoretical properties that make the earlier parallel models seem preferable. In either case, my adaptation of a parallel interactive model puts constraints on the interactions.) A critical feature of the Restricted-Interactive Model is that it places specific restrictions on interactions. Its interactions are restricted to occur only within the specific data structures of lexical formation (i.e., letters, phonemes, and words). It allows no influences from outside lexical data structures, no importation of knowledge, expectancies, and beliefs. Skilled word recognition is context-free.

What this means for an individual case of word reading can be illustrated as follows: Upon reading the English word, *pencil*, in the sentence, "John had nothing to write with so he asked the teacher for a *pencil*," connections between the reader's representation of the letters p–e–n–c–i–l and his representation of the word "pencil" including its pronunciation are activated. Interactive processes occur insofar as connections between units of several levels of lexical representations are mutually activated as a part of the identification of the word, between letters and phonemes, and between phonemes and words, begin to be activated immediately upon encountering the printed letters. Thus the letters *pen__* activate the phonemes /p/ /e/ /n/ and the word *pencil*. Moreover, activation of the phonemes increase activation of the word and activation of the word increases activation of the phoneme. It is these connections among letters and words and phonemes that are the *interactive* part of reading. (Note that this description includes the claim that letter–phoneme connections play a real role in identifying the word. (See Perfetti, Bell, & Delaney, 1988, and van Orden, 1987, for evidence that this is the case.)

The restricted part of word identification is this: Although the reader can expect a word such as "pencil" to occur at the end of the example sentence, this expectation has only a delayed effect on identifying the word. It can confirm what the word identification process has proposed, but the identification process itself is initially restricted to the data structures of words: letters, words, and phonemes. This is what it means to claim that word identification is context free for the skilled reader. Context confirms the meanings that are obtained from the words, but only modestly, if at all, influences the identification itself. This conclusion is central to accounts of reading skill that emphasize the rapid context-free identification processes of the fluent reader and the slower context-dependent processes of the slower less able reader (Perfetti, 1985; Stanovich, 1980).

THE ACQUISITION OF WORD REPRESENTATIONS

The central concern is how the child comes to acquire expertise in lexical representation. It is the reader's representation of words and word parts (e.g., letters) that enables the kind of rapid restricted-interactive process illustrated previously. The development of expert lexical representations includes two components. One component is the development of a *functional* lexicon and the second is the development of an *autonomous* lexicon. It is the autonomous lexicon that has the key properties of the Restricted-Interactive Model I described earlier. The functional lexicon is simply all the lexical entries that can be accessed through reading but do not yet have this autonomous status. At any given point in learning to read, some lexical entries have moved into the autonomous lexicon. This distinction between functional and autonomous is slightly different from the general distinction between accurate word recognition and "automatic" word recognition. However, it is parallel to this distinction and can be roughly captured by it. One particular implication of the functional–autonomous distinction is different, however: It is lexical items, not children, that become autonomous. They do this on a word-by-word basis, although in principle a change in abstract spelling knowledge can effect a change over a wide portion of the lexicon, perhaps causing entire word families to become autonomous. Nevertheless, the general claim that the process is word by word entails that a question such as "at what age does a child come to be an automatic decoder" is not quite the right one. Instead, the question is how large is the child's autonomous lexicon? How large is his functional lexicon?

Decoding and Word Identification

The key developments in the acquisition of these lexicons are the increase in the quantity of words represented and the increase in the quality of representations. Lexical representation quality depends on two principles of quality: (1) *Precision* and (2) *Redundancy*.

Precision. The precision principle is that fully specified representations are superior to partially specified ones. The advantage of a fully specified or precise representation is that its relationship to appropriate input features is deterministic. In the case of reading, this means that a particular spelling will activate a specific word to quickly bring about the recognition of that word rather than some other word. Contrasting with precise representations are *variable* ones. Whereas precise representations contain specific letters ("constants") in each letter position of a word, variable representations contain "variables" in some letter positions.

Figure 3.1 illustrates this distinction for three hypothetical levels of skill for three "irregular" words from a sight vocabulary list commonly used in the United States. Although the words are "irregular" in that their spellings do not reflect regular phoneme correspondences, the principles of precision and redundancy apply to all words, both "regular" and "irregular." The asterisks indicate variable representations, essentially cases in which the child's spelling knowledge is incomplete. There are certain nonarbitrary choices re-

LEVEL 1	LEVEL 2	LEVEL 3
ir*n	iron	iron
t*g*	t*ng**	tongue
uk*	ukil*	uk*l*l*

Fig. 3.1.   Change in representation precision over three hypothetical skill levels in the acquisition of reading for the words *iron*, *tongue*, and *ukulele*. Asterisks denote free variables in the representation. For example, at level 1, the reader's representation for *tongue* does not include precise knowledge concerning the second letter nor concerning how many letters follow the *n*.

flected in the figure. Early representations are more likely to include initial letters than medial or final ones (Marchbanks & Levin, 1965; Williams, Blumberg, & Williams, 1970). Vowels are more likely to be variables than consonants, consistent with the greater difficulty in reading complex vowels (Liberman et al., 1971). An important point is that phonemic values play a large role in determining which letters get represented, a fact we get from children's spelling errors (e.g., Read, 1971; Treiman, 1985). (The concept of a variable representation has some interesting complexities that are beyond what I can discuss here. Suffice it to say that variable representations reflect partially known and unknown spellings.)

Redundancy.   The second principle of representation quality is the redundancy principle, which is that representations that include redundant connections (information sources) are superior to nonredundant ones. There are two benefits of redundant connections: (1) They allow multiple parallel processes to aid rapid recognition and (2) they provide fall-back routes to identification when one information source is impoverished or noisy. Two things happen to the lexicon to increase redundancy. First, at the subword level, context-dependent grapheme–phoneme connections get strengthened. (These represent emergent decoding rules.) Second, at the word level, there is a bonding of orthographic and phonemic representations. These two developments are essentially the same thing at two different levels (hence "redundant"). (The bonding suggestion is similar to the "amalgamation" concept proposed by Ehri, 1980, perhaps differing in representation details from her proposal.) To illustrate just one consequence of this redundancy, the letter string *i–r–o–n*, with word level redundancy, is sufficient to trigger a bonded representation *iron–ayrn*; that is, the bonded lexical representation assures that the encoded letters arouse a phonemic representation as part of lexical access, regardless of sublexical phoneme activation. Furthermore, the phoneme string /ayrn/ is also sufficient to bring about lexical access as these phonemes are activated by their connections with letters. Lexical access, therefore, is overdetermined, a consequence that is helpful both for bootstrapping the identification of unfamiliar words and for producing the rapid recognition of familiar ones. This development of precision and redundancy is illustrated in Fig. 3.2 over three stages of acquisition. These figures show increasingly specified lexical representations and increasing redundant connections. Finally, before turning to the question of how this representation theory is related to phonemic awareness, let me make clear what the concept of representational quality implies for both acquisition and its measurement. The main point for acquisition is that quality of word representation is the critical development, not such things as "access strategies" (rules, analogies, etc.). For measurement, the implication is that spelling facility is the measure of quality. Under idealized conditions of spelling

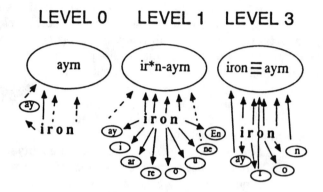

Fig. 3.2. Development of redundant phonemic information over three hypothetical levels of reading acquisition. The levels are not necessarily identical to those of Figure Fig. 3.1. Represented information is in circles. Thus each level represents the word *iron*, but the form of the representation begins as a phonemic object at Level O, includes variable orthographic information at level 1, and at level 3 includes a fully specified orthographic representation "bonded" to the phonemic representation. (An analogy to chemical bonding is intended.) Meanwhile, the representation of phonemes changes in two directions, beginning impoverished at level O, proliferating at level 1, and by level 3 reducing to mainly those that are sensitive to the orthographic context imposed by the word *iron*. The solid arrows indicate strong activation patterns, the dashed arrows, weak ones.

production and spelling recognition, the spelling of a given word by a child is the quality of its representation in terms of precision.

Phonological Knowledge

Phonological knowledge is clearly critical in skilled reading. The heart of lexical access in the Restricted-Interactive Model is the activation of a phonologically referenced name code. The question is, what is the role of phonological knowledge in acquiring this skill?

The issue, simply put, is whether explicit reflective phonological knowledge is necessary to learn to read an alphabetic orthography. The answer depends in part on a distinction between computational and reflective knowledge: Computational knowledge is represented by connections between letters and phonemes that are used in word identification. Reflective knowledge is represented by the conscious manipulation of the components of spoken words. Some computational phonological knowledge is necessary to gain a functional lexical representation system of any size and hence is critical in reading acquisition. Furthermore, explicit reflective knowledge, or "awareness," certainly is a sign of a more powerful learning mechanism than is implicit knowledge. However, explicit reflective phonological knowledge is not necessary to begin the acquisition of a functional representation system. All that is necessary is the ability to represent some of the graphemes of a word and to use these to compute the word's phonological representation. It is better to say that the child can compute the *word* on the basis of some of the graphemes and that the phonological representation comes with the word. Because the essence of a grapheme string is its orthography, not its pronunciation, it is possible, in principle, to acquire some word representations in ignorance of phonemic connections to their letters. Thus it is possible that initial progress in acquisition could be based only on visual information (Gough & Hillinger, 1980). However, this visual-only stage probably is very short-lived or perhaps nonexistent in any pure form. Children do acquire phonemic mappings to letters and this serves the acquisition of word representations. Indeed, Ehri and Wilce (1985) have shown that children just starting to read are disposed to take advantage of grapheme–phoneme connections, even when their knowledge of phoneme values is little more than letter names. But taking advantage of these connections is to use essentially *computational* knowledge rather than *reflective* knowledge.

Thus the very early computational use of phonemic information characterizes learning how to read. Furthermore, we know that providing children with phonemic instruction can improve their reading. Bradley and Bryant's (1983) study showed that training backward readers in an implicitly phonemic task improved their reading performance. Treiman and Baron (1981) also report effective training based on segmentation knowledge. Such studies demonstrate a causal connection between phonemic knowledge and reading skill and strengthen the conclusion from many correlational studies that show beginning reading success is predicted by prereading measures of phonological knowledge (e.g., Lundberg, Olofsson, & Wall, 1980; Mann & Liberman, 1984; Stanovich, Cunningham, & Cramer, 1984; see Wagner & Torgesen, 1987, for a review). Nevertheless, explicit reflective phonemic knowledge is not a prerequisite to reading. To support this claim, I refer to a study reported in Perfetti, Beck, Bell, and Hughes (1987). This longitudinal study found that first-grade children showed progress in simple word and pseudoword reading (before) they showed progress in a task of *explicit* phonemic awareness. (The task was phoneme deletion in which the child produces, for example, cat without the /k/ or without the /t/.) Because progress on a simple computation-type synthetic phonemic task ("blending" phonemes into words and syllables) preceded progress in word reading, we concluded that the relationship between explicit phonemic knowledge and reading, in a sense, is reciprocal. Some rudimentary phonemic knowledge—not reflective analytic knowledge—is causally necessary for progress in word reading. However, a deeper reflective kind of phonemic knowledge—the kind most researchers have in mind when they refer to "phonemic awareness"—has a more complex reciprocal relationship. At least some of this reflective awareness comes through experience with alphabetic stimuli, although it probably has its origins in preliterate speech play. The typical child does not have easy access to this reflective knowledge based only on his spoken language experience.[1] Children begin to treat words as having separable constituents when they notice that printed words have such constituents in the form of letters. When they also notice that these alphabetic symbols have speech sounds, they are in a good position to develop reflective phonemic awareness. With this development comes the potential for further gains in reading. Indeed Perfetti et al. (1987) found that gains in awareness, although initially preceded by gains in reading, then were followed by further gains in reading. In short, the pattern of time-lag correlations in that study supports a reciprocal relationship between explicit and analytic phonemic knowledge and learning to read.

Downgrading phonological awareness from causal status to reciprocal status does not diminish its importance for reading. Indeed, it allows it to be seen as a *central* component of reading instead of as a *prerequisite*. The problem with prerequisites is that they appear peripheral rather than central. They are things to get out of the way so that the learner can get to the heart of the matter. The other problem with prerequisities is that there is an implication that they must be met before progress is made. If phonemic awareness and learning to read are reciprocal, phonemic awareness is no longer a prerequisite that has to be met (and cannot be met by most children), but an achievement of learning that then facilitates further learning. The "glue" for the redundant lexical representation and, perhaps more important, the knowledge for a fully specified lexical representation both depend in part on phonemic knowledge.

CONTRADICTIONS AND SYNTHESIS

The claim that phonemic knowledge and learning to read are reciprocal may not seem consistent with the evidence that phonemic awareness is causally

---

[1] Actually, I would stress the accessibility of the knowledge as the problem. Very young children show speech play that indicates experimentation with the meaningless sounds of language even before their speech is very well developed. In fact, MacLean, Bryant, and Bradley (1987) have shown that a child's preschool knowledge of nursery rhymes is predictive of phonemic awareness and later reading achievement.

related to reading. The evidence from training studies (Bradley & Bryant, 1983; Treiman & Baron, 1983) and carefully controlled correlational studies (Maclean, Bryant, & Bradley, 1987; Stanovich, Cunningham, & Feeman, 1984) is quite substantial. There is also evidence that segmentation training, which should promote awareness of phonemes, improves reading skill of less able readers (Vellutino & Scanlon, 1987). The reciprocity hypothesis (i.e., that reflective phonemic knowledge and reading competence develop in mutual support) is not a denial of a causal role for phonemic awareness. It is instead a suggestion that the causal connection is only half the picture. The other half is that advancement in reading promotes increased reflective phonemic awareness, which in turn promotes further gains in reading, which is longitudinal data reported by Perfetti et al. (1987).

Let me illustrate how this picture can be pieced together. Many preschool children, but not all, have speech experiences that promote reflective awareness of phonemes. Word games such as piglatin and nursery rhymes that emphasize speech sounds are examples. In their study, Maclean et al. (1987) found that about 20% of 3-year-old children could indicate their awareness of simple word rhymes and a somewhat larger percentage could indicate their awareness of initial consonant segments. What was important in the child's eventual acquisition of such phonemic knowledge and, in fact, reading acquisition, was whether the child knew some nursery rhymes at age 3. Now, this is an interesting piece of the picture. It appears that, quite independently of any other factor, including IQ, children who know nursery rhymes at age 3 acquire both more phonological awareness and more success at reading words. On the other hand, it is important to keep in mind that most children in the Maclean et al. study did not show early abilities (at age 3) in the detection of rhymes and word-initial segments, and that very few children could demonstrate their implicit phonemic knowledge in certain more demanding tasks. Thus the implicit knowledge the child has, if it is a "unitary" knowledge at all, is not equally accessible to all procedures of access. It is very likely that those phonemic procedures that provide most success are those that have the smaller reflective component and the largest computational component. To decide that two words rhyme is largely computational in the sense that vowel and syllable endings have only to be encoded and compared. They do not have to be manipulated. A more reflective and analytic task is likely to produce less success until the child is able not only to compute phonemic patterns but also to have direct controlled access to them. Presumably, increased abilities in controlled access can develop in a number of linguistically based ways. The most common way, however, is probably through experience with word reading, which will promote awareness of letter–word connections and may bring about a parallel awareness in word listening (i.e., an increased awareness of segment-word connection). Thus, the course of normal development that leads to successful reading can be summarized as follows. There seems to be some preliterate experiences with speech sounds, "noticing and producing rhymes especially," that direct the child's attention to relevant speech facts. The child's knowledge of speech sounds remains, during the preliterate period, largely implicit and difficult to access under many conditions. However, if the child has such knowledge, this enables some critical connections to be made during his or her early encounters with alphabetic print. At least parts of the words that the child encounters can be connected with speech sounds, whether they are letter names, phonemes, or even syllables. The alphabetic principle, that meaningless units of print map onto meaningless units of speech, is within the grasp of such a child. As children advance a bit in reading, they achieve a more controlled and reflective knowledge of the sound structure of words. This occurs because learning to read words has forced their attention to word parts, both parts of written words, the letters, and corresponding parts of spoken words, the phonemes. As the children become more analytic about speech sounds and more able to access and control the segments of spoken words, they are increasingly able to read new words. Thus can we describe the normal progress of learning to read as a tandem, reciprocal growth of speech knowledge and print knowledge. For the child who, for some reason, has not had this advantageous course of development, there is a problem in acquiring fundamental reading competence.

For the child who prior to school has missed the opportunity to notice and produce rhymes, or who has simply not demonstrated even dim awareness of spoken language structure, then prognosis for reading advancement is poorer. However, the training studies have demonstrated that children can have their awareness of speech sounds increased by training and that this training can bring about gains in reading competence. The effect of such training, on my account, is not simply to give children access to phonemic knowledge. Such training affects the child's computational knowledge (i.e., the ability to make connections between letters, which they have already learned about, and phonemes, about which they have had only dim and inaccessible knowledge at best). Thus training helps make clearer the structure of words: Spoken words contain phonemes; written words contain letters; letters and phonemes correspond.

However, even the evidence of the training studies does not necessarily mean that explicit phonemic knowledge is a strong prerequisite to reading. It does demonstrate that there is an enabling relationship between the two abilities. Phonemic knowledge, of some kind, enables reading competence. The more reflective and analytic the child's knowledge, the more rapid will be his or her progress in reading. However, normally a basic and nonanalytic knowledge is enough to get the reading process off to a good start.

CONCLUSION

I have given a simplified account of the development of reading competence and the relationship between reading acquisition and explicit phonemic knowledge. Skilled reading is described by a Restricted-Interactive Model in which word representations acquire rich connections between phonemic and graphemic segments (redundancy) with reliable precise spellings (precision) uninformed by rules. Decoding is a mechanism to help increase the size of this lexicon by allowing recognition of new words, but it changes its character as words move from the *functional* lexicon to the *autonomous* lexicon. Computational phonemic knowledge plays a critical role in decoding and helps build up the functional lexicon. Moreover, it is clear that some preliterate knowledge of speech sounds is important in enabling the child to acquire competence in reading. Furthermore, a child lacking such knowledge can benefit from instruction in phonemic awareness. However, reflective phonemic knowledge is not a prerequisite to word reading. Rather the two abilities naturally develop in tandem and gains in either one should facilitate gains in the other. The relationship is mutually enabling and more than one-directional.

ACKNOWLEDGMENT

I am grateful to the Netherlands Institute for Advanced Studies in the Humanities and Social Sciences (NIAS), where I was a fellow during the preparation of this manuscript in 1988. Parts of the research discussed in the chapter were supported by the Learning, Research, and Development Center, University of Pittsburgh. Some of the ideas of the chapter also appear in a chapter titled, "The Representation Problem in Reading Acquisition," which appears in a forthcoming book, *Reading Acquisition*, edited by Philip B. Gough, Linnea Ehri, and Rebecca Treiman to be published by Lawrence Erlbaum Associates.

REFERENCES

Bradley, L., & Bryant, P. E. (1983). Categorizing sounds and learning to read—a causal connection. *Nature, 301*, 419–421.

Ehri, L. C., (1980). The development of orthographic images. In U. Frith (Ed.), *Cognitive processes in spelling*. London: Academic Press.

Ehri L. C. & Wilce, L. S. (1985). Movement into reading: Is the first stage of printed word learning visual or phonetic? *Reading Research Quarterly, Winter*, 163–179.

Gough, P. B., & Hillinger, M. L. (1980). Learning to read: An unnatural act. *Bulletin of the Orton Society, 20*, 179–196.

Liberman, I. Y., Shankweiler, D., Orlando, C., Harris, H. S., & Berti, F. B. (1971). Letter confusion and reversals of sequence in the beginning reader: Implications for Orton's theory of developmental dyslexia. *Cortex, 7*, 127–142.

Lundberg, I., Olofsson, A., & Wall, S. (1980). Reading and spelling skills in the first school years predicted from phonemic awareness skills in kindergarten. *Scandinavian Journal of Psychology, 21*, 159–173.

Maclean, M. Bryant, P., & Bradley, L. (1987). Rhymes, nursery rhymes, and reading in early childhood. *Merrill–Palmer Quarterly*, Special Issue, *Children's Reading and the Development of Phonological Awareness* (Vol. *33*, No. 3, 255–281) K. Stanovich (Ed.).

Mann, V. A., & Liberman, I. Y. (1984). Phonological awareness and verbal short-term memory. *Journal of Learning Disabilities, 17*, 592–599.

Marchbanks, G., & Levin, H. (1965). Cues by which children recognize words. *Journal of Educational Psychology, 56*, 57–61.

McClelland, J. L. (1986). Resource requirements of standard and programmable nets. In D. E. Rumelhart, J. L. McClelland, & The PDP Research Group, *Parallel distributed processing; Explorations in the microstructures of cognition, Vol. 1, Foundations*, 460–487.

Perfetti, C. A. (1985). *Reading ability*, New York: Oxford University Press.

Perfetti, C. A., Beck, I., Bell, L., & Hughes, C. (1987). Phonemic knowledge and learning to read are reciprocal: A longitudinal study of first grade children. *Merrill-Palmer Quarterly*, Special Issue, *Children's reading and the development of phonological awareness* (Vol. 33, No. 3, pp. 283–320.) K. Stanovich, (Ed.).

Perfetti, C. A., Bell, L., & Delaney, S. (1988). Automatic phonetic activation in silent word reading: Evidence from backward masking. *Journal of Memory and Language, 27*, 59–70

Read, C. (1971). Pre-school children's knowledge of English phonology. *Harvard Educational Review, 1*, (No. 1).

Rumelhart, D. E., & McClelland, J. L. (1981). Interactive processing through spreading activation. In A. M. Lesgold & C. A. Perfetti (Eds.), *Interactive processes in reading* (pp. 37–60). Hillsdale, NJ: Lawrence Erlbaum Associates.

Stanovich, K. E. (1980). Toward an interactive-compensatory model of individual differences in the development of reading fluency. *Reading Research Quarterly, 16*, 32–71.

Stanovich, K. E., Cunningham, A. E., & Cramer, B. B. (1984). Assessing phonological awareness in kindergarten children: Issues of task comparability. *Journal of Experimental Child Psychology, 38*, 175–190.

Stanovich, K. E., Cunningham, A. E., & Feeman, D. J. (1984). Intelligence, cognitive skills, and early reading progress. *Reading Research Quarterly, 19*, 178–303.

Treiman, R. (1985). Phonemic awareness and spelling: Children's judgments do not always agree with adults'. *Journal of Experimental Child Psychology, 39*, 182–201.

Treiman, R. A., & Baron, J. (1981). Segmental analysis ability: Development and relation to reading ability. In T. G. Waller & G. E. MacKinnon (Eds.), *Reading research: Advances in theory and practice* (Vol. 3, pp. 159–198). New York: Academic Press.

Treiman, R., & Baron, J. (1983). Phonemic-analysis training helps children benefit from spelling–sound rules. *Memory and Cognition, II*, 382–389.

Van Orden, G. C. (1987). A Rows is a ROSE: Spelling, sound and reading. *Memory and Cognition, 15*, 181–198.

Vellutino, F. R., & Scanlon, D. M. (1987). Phonological coding, phonological awareness, and reading ability: Evidence from a longitudinal and experimental study. *Merrill-Palmer Quarterly*, Special Issue, *Children's reading and the development of phonological awareness*, (Vol. 33, No. 3, 321–363), K. Stanovich (Ed.).

Wagner, R. K., & Torgesen, J. K. (1987). The nature of phonological processing and its causal role in the acquisition of reading skills. *Psychological Bulletin*.

Williams, J. P., Blumberg, E. L., & Williams, D. V. (1970). Cues used in visual word recognition. *Journal of Educational Psychology, 61*, 310–315.

II Starting to Learn to Read

4 The First Stages of Word Recognition

Philip B. Gough
Connie Juel
University of Texas at Austin

Let us suppose that reading consists of two things. One is word recognition; the reader must grasp what word each letter string represents. The other is comprehension; the reader must then decide what those words collectively mean. Both things are necessary; neither is sufficient. If we let R represent reading, D word recognition, and C comprehension, then this idea can be stated as an equation: $R = D \times C$.

This is a simple view of reading, and it is probably overly simple. For one thing, the *processes* of word recognition and comprehension are not independent. We know that context can strongly influence word recognition, and many take this fact as evidence that the processes of word recognition and comprehension are not independent, but instead interact to produce skilled reading.

But there is some reason to believe that the *skills* of word recognition and comprehension do make independent contributions to reading achievement. It is true that word recognition and linguistic comprehension skills are not themselves independent; instead, they are correlated: the child who is good at one tends to be good at the other, and the poor decoder tends to be a poor comprehender. But, as Gough and Tunmer (1986) point out, the two skills can be dissociated. On the one hand, hyperlexic children can decode very well, but their listening comprehension is mediocre or worse (Healy, 1982). In contrast, dyslexic children typically show poor decoding skills in the presence of normal (or even superior) listening comprehension (Vellutino, 1979).

Moreover, the formula $R = D \times C$ has been shown to be a remarkably accurate description of individual differences in reading achievement in at least one population. Hoover and Gough (1990), using data collected in a study of 210 bilingual firstgraders in Texas, found that the product of the child's decoding skill (his ability to read aloud pseudowords) and his listening skill (his ability to answer oral questions about a passage read to him) correlated with reading achievement .84.

There is evidently some merit to the simple view that reading equals word recognition times linguistic comprehension, $R = D \times C$. On this view, reading acquisition must involve growth in both word recognition and in linguistic comprehension. But it first must involve growth in word recognition.

The five- or six-year-old has half of what it takes to be a reader. That child can understand the spoken language. What the child lacks is the ability to recognize written words, and learning this skill is the primary goal of the firstgrader.

Our concern, then, is with how the child learns to recognize printed words. We would note that this is not the question of how to teach the child to read. How we teach a child and how the child learns are surely related. How well we teach a child must be judged by how well he learns, and how we teach the child may affect how he learns, but teaching and learning are different things. Moreover, studies of emergent literacy (e.g., Teale & Sulzby, 1986) have shown us that children often learn much about reading well before they receive any explicit instruction. So what interests us is the process within the child by which he learns to recognize words, whether before or after formal instruction begins, and no matter what form that instruction takes.

THE FIRST STAGE

We begin with the first words. Whether at home or in school, at some point the child learns to recognize his first words. How does this happen?

We share with many scholars (e.g., Samuels, 1976) the assumption that first words are mastered through paired-associate learning, i.e., in the same way that a college student might learn a list of arbitrary pairs in a verbal learning experiment. We mean by this, not that children must learn through repetition and drill, but rather that they learn by the same processes the sophomore uses to remember that an arbitrary response (e.g. "4") is associated with an arbitrary stimulus (e.g., *gex*).

We assume that this process is *selective* association. Confronted with the task of learning that a certain response goes with some stimulus, the learner examines the stimulus, and *selects* from it some cue, some aspect, some property which might distinguish it from the other stimuli from which it must be distinguished. The cue sampled might be the left-most letter or the right; it might be the font; it might be the fact that *gex* has three letters. But whichever cue the learner notices, the response is *associated* with that cue and that cue only. When the learner next encounters that cue, he retrieves the associated response. If it is correct, he retains that association, if it is wrong, he discards that association and selects another cue.

Our conjecture is that the child learns to recognize his first words by just such a process. When the child first encounters a printed word, that word is a seemingly random collection of visual shapes, often themselves unfamiliar, and almost always meaningless. But the child wants to remember that it stands for a word, a spoken word. So the child examines the word for anything he might remember, anything with which to associate the spoken word. Any cue which will distinguish the word will suffice. It might be a character, or a matching pair of characters, or even the font in which the characters appear; if the child knows the names of some letters, it might be the name of one of them (cf. Ehri & Wilce, 1985). Or it might be a property of the whole word; it might be its color, or its length, or even the resemblance of the whole to some familiar object. Whatever the child might notice, the child will associate the word with that cue, and with that cue only. The child will select that cue, and so his association will be selective.

We think that this hypothesis explains many observations about beginning word recognition (see Gough & Hillinger, 1980). It offers an explanation of why it is easy for the child to recognize a few words and why those words tend to be visually distinctive (rather than short, or regular). It helps explain why children can learn dissimilar words more easily than similar words, but will make more overgeneralization errors (e.g., calling *dinosaur dog*) with those words. And it explains the early reader's seeming inconsistency. But the strongest evidence can be found in two unpublished experiments carried out by Gough.

In one study, 32 4- and 5-year-olds were asked to learn four words, presented on flash cards. The method was the usual one of random presentation with anticipation and correction; the only thing unusual was that one of the four cards bore a thumbprint in the lower left corner. The child worked through the cards until he got all four words right twice in a row.

Gough found that every child learned the item with the thumbprint faster than the other three. Evidently the child quickly attended to, and associated the word with, the conspicuous extraneous cue. But at the same time, the child selected that cue, and ignored all others, for when the child was shown a card bearing the same word without the thumbprint, few of the children could correctly identify the word (although almost all could tell you what word went with the thumbprint presented by itself, and most would incorrectly label another word when it was accompanied, for the first time, by the thumbprint.)

This first study showed that the child will learn to recognize a word by selecting an extraneous cue, ignoring the word itself. This certainly suggests

that if a word is accompanied by a salient extraneous cue, the child will select that cue and will not come to recognize the word without it. But most
words are unaccompanied by such cues. Gough's next study concerned
whether beginners selectively associate to cues within these words.

He taught 32 preschoolers, with flashcards, to read four 4-letter words
like *duck* and *pony* until they got all four right twice in a row. Next he asked
them whether they could recognize each word when part of it was hidden.
He then showed them, in random order, the first half and the last half of each
word (e.g., *du—*, *—ny.*) Gough then tallied, in a 2 × 2 table, whether they
recognized the first half or not, and whether they recognized the second half
or not.

The selective association hypothesis does not tell us what cue a child
might select. Nor does it tell us that the child will select a cue which might
be found in the left or right half of a word. But it does tell us that if the child
selects a cue from one half, he should not recognize a cue from the other.
Thus, it predicts a negative correlation between the child's recognition of the
two halves of each word.

That is what Gough found. If the child recognized one half of the word,
he was not likely to recognize the other, and vice versa: the child who failed
to recognize the first half of a word knew the second half twice as often as
the child who did recognize the first, while the child who did not recognize
the second half knew the first half one-and-a-half times as often as the child
who did.

Selective association is a useful technique for learning arbitrary associations, and the child could master many words in this way. But there are two
major problems with it.

First, although it is easy, in the beginning, to find a partial cue which distinguishes each word, as the number of words grows, finding a unique cue
becomes more and more difficult. So although it is easy to recognize the first
words in this fashion, with each additional word the task becomes harder and
harder.

At least as important is the novelty problem. Selective association may
give the child an effective procedure for identifying many words. But each
of those words must have been seen before: the child must have selected an
identifying cue from each word. We can teach a child to read dozens, perhaps even hundreds (though see above), of sight words. But in any but the
most tightly controlled text, the child will encounter novel words, words
which the child has not seen in print before.

Some theorists hold that context will enable the child to recognize these
words. Sometimes it will. But very often it will not, for many words are un-
predictable. When college students are asked to guess words in running text,
they can predict only one content word in ten (Gough, 1983). Moreover, the
predictability of a word varies with its frequency and (inversely) with its

length (Alford, 1980): the rarer and longer a word is, the less predictable it is. Thus, context will help the child recognize short, familiar words. But those are just the words where the child does not need help; context will let the child down precisely where he needs help most.

What the child needs is a way to recognize novel words on the basis of their form, rather than their context.

THE TRANSITION

The first-grade child already knows, in their spoken or phonological form, most of the words that he will encounter in print for the next 3 years. What he doesn't know is their printed form. If he had a means of converting the novel printed word into phonological form, then he could recognize it.

In an alphabetic language, such a means is afforded by knowledge of the letter-sound correspondences of the language, or what we call its orthographic *cipher*.

It is, of course, this cipher that advocates of phonics hope to teach through direct instruction. But it is our conjecture that the rules we teach in phonics are not the rules of the cipher. The rules of phonics are explicit; the teacher, and the child can state them, in words. In contrast, the rules of the cipher are implicit. Moreover, the rules taught in phonics are relatively few, numbering perhaps 75 to 100. But text-to-speech computer programs show us that the rules of the cipher (in English, at least) number over 500. Finally, the rules of phonics are slow and laborious, while the cipher is fast and (seemingly) effortless. The difference between a child sounding out and blending a word, and the skilled reader pronouncing a novel word or pseudoword as easily as his name, seems to us to vividly demonstrate the difference we claim.

The second point is that we are not committed to the idea that the cipher consists of a set of rules. It could equally well consist of an analogical mechanism. The nature of the cipher is a fascinating theoretical question. We do not know what it is, but we do know how to measure it: the child's mastery of the cipher is directly reflected in his ability to pronounce pseudowords.

We argue, then, that the cipher is not taught; rather, it must be discovered. It is not memorized. Instead, it is internalized by a process we have called cryptanalysis.

In order to perform this cryptanalysis, we have argued that the child needs four things. First, he needs cryptanalytic intent. He must grasp that there is a system of correspondences to be mastered. Second, he must become aware of the letters that figure in those correspondences. He can no longer select from among the letters in words; he must register every letter in each word.

Third, he must be equally aware of the other half of those correspondences; he must realize that each spoken word can be decomposed into phonemes. Finally, he needs data, in the form of printed words paired with their spoken equivalents.

Taken together, the first three prerequisites comprise the alphabetic principle. Most children understand that printed words are made of letters, and most children understand that those letters correspond, in some way, to the spoken word. But most beginning first graders do not understand that spoken words are constituted of phonemes.

Our research (Juel, Griffith, & Gough, 1986), like that of many others (e.g., Bradley & Bryant, 1983; Tunmer & Nesdale, 1985) suggests that phonemic awareness is the key to the transition. It is a necessary condition, but not a sufficient one; it unlocks the door, but it does not open it. For that, the child must master the cipher. The child must discover what letters correspond in what way to what phonemes. Given that he does so, he will read words in a new way.

Our claim, then, is that children who have mastered the cipher recognize words in a fundamentally different way than those who remain in the first stage, who still must recognize words by means of selective association. We have found abundant evidence for this in children's oral reading, and in their spelling.

THE CIPHER STAGE

To decide whether children have mastered the cipher, we measure their ability to read aloud pseudowords, often using the Bryant Test of Decoding (Bryant, 1975). The Bryant Test consists of 50 pseudowords, beginning with CVCs (the first 35 items are monosyllables) and steadily increasing in difficulty. We measure their oral reading by asking each child to read aloud a children's story.

Knowledge of the cipher is certainly related to the speed and accuracy with which children read orally. For example, Gough, Juel, and Roper-Schneider (1983) found that score on the Bryant correlated .55 with the number of words read correctly per second by a group of 63 firstgraders. Moreover, it determines how word frequency will influence this index.

Children who do not have the cipher (i.e., those with low scores on the Bryant test) must be reading by selective association. Therefore, they must rely much more heavily on word familiarity than do cipher readers. To test this, we measured the effect of word frequency on oral reading accuracy for each child. Knowing how far that child had reached in his basal reader, we computed an individual regression of oral reading errors on word frequency.

Gough, Juel, and Roper-Schneider (1983) found that the slope of this regression correlated.69 with score on the Bryant. Thus, as our hypothesis predicts, familiarity plays a much smaller role in cipher reading than it does in reading by selective association.

Knowledge of the cipher not only influences accuracy (and its dependence on frequency); it also affects the quality of those errors.

On our hypothesis, the child who does not have the cipher recognizes words by means of selective association. If he makes an error, it is a failure of association; either he selects the wrong cue, or he finds no cue at all. In the former case, he will produce the wrong word; in the latter case, he must guess. In either case his error must be a word. In contrast, the cipher reader is held to recognize words using the cipher. Thus, his errors result from misapplication of that cipher. This may result in a word error (e.g., in misreading *fate* as *fat*). But it can just as well result in a nonword (e.g., in misreading *keep* as *kep*). We predicted, then, that the proportion of the child's errors that are nonwords will increase with the child's knowledge of the cipher, and Gough, Juel, and Roper-Schneider (1983) found this correlation to be significant.

The cipher reader makes more nonword errors than the selective reader. But the cipher reader will also make word errors, resulting from either the use of context or from misapplication of the cipher. In the latter case, the word errors will bear little relationship to the child's prior reading.

The selective association reader will also use context. But he has another source for word errors. In the absence of a familiar cue, he may just reach into memory for one of his "reading words" and try that. We predicted, then, that if we examine the child's word errors and ask what proportion of them are words that the child has previously encountered in the pages of his basal, that proportion will decrease with knowledge of the cipher. We found just this. The proportion of the child's word errors that are drawn from previously read text correlated significantly (-.41) with score on the Bryant.

The distinction between children who do and do not have the cipher correctly predicts a number of differences in the way beginners read. It also predicts differences in the way they spell.

Consider how the selective reader must spell. Asked to spell *camel*, the child who has learned that it's the one with the humps will (assuming associative symmetry) remember the *m*. He may also remember that the *m* is in the middle. But that is all. So he might spell *camel* with an *m* in the middle and some other letters around it (e.g., *bimot*). His spelling errors, then, may bear little resemblance (and only accidental *phonetic* resemblance) to the target word.

This is not to say that the child without the cipher must spell inaccurately. We note that he might use as his cue the whole word, and thus commit that to memory, just as he probably does with his first name. So this reader can spell words correctly. But his errors will tend to be nonphonetic.

In contrast, we assume that the child who has internalized the cipher will use it in his spelling. Asked to spell *camel*, he will attend to its phonemes and try to represent them in letters. Thus, he is apt to spell it *kaml*.

We predicted, then, that the proportion of the child's spelling errors that are phonetic will increase with his knowledge of the cipher. Juel, Griffith, and Gough (1985) found that children with the cipher made 10 times as many spelling errors that were homophonous with the target as did children who could not read pseudowords.

If a child does not know the cipher, his spelling must derive from something other than the phonological form of the word. Correct letters might come from his selective association, or they might come from his visual memory. But incorrect letters must be randomly derived. This led us to the prediction that, given a misspelled word, the proportion of its letters that are intrusions (i.e., letters not drawn from the target word) would *decrease* with the child's knowledge of the cipher. We indeed found a significant negative correlation of proportion of intrusions with score on the Bryant.

Code readers spell with more intrusions than do cipher readers. These intrusions do not derive from the target's phonology. From whence do their errors come?

One source is memory. If the selective association reader fails to remember his cue for a word, he may simply pull from memory a string of letters that he remembers. Such a string might well be another word. Thus, we reasoned that such a reader may simply substitute the wrong word for a target word in a spelling task. Juel, Griffith, and Gough (1985) found that children who do not know the cipher make significantly more real word substitutions in a spelling task than do cipher readers.

The last source is perhaps the most theoretically interesting, for it corroborates the view that it is the lack of the cipher that accounts for the code reader's spelling problems. When the code reader remembers the printed page and visualizes its contents, he will see letters, but he will also see other shapes, like numbers, ampersands, parentheses, and other punctuation marks. The cipher reader knows that these are not parts of words, for words are spelled with the alphabet. But the code reader, we think, does not even grasp the alphabetic principle. Thus, we wondered whether his misspellings would include nonalphabetic material, and this is what we observed: Juel, Griffith, and Gough (1985) found that firstgraders who could read no pseudowords include in their spellings numbers and other nonalphabetic symbols more than ten times as often as cipher readers.

We conclude that mastery of the cipher alters the child reader: It changes how he recognizes words, and it changes how he spells them. These changes last: We have evidence (see also Stanovich, 1986) that children who have mastered the cipher in the first grade will be successful readers by the time they reach the fourth, while those who have not mastered the cipher remain poor readers 3 years later.

In a longitudinal study of 54 children from first through fourth grade, Juel (1988) found that there was a.88 probability that a child at the bottom quartile on the IOWA Reading Comprehension subtest at the end of first grade, would be a poor reader at the end of fourth grade. Of 24 children who remained poor readers through four grades, only two had average decoding skills. At the end of fourth grade, the other 22 children were at least one standard deviation below their average and good reader peers on the Bryant pseudoword test. These 22 children could not decode all the monosyllable pseudowords (e.g., *dit, cleef, yode*) on the Bryant.

Most of the children who became poor decoders entered first grade with little phonemic awareness. Although their phonemic awareness steadily grew in first grade, they left first grade with less phonemic awareness than the children who became average or good readers possessed upon *entering* first grade. This appeared to contribute to a very slow start in learning the cipher (Juel, Griffith, & Gough, 1986). Nine of the poor readers could not read a single pseudoword on the Bryant at the end of first grade. By the end of fourth grade the poor decoders still had not achieved the level of decoding that the average/good readers had achieved by the beginning of second grade.

The poor decoders expressed a dislike for reading and read considerably less than the good decoders both in and out of school (Juel, 1988). They thus lost the opportunity to gain vocabulary, complex syntax, knowledge of text structures, concepts, and general knowledge that comes from wide reading. The children who were good decoders made considerable growth in listening comprehension through the 4 years, while the poor decoders made little growth. By fourth grade the poor readers were mainly children who were neither competent decoders not competent listeners. Given the simple view of reading (that it is composed of word recognition and comprehension), it is easy to see why these children were poor readers in fourth grade.

What seems essential is to insure that children learn to decode in first grade. If decoding skill does not arrive then, it may be very hard to change the direction that reading achievement takes: Poor decoding skill leads to little reading and little opportunity to increase one's basic vocabulary and knowledge, leaving a shaky foundation for later reading comprehension.

We conclude, then, that early mastery of the cipher is the critical step in reading acquisition. This is not to say that word recognition skill is finished with mastery of the cipher. Knowing the cipher will not enable one to recognize (or spell) exception words (e.g., *tongue*, or *island*, or *colonel*), nor will it alone determine the pronunciation (or spelling) of a large number of polyphonous forms (like *bass*, and *great*, and *chord*). Thus, the child must internalize not only the cipher, but also a great deal of word-specific information. But with the acquisition of the cipher, the first stage of word recognition is over. What the child must now do is read.

REFERENCES

Alford, J. A., Jr. (1980). *Lexical and contextual effects on reading time*. Unpublished doctoral dissertation, University of Texas at Austin.

Bradley, L., & Bryant, P. E. (1983). Categorizing sounds and learning to read—a casual connection. *Nature, 301*, 419–421.

Bryant, N. D. (1975). *Diagnostic test of basic decoding skills*. New York: Teachers College, Columbia University.

Ehri, L. C., & Wilce, L. S. (1985). Movement into reading: Is the first stage of printed word learning visual or phonetic? *Reading Research Quarterly, 20*, 163–179.

Gough, P. B. (1983). Context, form, and interaction. In R. Rayner (Ed.), *Eye movements in reading* (pp. 203–211). New York: Academic Press.

Gough, P. B., & Hillinger, M. L. (1980). Learning to read: An unnatural act. *Bulletin of the Orton Society, 30*, 179–196.

Gough, P. B., (in press). A simple view of reading. In R. Hoffman & D. Palermo (Eds.), *Cognitive psychology: The state of the art*. Hillsdale, NJ: Lawrence Erlbaum Associates.

Gough, P. B., Juel, C., & Roper-Schneider, D. (1983). Code and cipher: A two-stage conception of initial reading acquisition. In J. A. Niles & L. A. Harris (Eds), *Searches for meaning in reading/language processing and instruction* (pp. 207–211). Rochester, NY: The National Reading Conference.

Gough, P. B., & Tunmer, W. E. (1986). Decoding, reading, and reading disability. *Remedial and Special Education, 7*, 6–10.

Healy, J. (1982). The enigma of hyperlexia. *Reading Research Quarterly, 17*, 319–338.

Hoover, W. A., & Gough, P. B. (1990). The simple view of reading. *Reading and Writing, 2*, 127–160.

Juel, C. (1988). Learning to read and write: A longitudinal study of fifty-four children from first through fourth grade. *Journal of Educational Psychology, 80*, 437–447.

Juel, C., Griffith, P. L., & Gough, P. B. (1985). Reading and spelling strategies of first grade children. In J. A. Niles & R. Lalik (Eds.), *Issues in literacy: A research perspective* (pp. 306–309). Rochester, NY: National Reading Conference.

Juel, C., Griffith, P. L., & Gough, P. B. (1986). Acquisition of literacy: A longitudinal study of children in first and second grade. *Journal of Educational Psychology, 78*, 243–255.

Samuels, S. J. (1976). Modes of word recognition. In H. Singer & R. B. Ruddell (Eds.), *Theoretical models and processes of reading* (pp. 270–282). Newark, DE: International Reading Association.

Stanovich, K. E. (1986). Matthew effects in reading: Some consequences of individual differences in the acquisition of literacy. *Reading Research Quarterly, 21*, 360–406.

Teale, W., & Sulzby, E. (1986). *Emergent literacy: Writing and reading*. Norwood, NJ: Ablex.

Tunmer, W. E., & Nesdale, J. R. (1985). Phonemic segmentation skill and beginning reading. *Journal of Educational Psychology, 77*, 417–427.

Vellutino, F. R. (1979). *Dyslexia: Theory and research*. Cambridge, MA: MIT Press.

5 Learning to Read and Spell Words

Linnea C. Ehri
University of California, Davis

IMPORTANCE OF WORD READING

One of the most important capabilities to be acquired in learning to read is learning to recognize words accurately, automatically, and rapidly (Ehri, 1978, 1980a, 1980b; LaBerge & Samuels, 1974; Perfetti, 1985; Stanovich, 1980). From eye-movement data (Carpenter & Just, 1981; McConkie & Zola, 1981), we know that when mature readers read text they do not pass over words and look only at those that they cannot predict from context. Rather their eyes fixate on most of the words. Less mature readers fixate on every word, often more than once. McConkie and Zola (1981) placed a few misspelled words in text and found that these words disrupted readers' eye movements, even when the errors were visually similar to correct forms (e.g., fraoture for fracture) and even when the misspelled words were highly predictable from their preceding contexts (e.g., The athlete suffered a compound fraoture). These findings indicate that readers do not often skip words they can predict, and they sample more than just a few letters in most words. Oral reading errors also indicate that the units processed in text are words. The most common error is to substitute other words for those appearing in print. This happens much more often than omitting words or inserting extra words (Weber, 1970).

How do readers identify words as they are reading? Our view and that of others is that readers utilize various knowledge sources stored in memory to process words. Semantic and syntactic information drawn from their world knowledge, their linguistic knowledge, and their memory for the text already read enables readers to form expectations about upcoming words in text, at least about a word's form class and semantic features if not the word itself. This information is coordinated with graphemic information when readers' eyes fixate on particular words. Two knowledge sources may be used to process graphemic information. To read words that have been read before, readers access their sight word vocabulary, that is, their knowledge about the printed forms of specific words stored in their lexicons. To read unfamiliar words, readers utilize their knowledge about regularities of the spelling system such as letter–sound correspondences, spelling patterns symbolizing morphemes, and common letter sequences symbolizing syllables. This knowledge enables readers to transform and blend letters into pronunciations that they can recognize as words (Marsh, Friedman, Desberg, & Saterdahl, 1981; Venezky, 1970). Readers can read unfamiliar words also by using their print lexicons and applying an analogy strategy (e.g., reading "slough" by analogy to the known printed word "rough"; (Glushko, 1979, 1981; Goswami, 1986; Kay & Marcel, 1981; Marsh, Friedman, Welch, & Desberg, 1981).

One of the issues dividing researchers is the question of whether individual words are read fully or only sampled during text reading (Stanovich, 1980). The main objection to individual word reading appears to be that it consumes too much attention, effort, and time to execute (Goodman, 1970). However, if one examines the nature of word-reading skill and the course of its development, one finds that this is not true.

Learning to read individual words is thought to pass through three successive phases (Ehri & Wilce, 1979b, 1983; LaBerge & Samuels, 1974). During Phase 1, an unfamiliar word is recognized with increasing *accuracy* as readers attend to letter–sound relations each time they read it. In Phase 2, as a result of more practice, a familiar word comes to be recognized *automatically* as a whole, without attention and without deliberate processing of component letter sounds. In Phase 3, the word comes to be recognized with increasing *speed* as identification processes are consolidated in memory. It is following Phase 2 when readers can recognize words automatically that the words become easy to recognize in text, because recognition requires little effort.

To experience what it means to recognize words automatically, try labeling the pictures in Fig. 5.1. Name the pictures as rapidly as you can. Ignore the words printed on the pictures. You will find that the distracting words are hard to resist and they definitely slow you down (Rosinski, Golinkoff, & Kukish, 1975). Guttentag and Haith (1978) used this task and found that children as young as the end of first grade process known words automatically. The point is that if readers can recognize words this easily when they are wishing to ignore them, then they certainly can recognize the same words easily when they encounter them in text. Thus, individual word reading is not an obtrusive or time-consuming process.

From our findings and those of others, it is clear that learning to process graphemic cues accurately, automatically, and rapidly is one of the hardest

FIG. 5.1. Pictures printed with semantically related words that create interference in a task requiring subjects to name the pictures as
rapidly as possible and to ignore the printed words. Source: Ehri
(1987). Reprinted by permission of the *Journal of Reading Behavior.*

parts of learning to read. It is a part that consumes substantial learning time.
It is a skill that clearly separates good readers from poor readers (Stanovich,
1980). One aim of our research has been to understand how beginners become skilled at graphemic cue processing.

Development of Reading Skill

Chall's (1979, 1983) portrayal of the initial stages of learning to read provides a global view of development. Stage 0 covers the prereading period
from birth until children become able to read print. During this stage, children acquire oral language skill. They observe and participate in many literate activities such as listening to storybooks and letters from relatives. They
acquire concepts about reading and writing, for example, what print looks
like, where it is found, how it sounds when it is read aloud, how to write
their names, and so on. They begin to learn the shapes and names of alphabet

letters and how letters differ from numbers. They learn to identify signs in their environment such as McDonald's, Coca Cola, and Stop. They practice writing by scribbling or by copying print, or by inventing their own spellings to label drawings or create messages (Mason & Allen, 1986).

Stage 1 is the initial reading and decoding stage. Children learn how to segment meaningful language into words and phonemes. They learn how letters symbolize phonemes in words. Letter knowledge and phonemic segmentation skill are the two best predictors of beginning reading achievement, better even than measures of intelligence (Share, Jorm, Maclean, & Matthews, 1984). Beginners acquire a sight vocabulary and use this to read simple text. In addition, they learn how to phonologically recode words, that is, to transform printed words into pronunciations. Biemiller's (1970) research indicates that when beginners first learn to read text, they may ignore graphic cues and use context cues to guess at unfamiliar words. However, those readers who progress in learning to read learn how to decode letters and how to process graphic cues in concert with syntactic and semantic information.

During Stage 2, readers acquire fluency in their reading. They become able to process a growing number of words automatically, and their text-reading speed increases. Stage 3 emerges when readers have mastered the mechanics of the reading process and can use reading as a primary means of acquiring new information. Whereas during the earlier stages, readers learn to read, at this stage, they read to learn (Chall, 1979, 1983).

Movement into Reading

Chall's (1979, 1983) view of the beginning stages of reading provides the background for specific questions we have addressed about the learning process. One question is, how do prereaders move into Stage 1? What knowledge sources, skills, and experiences enable them to begin reading words by processing graphic cues without any help from pictures or other context cues? One explanation is that this ability evolves naturally and spontaneously out of children's prereading experiences, the same way that their oral language develops (Goodman & Goodman, 1979; Goodman & Altwerger, 1981; Harste, Burke, & Woodward, 1982). According to this view, during Stage 0, children become able to identify print in their environment. Acquiring print-meaning associations for environmental labels and signs provides the foundation for learning about the graphic system. First, children become aware that print is different from nonprint. Although they are not able to read the words themselves in signs, they can point to the place where it says "McDonald's," "Stop," or "milk." As a result of repeated exposure to these labels and signs, the print itself gradually becomes decontextualized and can be recognized from graphic cues alone.

An alternative explanation is that, to begin processing graphic cues to read words, children must acquire certain prerequisites such as letter knowledge and phonemic awareness (Bradley & Bryant, 1983; Ehri, 1979, 1983; Fox & Routh, 1975, 1976; Gough & Hillinger, 1980; Liberman & Shankweiler, 1979; Morais, Cary, Alegria, & Bertelson, 1979; Tunmer & Hoover, in preparation). Prereaders who lack such knowledge may appear able to read signs in their environment, but they are "reading" the environment, not the print (Mason, 1980). According to this view, for prereaders to shift attention from environmental cues to the print itself, they need to learn the alphabet. To recognize how print tracks speech, they need to become aware of sounds in words. Because there are so many letter shapes to be learned and associated with meaningless, arbitrary sounds, and because the sounds are folded into adjacent sounds and are hard to distinguish as units, children need instruction and practice in these prerequisites before they can begin reading words and text independently. Reading skill is not picked up simply through exposure to print.

We performed a study to see whether environmental print experiences enable young children to process graphic cues (Masonheimer, Drum, & Ehri, 1984). We selected 102 preschoolers 3–5 years old who were *experts* at reading signs and labels in their environment. These were children who could identify correctly at least 8 out of 10 signs in photographs, for example, a Pepsi label on a bottle, a McDonald's sign on a restaurant. We examined these experts' ability to read environmental print with and without context cues and also their ability to detect spelling errors in environmental print, for example, "Pepsi" misspelled "Xepsi." In addition, subjects' ability to name letters and to read high-frequency beginning-level words was measured.

We reasoned that if environmental print experiences lead to gradual decontextualization of graphic cues, then the scores of our "experts" on the word-reading task ought to be distributed normally. Results showed just the opposite, a bimodal distribution. Most of the children, 94%, read few if any words. The remaining 6% read most of the words. There were no children in the middle of the distribution. In naming letters, the nonreaders and readers differed greatly. Whereas all the readers could name at least 98% of the letters, very few nonreaders could name them this well. Nonreaders' mean was 62% correct.

In the environmental print reading tasks, the readers had no trouble reading labels either with or without contexts, and they spontaneously noticed misspellings. In contrast, the nonreaders could read the print only when it was accompanied by contexts and logos, not when it was presented alone. Moreover, they failed to notice incorrect letters in the print, even when they were asked whether there was anything wrong or strange about the print. When the misspelled labels were presented beside correct labels, only one-third of the nonreaders detected the misspellings.

These results provide little support for the view that children move closer to acquiring reading skill after they have accumulated substantial experience with environmental print. Why is this so? Why isn't reading acquisition like oral language acquisition? Our explanation is that during Stage 0 there is no "press" on children to look beyond the cues that are easiest to discern and most obvious. From a functional point of view, little purpose is served by attending to letters in the environment. All the information prereaders need can be obtained from nonalphabetic sources. Moreover, if letters are not familiar forms, there is even less reason to notice them.

If environmental print experiences are not sufficient to move prereaders into Stage 1 reading, then how do they become able to process graphic cues? We have suggested that one thing they need to have mastered is the alphabet (Ehri, 1983). Some evidence for this was uncovered in our print expert study. Whereas all of the readers could name practically every upper and lower case letter, only 6% of the nonreaders performed this well. We have observed this relationship in other studies too (Ehri & Wilce, 1985). Letter knowledge is one of the best predictors of beginning reading achievement (Chall, 1967; Share, Jorm, Maclean, & Matthews, 1984). Our explanation for the relationship is that knowledge of letter shapes and names or sounds provides children with the foundation for processing graphic cues in printed words. Knowing shapes helps children distinguish and remember the visual constituents of words. Knowing letter names helps them associate relevant sounds with letters because most of the names contain these sounds. Of course, knowing letter names is just a starting point because not all names contain relevant sounds and because there are many more sounds to be learned that are not found in the names.

How do beginning readers get started using graphic cues to read words? We have disagreed with Phil Gough over this question, and we have conducted studies to attempt to settle the issue. Gough and Hillinger (1980) propose that beginning readers pass through two stages in their use of graphic cues to read words. We will call children in the first stage *cue readers* and children in the second stage *cipher readers*. During the first stage, the mechanism of selective paired-associate learning is used to read words. Readers select a *visually distinctive cue* located in or around the printed word and associate this with the word in memory, for example, the tail on the final g in the spelling of "dog," or a thumbprint appearing next to the word. In most cases, the visual cues selected are unrelated to the meanings of the words, and they are never related to sounds. Gough and Hillinger (1980) speculate that children use visual cues in learning to read their first 40 or so words. In attempting to employ this technique with more and more words, cue readers run into trouble. It becomes harder to find a unique visual cue in each printed word to form an association. Different words sharing the same features are mistaken for each other (Otto & Pizillo, 1970). Because they are arbitrary, associations are often forgotten. As a result, learners are unable to read words reliably over time (Mason, 1980). The mounting confusion and frustration eventually results in a shift to cipher reading, the second stage of development.

Cipher reading becomes possible when readers master letter–sound mapping relations and phonemic segmentation. Upon seeing a word, cipher readers can apply their general knowledge of how orthography tracks speech to generate a pronunciation of the word that takes account of all its letters. Cipher reading enables readers to decode spellings they have never seen before and to read words accurately and consistently over time.

Our dispute with Gough is over his two-stage conception of the word-reading process. His view is that children use visual cues to read words until they become able to decipher words. Our view is that there is an intermediate stage between visual cue reading and deciphering. We call this stage *phonetic cue reading*. It is like visual cue reading in that only one or a few specific cues, not the entire spelling, is selected and associated with the word in memory. However, it is different from visual cue reading in that the cues are *letters* that link the spelling to the *pronunciation* of the word. Once learners know letter names or sounds, they can begin to form phonetic associations between printed words and their pronunciations in memory to read words. For example, beginners might learn to read the word "jail" by selecting the letters J and L and associating the names of these letters with sounds heard in the word's pronunciation. These associations are stored in memory and retrieved the next time the word is seen. Phonetic cue reading is an easier process than visual cue reading because the associations between spellings and pronunciations are systematic rather than arbitrary and thus are easier to remember. However, mistakes arise in both cases when new words having the same cues as the learned words are encountered, for example, misreading "house" as "horse."

Phonetic cue reading might be regarded as a primitive form of deciphering because phonetic cue readers use letter–sound relations to read words just as cipher readers do. The difference is that phonetic cue readers form associations out of only some of the letters, not all of them. Moreover, they can only read words that they have seen before and stored in memory. They lack sufficient knowledge of the orthographic system to decode unfamiliar words accurately.

We conducted a study to find out when during development beginning readers become able to use phonetic cues more effectively than visual cues in learning to read words (Ehri & Wilce, 1985). In this study, we taught prereaders and beginning readers to read two kinds of word spellings. One set

consisted of simplified phonetic spelling of words. All the letters corresponded to sounds found in the names of the letters. For example, JRF
spelled "giraffe." The other set consisted of visually distinctive spellings.
These spellings were created by varying the height and ascending or de-
scending positions of letters to give each word a unique contour. Also, each
word had unique letters not appearing in other words. However, none of the
letters in visual spellings corresponded to sounds in the words. For example,
WBc spelled "giraffe." In the word-learning task, children were told what
word each spelling symbolized and were given several trials to learn to read
the words.

To study word reading developmentally, we selected kindergartners and
divided them into three groups according to their word-reading ability: prereaders who read 0–1 beginning-level words on a list of 40 words, novices
who read 1–11 words, and veterans who read 11–36 words. Of particular
interest were the novice readers who could read only a few words, certainly
fewer than 40. We reasoned that if Gough is right, these children should find
it easier to learn to read words having distinctive visual cues than words having phonetic cues, whereas if we are right, they should learn the phonetic
spellings more easily than the visual spellings.

Results are displayed in Fig. 5.2. Statistical tests revealed that the novices
learned to read the phonetic spellings significantly faster than the visual
spellings. In fact, novices performed similarly to the more advanced beginning readers. These findings support our claim that children who have just
moved into word reading can use phonetic cues more effectively than visual
cues to read words. Interestingly, the subjects who found visual cues significantly easier to use than phonetic cues were the prereaders. This suggests
that Gough's portrayal of visual cue reading may apply more to *nonreaders*
than to novice beginning readers.

In this same study, we examined children's knowledge of alphabet letters
and found that the novices had mastered letter names but the prereaders had
not. These findings echo those in our print expert study and further support
our claim that one prerequisite for being able to process graphic cues effectively in words is knowing the shapes and names or sounds of alphabet letters.

We performed another study to validate the concept of phonetic cue reading and to explore how it differs from cipher reading (Ehri & Wilce, 1987).
We pretested kindergartners to select subjects who could not decode nonsense words but who knew letter–sound relations and could read a few real
words by sight. Half of the subjects were trained to read similarly spelled
nonsense words that included consonants and consonant blends preceding or
following vowels (e.g., SUS, LUS, SUST, BLIS). These were our cipher
readers. The other subjects rehearsed isolated letter–sound relations. These
were our phonetic cue readers. After training we compared cipher and cue

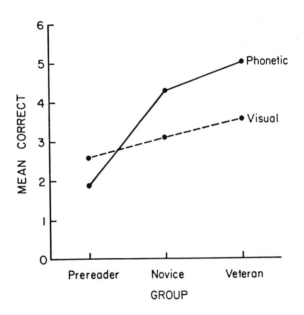

FIG. 5.2. Mean number of phonetic and visual spellings identified correctly in the word-learning task by prereaders, novices, and veteran beginning readers. Source: Ehri and Wilce (1985). Reprinted by permission of *Reading Research Quarterly*.

readers' skill in learning to read 15 similarly spelled real words (e.g., spin, stab, stamp, lap, lamp). Also their memory for spellings of these words was measured.

Results showed that training was effective. On a nonsense word decoding posttest, cipher readers were far superior to cue readers. Also, in learning to read the 15 real words, cipher readers clearly outperformed cue readers. Across 7 trials, cipher readers learned to read almost all of the words, whereas cue readers learned to read only about 30%. Whereas cipher readers showed consistent gains across trials, cue readers were erratic. Often they would read a word correctly on one trial and then fail to read it correctly on a later trial. Analysis of the words they read and then continued to read correctly revealed that cipher readers read twice as many words consistently (72%) as cue readers (35%) across trials.

It was not the case that cue readers were processing non-alphabetic visual cues. When they misread words, they produced a reasonable pronunciation for 52% of the letters they saw in the spellings. This indicates that cue readers were using letter–sound cues. However, they were not attending to as many graphemic cues as cipher readers who pronounced 66% of the letters in their misreadings.

Most of the cue readers' misreadings (81%) were other words that shared letters with the printed words on the list, particularly initial letters. The most common errors were misreading LAP as "lamp" and STAB as "stamp." This is evidence that cue readers were mixing up words on the basis of partial letter cues.

Interestingly, cue readers made some semantic errors, misreading "light" or "lantern" for LAMP, "bang" or "shot" for BLAST; "baby" for BIB. Some of these words were suggested by sentence contexts that had accompanied the word during the learning trials. No cipher reader produced any semantic misreadings of this kind. One explanation is that cipher readers' misreadings were controlled more by graphemic cues than cue readers' misreading. It may be that when readers begin attending primarily to letter–sound cues in reading words, semantically related words are suppressed because readers realize that sounds in the words do not match up well enough with spellings.

In recalling spellings of the words they read, cipher readers generally outperformed cue readers, particularly in spelling consonant clusters correctly (i.e., 70% vs. 12% correct). This shows that teaching beginners to decode consonant clusters enables them to spell these sounds even without direct spelling instruction, perhaps because decoding training teaches how to analyze consonant blends into two sounds. Without training, only one sound is detected (Treiman, 1985).

There was one spelling measure that did not distinguish cipher from cue readers statistically. This involved their memory for initial and final letters in words (i.e., 79% correct by cue readers vs. 90% correct by cipher readers). One reason why phonetic cue readers remembered initial and final letters so well may be because these served as the phonetic cues that they used during the word-reading task. The spellings of one cue reader provided extra support for this. She spelled 97% of the first and final letters correctly but few middle letters correctly. In addition, when she wrote these words, she capitalized the initial and final letters as they had appeared in the words she had seen, but she wrote most of the medial letters in lowercase, even though these too had been seen in capital letters. These behaviors suggest that this cue reader attended to and remembered boundary letters during the word-reading task but ignored medial letters.

Findings of this study show that acquiring the ability to decipher print offers clear advantages. It enables readers to learn to read similarly spelled words accurately and consistently and also to spell words. Also findings support our claim that there is another way to read words besides memorizing visual features and besides decoding letters into sounds. This way was exhibited by our phonetic cue readers who attempted to process a few salient letter–sound relations and store these associations in memory. This mechanism of word reading may explain how not only novice beginning readers but also older disabled readers are able to read words. We know from other studies that disabled readers have weak decoding skill and spelling skill yet they are able to read many real words (Ehri, 1986; Ehri & Wilce, 1983; Perfetti & Hogaboam, 1975). The explanation usually given is that poor readers remember visual cues in words (Gough & Hillinger, 1980). However, visual associations are harder to remember than phonetic associations. It may be that poor readers read words by processing and remembering phonetic cues. This possibility awaits further investigation.

Acquisition of a Print Lexicon. We have conducted other studies to examine how readers at the cipher stage become able to read specific words as sight words by storing their printed forms in lexical memory (Ehri, 1978, 1980a, 1980b, 1984, 1985). Our theory is that spellings of words are stored by amalgamating their orthographic identities with the other identities already present in memory: most importantly the phonological identity, but also the syntactic and semantic identities (Ehri & Roberts, 1979; Ehri & Wilce, 1980a). Amalgamation between the spellings of words and their phonological identities occurs when readers analyze how individual letters symbolize phonemic constituents in pronunciations. To do this, readers must know the particular phonemes that letters typically symbolize, and they must know how to segment pronunciations into phonemes in order to match up letters to these constituents. For example, in reading and remembering the word "rich," they must recognize how the graphemic units, R, I, and the digraph CH each symbolizes a phoneme in the pronunciation. To the extent that letters are processed in this way, spellings of individual words are retained in memory as the word's visual representation. This view contrasts with the alternative view, referred to as dual route theory, that the visual forms of words are stored in memory separately and independent of their pronunciations (Baron, 1977). We have conducted several studies to obtain evidence that spellings function as symbols for phonemes in memory.

We conducted a study to determine whether letters can aid in preserving nonsense sounds in memory when the letters provide an adequate printed symbol for the sounds (Ehri & Wilce, 1979a). A common example of spellings functioning as mnemonics for sounds is when people attempt to enhance their memory for an unfamiliar name by inquiring how the name is spelled. In this study, we used a paired-associate learning task. Young readers (first and second graders) were given several trials to learn four oral non-sense words such as "mav," "rel," "kip," and "guz." Recall of these responses was prompted by numbers. During study periods, children saw either correct spellings of the sounds, or misspellings, or they rehearsed the sounds orally. On test trials, only the numbers were presented and children recalled the sounds. We found that children learned the sounds fastest when they viewed correct spellings during study periods. Looking at misspellings made it especially hard to learn the sounds. Our interpretation is that memory was improved because the spellings were retained as visual symbols preserving the sounds in memory. In this study, we observed a very high correlation between young readers' ability to use letters mnemonically and the size of their print lexicons. This encouraged us in our belief that letter–sound symbolization underlies readers' ability to store printed words in memory.

We conducted several other studies whose results also indicated that spellings are stored in memory as symbols for the pronunciations of words. We found that silent letters in spellings (e.g., the T in "listen") are harder to remember than pronounced letters but that, once stored, are more salient in the memory representation, presumably because silent letters are singled out as exceptions by the letter–sound symbolization process (Ehri & Wilce, 1982). We found that the process of learning spellings of words influences learners' beliefs about the sounds that comprise words. For example, learners who know the spellings of "rich" and "pitch" think that "rich" has three sounds but "pitch" has four sounds, including an extra /t/ symbolized by the letter T and detected as a separate alveolar unit in articulation (Ehri & Wilce, 1980b). Speakers who know how "interesting" is spelled tend to think that the word has four syllables corresponding to the spelled syllables, whereas speakers who do not know the spelling perceive three syllables (Ehri, 1984, 1985). Although American speakers pronounce the alveolar flap in the middle of words such as "la dder," "le tter," "me dal," and "a ttic" identically as a sound closer to /d/ than to /t/, speakers who know the spellings of the words think that the sounds are different, either /t/ or /d/ depending upon how the sounds are spelled (Ehri & Wilce, 1986). According to our view, spellings influence speakers' beliefs about the sounds in words because speakers learned the spellings by interpreting letters as symbols for sounds. The spellings continue to sit in memory and indicate what sounds are in the words.

Studies by other researchers have also provided evidence for this idea. Seidenberg and Tanenhaus (1979) found that spellings influence subjects' performances in oral language tasks. They had subjects listen to a succession of nouns such as "glue" and "shoe" and decide whether each rhymed with the target word "clue." They found that subjects responded faster to words having spellings that were similar to the target word, in this case, "glue," than to words with different spellings, such as "shoe." Also, it was found that when words had similar spellings but did not rhyme, for example, "bomb" and"tomb," subjects took longer to make negative rhyming decisions than they did with words having different spellings and pronunciations, for example, "bomb" and "room." Spellings of words were neither shown nor mentioned so their effects had to come from subjects' memories.

There is evidence that printed language acts to constrain phonological drift, a term referring to changes in the pronunciations of words that occur in communities of speakers over time. According to Gelb (1952), English pronunciations have changed relatively little over the last four or five hundred years as a result of its writing system. This contrasts with dramatic shifts that occurred prior to that time. Also, this contrasts with rapid linguistic changes that are evident in modern primitive societies that lack a phonemic writing system. Gelb claims that some American Indian languages are changing so fast that people of the present generation have difficulty conversing with people three or four generations older. Further support for Gelb's claim is presented by Bright (1960) and Bright and Ramanujan (1962), who compared phonological drift in several South Asian Indian communities that spoke various dialects. They found less phonological drift in communities that had a written form of language than in communities that had only a spoken form. According to our theory, the reason why written language freezes pronunciations and inhibits phonological change is that spellings cast pronunciations into fixed phonemic forms. The letters specify which phonemes are there, and because speakers hold these in memory, they are reminded of the forms and adhere to them in their speech.

We interpret these studies to show that the process of learning to read and spell words is a major occurrence during the course of language development because it influences people's linguistic competence and functioning in important ways. During acquisition, print works its way into the minds of learners and influences how they perceive and process speech. Learning how the spelling system tracks speech enhances people's awareness of and ability to manipulate phoneme constituents in their language. Learning the spellings of specific words provides people with visual symbols of their pronunciations. The symbols sit in memory and influence how people conceptualize sounds in the words, how they say the words, and how they process relationships among spoken words. Thus, the study of how children learn to read and spell is important not only for applied reasons having to do with skill acquisition and school achievement but also for clarifying our basic understanding of how linguistic information-processing equipment develops.

SUMMARY

In this chapter we have argued that learning to read and spell words is a central part of becoming literate. During text reading, most words are processed, and skilled readers are able to do this effortlessly. How they become skilled at processing graphemic cues has been the focus of our research. Findings indicate that prereaders do not acquire graphemic skill by learning to read signs and labels in their environment. Rather, mastery of letters is required. Whereas prereaders use visual or context cues to identify words, as soon as children move into reading they shift to letter–sound cues. Initially, words are read by accessing remembered associations between a few letters in spellings and sounds in pronunciations. Later, when decoding skill matures, complete spellings are analyzed as phonemic symbols for pronunciations and are stored in memory. Various studies indicate that having visual "pictures" of spoken words in memory is an important part of a person's information-processing equipment. Spellings may influence how words are pronounced, what sounds people think are in words, how quickly people judge spoken word rhymes, how rapidly pronunciations change over time.

ACKNOWLEDGMENT

This chapter is a revised version of an article by L. C. Ehri that appeared in the *Journal of Reading Behavior*, 1987, Volume 19, pp. 5–31, entitled, "Learning to read and spell words." Parts are reprinted by permission.

REFERENCES

Baron, J. (1977). Mechanisms for pronouncing printed words: Use and acquisition. In D. LaBerge & S. J. Samuels (Eds.), *Basic processes in reading : Perception and comprehension* (pp. 175–216). Hillsdale, NJ: Lawrence Erlbaum Associates.

Biemiller, A. (1970). The development of the use of graphic and contextual information as children learn to read. *Reading Research Quarterly, 6,* 75–96.

Bradley, L., & Bryant, P. E. (1983). Categorizing sounds and learning to read—A causal connection. *Nature, 301,* 419–421.

Bright, W. (1960). Linguistic change in some Indian caste dialects. In C. A. Ferguson & J. J. Gumperz (Eds.), *Linguistic diversity in South Asia. International Journal of American Linguistics, 26,* 19–26.

Bright, W., & Ramanujan, A. K. (1962). Sociolinguistic variation and language change. In H. G. Lunt (Ed.), *Proceedings of the Ninth International Congress of Linguistics.* Cambridge, MA: Mouton.

Carpenter, P. A., & Just, M. A. (1981). Cognitive processes in reading: Models based on readers' eye fixations. In A. M. Lesgold & C. A. Perfetti (Eds), *Interactive processes in reading.* Hillsdale, NJ: Lawrence Erlbaum Associates.

Chall, J. (1967). *Learning to read: The great debate.* New York: McGraw–Hill.

Chall, J. S. (1979). The great debate: Ten years later with a modest proposal for reading stages. In L. G.

Resnick & P. A. Weaver (Eds), *Theory and practice of early reading* (Vol. 1, pp. 29–56). Hillsdale, NJ: Lawrence Erlbaum Associates.

Chall, J. S. (1983). *Stages of reading development*. New York: McGraw-Hill.

Ehri, L. C. (1978). Beginning reading from a psycholinguistic perspective: Amalgamation of word identities. In F. B. Murray (Ed.), *The recognition of words* (pp. 1–33). IRA Series on the Development of the Reading Process. Newark, DE: International Reading Association.

Ehri, L. C. (1979). Linguistic insight: Threshold of reading acquisition. In T. G. Waller & G. E. Mackinnon (Eds.), *Reading research: Advances in theory and practice* (Vol. 1). New York: Academic Press.

Ehri, L. C. (1980a). The development of orthographic images. In U. Frith (Ed.), *Cognitive processes in spelling*. London: Academic Press.

Ehri, L. C. (1980b). The role of orthographic images in learning printed words. In J. Kavanagh & R. Venezky (Eds.), *Orthography, reading and dyslexia*. Baltimore: University Park Press.

Ehri, L. C. (1983). Critique of five studies related to letter name knowledge and learning to read. In L. Gentile, M. Kamil, & J. Blanchard (Eds.), *Reading research revisited* (pp. 143–153). Columbus, OH: Merrill.

Ehri, L. C. (1984). How orthography alters spoken language competencies in children learning to read and spell. In J. Downing & R. Valtin (Eds.), *Language awareness and learning to read* (pp. 119–147). New York: Springer Verlag.

Ehri, L. C. (1985). Effects of printed language acquisition on speech. In D. Olson, N. G. Torrance, & A. Hildyard (Eds.), *Literacy, language and learning: The nature and consequence of reading and writing*. Cambridge, England: Cambridge University Press.

Ehri, L. C. (1986). Sources of difficulty in learning to spell and read. In M. I. Wolraich & D. Routh (Eds.), *Advances in developmental and behavioral pediatrics* (Vol. 7, pp. 121–195). Greenwich, CT: JAI Press.

Ehri, L. C., & Roberts, K. (1979). Do beginners learn printed words better in context or isolation? *Child Development, 50*, 675–685.

Ehri, L. C., & Wilce, L. S. (1979a). The mnemonic value of orthography among beginning readers. *Journal of Educational Psychology, 71*, 26–40.

Ehri, L. C., & Wilce, L. S. (1979b). Does word training increase or decrease interference in a Stroop task? *Journal of Experimental Child Psychology, 27*, 352–364.

Ehri, L. C., & Wilce, L. S. (1980a). Do beginners learn to read function words better in sentences or in lists? *Reading Research Quarterly, 15*, 451–476.

Ehri, L. C., & Wilce, L. S. (1980b). The influence of orthography on readers' conceptualization of the phonemic structure of words. *Applied Psycholinguistics, 1*, 371–385.

Ehri, L. C., & Wilce, L. S. (1982). The salience of silent letters in children's memory for word spellings. *Memory and Cognition, 104*, 155–166.

Ehri, L. C., & Wilce, L. S. (1983). Development of word identification speed in skilled and less skilled beginning readers. *Journal of Educational Psychology, 75*, 3–18.

Ehri, L. C., & Wilce, L. S. (1985). Movement into reading: Is the first stage of printed word learning visual or phonetic? *Reading Research Quarterly, 20*, 163–179.

Ehri, L. C., & Wilce, L. S. (1986). The influence of spellings on speech: Are alveolar flaps /d/ or /t/? In D. Yaden & S. Templeton (Eds.), *Metalinguistic awareness and beginning literacy*. Exeter, NH: Heinemann.

Ehri, L. C., & Wilce, L. S. (1987). Cipher versus cue reading: An experiment in decoding acquisition. *Journal of Educational Psychology, 79*, 3–13.

Fox, B., & Routh, D. K. (1975). Analyzing spoken language into words, syllables, and phonemes: A developmental study. *Journal of Psycholinguistic Research, 4*, 332–342.

Fox, B., & Routh, D. K. (1976). Phonemic analysis and synthesis as word-attack skills. *Journal of Educational Psychology, 68*, 70–74.

Gelb, I. J. (1952). *A study of writing*. Chicago: University of Chicago Press.

Glushko, R. J. (1979). The organization and activation of orthographic knowledge in reading aloud. *Journal of Experimental Psychology: Human Perception and Performance, 5*, 674–691.

Glushko, R. J. (1981). Principles for pronouncing print: The psychology of phonography. In A. M.

Lesgold & C. A. Perfetti (Eds.), *Interactive processes in reading* (pp. 61–84). Hillsdale, NJ: Lawrence Erlbaum Associates.

Goodman, K. S. (1970). Reading: A psycholinguistic guessing game. In H. Singer & R. B. Ruddell (Eds.), *Theoretical models and processes of reading* (pp. 497–508). Newark, DE: International Reading Association.

Goodman, K. S., & Goodman, Y. M. (1979). Learning to read is natural. In L. B. Resnic & P. A. Weaver (Eds.), *Theory and practice of early reading* (Vol. 1, pp. 137–154). Hillsdale, NJ: Lawrence Erlbaum Associates.

Goodman, Y. M., & Altwerger, B. (1981). Print awareness in preschool children: A working paper. *A study of the development of literacy in preschool children.* Occasional Papers No. 4, Program in Language and Literacy, University of Arizona.

Goswami, U. (1986). Children's use of analogy in learning to read: A developmental study. *Journal of Experimental Child Psychology, 42,* 73–83.

Gough, P. B., & Hillinger, M. (1980). Learning to read: An unnatural act. *Bulletin of the Orton Society, 30,* 180–196.

Guttentag, R. E., & Haith, M. M. (1978). Automatic processing as a function of age and reading ability. *Child Development, 49,* 707–716.

Harste, J. C., Burke, C. L., & Woodward, V. A. (1982). Children's language and world: Initial encounters with print. In J. Langer & M. Smith-Burke (Eds.), *Bridging the gap: Reader meets author* (pp. 105–131). Newark, DE: International Reading Association.

Kay, J., & Marcel, T. (1981). One process not two in reading aloud: Lexical analogies do the work of nonlexical rules. *Quarterly Journal of Experimental Psychology, 33,* 397–413.

LaBerge, D., & Samuels, S. J. (1974). Toward a theory of automatic information processing in reading. *Cognitive Psychology, 6,* 293–323.

Liberman, I. Y., & Shankweiler, D. (1979). Speech, the alphabet and teaching to read. In L. B. Resnick & P. A. Weaver (Eds.), *Theory and practice of early reading* (Vol. 2, pp. 109–132.). Hillsdale, NJ: Lawrence Erlbaum Associates.

Marsh, G., Friedman, M., Welch, V., & Desberg, P. (1981). A cognitive-developmental theory of reading acquisition. In G. E. Mackinnon & T. G. Waller (Eds.), *Reading research: Advances in theory and practice* (Vol. 3, pp. 199–221). New York: Academic Press.

Mason, J. (1980). When *do* children begin to read: An exploration of four-year-old children's letter and word reading competencies. *Reading Research Quarterly, 15,* 203–227.

Mason, J. M., & Allen, J. (1986). A review of emergent literacy with implications for research and practice in reading. In E. Z. Rothkopf (Ed.), *Review of research in education* (Vol. 13, pp. 3–47). Washington DC: American Educational Research Association.

Masonheimer, P. E., Drum, P. A., & Ehri, L. C. (1984). Does environmental print identification lead children into word reading? *Journal of Reading Behavior, 16,* 257–271.

McConkie, G. W., & Zola, D. (1981). Language constraints and the functional stimulus in reading. In A. M. Lesgold & C. A. Perfetti (Eds.), *Interactive processes in reading* (pp. 155–175). Hillsdale, NJ: Lawrence Erlbaum Associates.

Morais, J., Cary, L., Alegria, J., & Bertelson, P. (1979). Does awareness of speech as a sequence of phones arise spontaneously? *Cognition, 7,* 323–331.

Otto, H., & Pizillo, C. (1970). Effect of intralist similarity on kindergarten pupils' rate of word acquisition and transfer. *Journal of Reading Behavior, 3,* 14–19.

Perfetti, C. A. (1985). *Reading ability.* New York: Oxford University Press.

Perfetti, C. A., & Hogaboam, T. (1975). Relationship between single word decoding and reading comprehension skill. *Journal of Educational Psychology, 67,* 461–469.

Rosinski, R. R., Golinkoff, R. M., & Kukish, K. S. (1975). Automatic semantic processing in a picture–word interference task. *Child Development, 46,* 247–253.

Seidenberg, M. S., & Tanenhaus, M. K. (1979). Orthographic effects on rhyme monitoring. *Journal of Experimental Psychology: Human Learning and Memory, 5,* 546–554.

Share, D. L., Jorm, A. F., Maclean, R., & Matthews, R. (1984). Sources of individual differences in reading acquisition. *Journal of Educational Psychology, 76,* 1309–1324.

Stanovich, K. E. (1980). Toward an interactive-compensatory model of individual differences in the development of reading fluency. *Reading Research Quarterly, 16,* 32–71.

Treiman, R. (1985). Phonemic analysis, spelling and reading. In T. Carr (Ed.), *New directions in child development: The development of reading skills* (27, pp. 5–18). San Francisco: Jossey-Bass.

Tunmer, W. E., & Hoover, W. (in preparation). Cognitive and linguistic factors in learning to read. In P. Gough, L. Ehri, & R. Treiman (Eds.), *Reading acquisition.* Hillsdale, NJ: Lawrence Erlbaum Associates.

Venezky, R. L. (1970). *The structure of English orthography.* The Hague: Mouton.

Weber, R. (1970). A linguistic analysis of first-grade reading errors. *Reading Research Quarterly, 5,* 427–451.

6

Experimental Analysis of the Child's Discovery of the Alphabetic Principle

Brian Byrne
Department of Psychology
The University of New England
Armidale, Australia

Educators who design programs to teach children to read, or indeed programs to teach anyone anything, make assumptions about the nature of the acquisition process, about how learning takes place. These amount to theories of learning. They may not be very explicit but they do guide curriculum design. It is one of the tasks of experimental psychology to examine learning processes in detail, and in this chapter I want to show how I have attempted to inspect the acquisition processes operating at the very earliest stages of reading acquisition. In doing so I hope to make clear what a theory of learning must do, and I hope to demonstrate that some of the assumptions made about the processes of learning to read may be unfounded.

EXPLAINING LEARNING

A full explanation of how anything is learned should specify the final state, the initial state, and the transition between them. The final state for the skilled, mature reader includes a variety of strategies for extracting meaning from print—direct access from the print sequence to the mental lexicon as well as the ability to pronounce previously unencountered and uncommon words on the basis of known letter–phoneme relations and a phoneme blending routine. Most of the attention of this chapter is on *decoding*, the term often given to this latter set of skills. It is clear that somewhere in the course of reading acquisition it must be learned.

The initial state, as far as reading is concerned, includes the child's useable knowledge of the units of speech that an alphabetic orthography represents, that is, phonemes. Work by other researchers reported in this volume (e.g., Liberman, Treiman) has shown that the preliterate child has only limited access to the phonemic principle: Liberman, Shankweiler, Fischer, and Carter (1974) discovered that young children could segment words into syllables but not into phonemes; Treiman and Breaux (1982) demonstrated that preliterate children could not readily group words on the basis of a common phoneme, suggesting that they were not aware of the identity of, say, the initial segments in *bat* and *big*. Because mature readers know that alphabetic writing systems are based on the segmental structure of speech and on the identity of segments in various words, the question to be faced is how the knowledge is acquired.

Acquiring the Alphabetic Principle: Competing Hypotheses

There are at least two learning theories for how novice readers become aware of the systematic basis of an alphabetic orthography. One is that they deduce it from learning pairings of print and speech at the word level. A competing hypothesis is, simply, that they will only discover it if told about it. To a point, these assumptions about the learner are embodied in two contrasting curriculum styles, known as "whole word" and "phonics." In the experiments that follow I have attempted to put to the test the assumption that the child will deduce the basic facts of alphabetic writing from learning whole words. To anticipate, the data I have gathered does not support the proposition that deduction of that kind will take place readily.

The Basic Experiment

In the basic experiment preschool children with no knowledge of reading or of the sounds of individual letters are taught to read just two English words, FAT and BAT. The question at stake is whether the children deduce that the letter F represents the phoneme /f/, and B, /b/, on the basis of their word knowledge. In principle they should be able to—F and B are the distinctive visual elements,and /f/ and /b/ the distinctive speech elements, and because they can now reliably link FAT and BAT with their spoken forms, linking the distinguishing elements is a possibility. This is what "whole word" curricula assume will happen, that is that the child will deduce the basic alphabetic principle from learning how to pronounce word-length print sequences. This amounts to attributing strong deductive powers to the child in this domain.

Here is the training procedure in a little more detail (for a full account, see Byrne, in preparation). Children were first screened for knowledge of letters (and words), and any who knew more than the names of a few letters were not tested further. The 11 selected preschoolers (average age, 53 months) first had to learn to place a card with FAT printed on it next to a picture of a fat boy, and one with BAT next to a picture of a bat. Once they could do this reliably, the pictures were removed and the children were asked to read the words on the cards ("fat" and "bat"), presented in random order. The training was considered complete once each child could read the words successfully on five successive presentations of the pair of words. For most children training was complete in a single session of about 10–15 minutes, whereas others needed two such sessions.

To discover if the children had deduced the sounds for F and B, they were asked, as an example, whether the printed word FUN said "fun" or "bun." They should be able to choose reliably if they had made the deduction even though they had never seen the word FUN before. This transfer procedure went as follows:

The experimenter drew a sketch of a (hamburger) bun and told the child what it was ("a bun"). Then some party balloons were drawn, and the child was told they were "fun." Immediately following, the printed word FUN was shown. The child was told it said bun or fun and asked to say which. The test sequence comprised eight such forced choices, each time using a pair of pictures and one word. The other items were the words BIG (drawing of a very tall house) and FIG (a fig), BELL (a bell) and FELL (a stick man on his back), and BIN (a garbage can) and FIN (shark with a prominent fin). On the first pass through the words FUN, BIG, FELL, and BIN were tested; then, using the same picture pairs, the words BUN, FIG, BELL, and FIN.

The results of this test procedure were quite clear—the children could not reliably choose the correct word, even though they were always ready to offer an answer rather than say they did not know. The average performance of 53% correct was not significantly different from the guessing rate of 50%. Hence I concluded that they had not deduced that the phonemes /f/ and /b/ correspond to F and B, respectively. This was despite being able to read a pair of words whose only distinguishing features were those sounds and those letters. Thus even though this is a very limited test of the hypothesis that young readers will work out how an alphabetic writing system operates at the letter level from learning to use it at the word level, it is not encouraging for that hypothesis.

Some Control Experiments

In experimental psychology we are alert to the fact that any set of results invites more than one explanation, and the standard tactic is to conduct further experiments to see which explanation is the best one available. One possibility with the basic experiment is that the testing technique, the forced-choice procedure with fun, bun, etc., is not a sensitive measure of the child's knowledge, that is, our young subjects *could* be deducing that F says /f/ etc., but the transfer technique does not indicate this because it is perhaps too complex a task for the children. To test this possibility we reran the transfer part of the experiment with older, kindergarten children who already knew what F and B said. They could not read any of the test words (FUN, BUN, FIG, etc.), so their responses could only be based on the relevant letter–phoneme knowledge. It turned out that all these children could successfully choose the words (fun, big, etc.), showing that if children have a firm grasp of letter–phoneme relations they can use this knowledge to solve the problem posed by the transfer test. Thus it is fair to conclude that the children in the basic experiment did not gain a firm grasp of the pronunciations of F and B as a result of the training conditions (learning to read FAT and BAT).

Another control experiment was concerned with the deductive powers of 4-year-old children for linguistic symbols standing for components of language above the phoneme level. One of the claims that exists in the literature is that young children have a particularly difficult time in isolating the phoneme as a linguistic unit, more difficult than the syllable or the word (the research of Liberman et al., 1974, mentioned earlier, makes this point). Thus it might be concluded that the results of the basic experiment are due to the opacity of the phoneme—children could hardly deduce that F represents /f/ if they do not have a clear idea of the separate identity of /f/ in the first place. But it may be, instead, that it is not phonemic awareness in particular but deduction of this kind in general that is deficient in children of such tender age. A test of this is to check the deductive process if the units are words rather than phonemes. This can be achieved by having preliterate children learn to read phrases like LITTLE BOY and BIG BOY and then test at transfer using items like LITTLE FISH—does it say "little fish" or "big fish"? If the children can do this successfully, it means that they *can* learn that symbols represent units of language (in this case that LITTLE stands for "little" and BIG for "big") and use this information in the transfer procedure, as long as the units are words rather than phonemes.

This is exactly what happened. Twelve preschoolers, mean age 52 months, were used and achieved a transfer performance of 69%, significantly above the chance performance of 50%. It appears, therefore, that deductive powers are established in young children sufficient to learn linguistic symbols, but not if phonemes are the symbols.

In other experiments reported in full in Byrne (in preparation), it has been demonstrated that the superior performance for word symbols is not due to the greater visual distinctiveness of whole words over single letters in ordinary printing. A series of studies was conducted using an invented symbol system (colored geometric forms) that was used uniformly to represent phrases like little boy, big boy, *and* words like fat, bat. The pattern of results remained the same as when actual English orthography was used—relations between the symbols and phonemes were not detected, whereas the children did notice the correspondences between the same symbols and whole words.

Extension Experiments

One cannot assume that the results reported so far are perfectly general. For instance, the letters F and B and their corresponding phonemes may be peculiarly problematic for children. Perhaps using other segments would result in improved deductive performance. This was tested, at least partly, by changing the word pair learned from FAT and BAT to SAT and MAT. The shift to S and M was not simply random. In the screening for letter knowledge, done to exclude children with more than the most fragmentary knowledge of letter–sound relations, it was noted that these letters were the best known, S in particular. Therefore it was possible that the sounds /s/ and /m/ were rather more obvious to children when embedded in words than other phonemes, including /f/ and /b/. If this were the case, the best chance for deductive learning of the links between letters and sounds might therefore exist if S and M were the distinguishing features (amongst children who did not already know these letters' sounds, of course).

But this change turned out not to help. Using SAT and MAT as the training items, and words like SUM, MUM, SOW, MOW for transfer testing, 13 preliterate children (mean age, 55 months) were subjected to the procedure of the basic experiment and produced a mean transfer performance score of 47% clearly not better than mere guessing. Thus failure to deduce letter–phoneme links from learning to read whole words appears not to be restricted to particular phonemes.

A second experiment designed to extend the basic finding involved an increase in the size of the training set to four words. One clear limitation to the generality of the work as so far described is that the children have only learned to read two items, and whereas the information about the correspondence between the distinctive letters and their respective phonemes exists in the array, there is not much pressure on the children to observe those links. For example, the young learners could, and probably do, create associations between the distinguishing letter (e.g., F and B) and the speech items as wholes ("fat" and "bat"). But if there are four items, say FAT, BAT, FIN, and BIN, then this learning strategy would fail. F, for example, appears in two words and cannot be the sole distinguishing stimulus for both. There is therefore some pressure on the child to discover the most basic mapping between print and speech, to realize in fact that F says /f/. A further reason for increasing the learning set is to move somewhat in the direction of what happens in real classrooms,where children learn to read many words over many months. (Note, however, that in some recent work from Seymour and Elder, 1986, it was shown that even after a year's tuition in a whole-word method most of their children could only read words they had been taught, that is, they had not discovered enough about the alphabetic principle to be able to decode new words. The correspondence between their findings and the results of these experiments described so far, both of which indicate that learning whole words does not necessarily lead to insights into the alphabetic principle, suggest that the lack of classroom realism in the present research using small word families does not inherently undermine the applicability of the results to the educational setting.)

Learning to read the four words FAT, BAT, FIN, and BIN proved to be quite difficult for some of the preschoolers. Of the 14 selected, only 10 could reliably read them after 4 days of training (a few of the children did learn very quickly, however). So the attempt to put pressure on the children by making the acquisition more difficult was apparently successful. Despite this, at the transfer stage there was no evidence that the subjects had discovered the letter–phoneme relations. When asked to choose whether FUN said fun or bun, for instance, the children could only guess. Remember that they had learned to read two words with F in them (FAT and FIN), but the extra exposure did not result in the appropriate deduction. (This suggests that any method of teaching reading that relies on children gaining insight into the fundamental principle of the alphabetic system by learning a small list of related words does not work immediately, at least without instruction from a teacher about what the words have in common. It is an empirical question as to how much exposure is necessary for that technique to bear fruit, but it seems to be more than the logical minimum of two words with a common letter.)

One final variant of the basic experiment is worth reporting because it clearly reinforces the primary message of these experiments—that it is very difficult for preliterate children to discover how letters represent phonemes from learning to read whole words because of special problems associated with phonemes as detectable linguistic units.

The experiment was conceived in an attempt to ease the preliterate child into acquisition of letter–phoneme links via successful performance in the transfer stage at a more transparent linguistic level. The basic design was to test a group of children on the LITTLE BOY, BIG BOY task as reported earlier, and then to take the successful subjects through the FAT, BAT condition. To this end, 13 children were selected from a local kindergarten class (mean age, 63 months). They were screened in the usual way for letter knowledge, which was minimal and included none of the critical letters. The subjects were older than their counterparts in the earlier experiments, a deliberate move to try to ensure a higher level of performance at transfer. Successful generalization, on LITTLE FISH, BIG FISH, etc., was defined as 7 or 8 out of 8 correct. Of the 13 children, 10 reached this criterion, 3 scoring 7 and the rest 8. These 10 were then taught to read FAT and BAT (in both training conditions, geometric forms were used rather than actual English print). Following this, the transfer procedure was used to test for deduction of symbol–phoneme relationships.

Mean transfer performance on FUN, BUN, etc. was only 45%. The highest score was 5 out of 8. Thus, being successful in transfer at the word level is of no assistance when it comes to the phoneme level. The failure of these particular children to deduce symbol–sound relationships could not have been due to a generalized failure in this kind of task. There really is something opaque about the phoneme.

THE ACQUISITION PROCESS FOR READING

I believe that the research I have reported sheds some light on the acquisition strategy children adopt as they learn to read their first few words. They learn to associate some distinguishing feature of a printed word with its spoken counterpart as a whole. They do not readily detect correspondences at the more basic phonemic level. Theories of the child-as-learner that assume that deduction of letter–phoneme relations will readily follow whole-word learning are in error, at least for children of the age used here and for the training and testing conditions in place in these experiments. The research of Seymour and Elder (1986), cited earlier, indicates that this "nonanalytic" acquisition strategy will in fact persist over much longer time periods and in natural classroom settings. Children who fail to supplement rote learning of whole words with discovery of the alphabetic principle are clearly headed for trouble as far as reading is concerned. There is a limit the number of print sequences one can commit to memory, and available data tell us that a substantial proportion of children with reading difficulties have not abandoned the whole-word strategy and have reached the limits of their memories (Boder, 1973; Johnston, 1985; Snowling, 1980).

Discovering the Alphabetic Principle

If deduction of the basic structure of alphabetic orthography does not automatically occur once the child has learned to read families of related words, how can discovery of this principle be fostered? One suggestion that has been made is that the learner needs to be made aware of the segmental nature of the speech stream, that is, of the existence of phonemes (see Gleitman &

Rozin, 1977, for one of the earlier statements of this hypothesis). I close this chapter with a brief account of how this idea can be tested using the techniques I have been describing. The experiments have been done in conjunction with Ruth Fielding-Barnsley, and are reported in full in Byrne and Fielding-Barnsley (1989).

The basic structure of these experiments is to provide preliterate children with increasing amounts of information about phonemic structure and how letters represent phonemes in the hope that a point will be reached when the children have a clear grasp of the alphabetic principle. The interest is, of course, where that point lies.

We began with 12 children, screened in the usual way to ensure minimal or nonexistent knowledge of the alphabet. They were first subjected to a new training routine that aimed to alert the children to the separability of the initial sounds in all the training and transfer items of the SAT, MAT set. The child was required to break each word up ("s...at," "m...at," "s...ow," "m...ow," and so on). The experimenter exemplified the segmentation and provided feedback on performance. We discovered that only 8 of the 12 children could segment the words successfully. All 12 children were then taught to read SAT and MAT and subsequently tested in the transfer task ("does SOW say sow or mow," etc.) to see if those who had learned to segment could now perform well at transfer. Our reasoning was that awareness of the separate status of /s/ and /m/ might result in the deduction that these segments are represented by separate visual symbols. As it turned out, however, not 1 of the 8 successful segmenters performed to criterion (7 out of 8) on the transfer task. Nor did the other 4 children. It seems that awareness of segmental structure of the words being learned does not guarantee the emergence of insight into the alphabetic principle.

We then trained a second aspect of phonemic awareness, segment identity. Because a child can segment, say, sat and sum, it does not follow that he or she is aware of the identity of the two initial segments (see Treiman & Breaux, 1982). But recognition of identity is part of the alphabetic principle, and it may be necessary to train this knowledge. Our training procedure involved the children telling us which word out of a pair (e.g., "sum" or "mum") starts with the same sound as "sat." After working through all the training and transfer words, with feedback, we again discovered that only some of the preschool children were successful—5 out of the 12. Four of these were also the successful ones on the segmentation task. We now retrained the basic reading items, SAT and MAT, and reran the transfer procedure. But for a second time we were faced with continued failure at transfer even among the 4 children who passed at both phonemic awareness tasks. So knowing the segmental structure of words and the identity of the segments (e.g., the /s/ in"sat" and "sum") does not translate into ability to link this knowledge with visual symbols that represent the segments.

Finally, we trained all these 12 children directly in symbol–phoneme relations. We taught them which symbol represented /s/ and which represented /m/, something all easily learned. Then we tested with the transfer procedure for a third time. Now we obtained a very interesting result. All 4 of the children who succeeded in both phonemic awareness tasks performed perfectly at transfer. One each of the children who succeeded at one of the two awareness tasks but not the other also performed well at transfer. But none of the remaining six children, all those who did not profit from either of the phonemic awareness tasks, performed to criterion at transfer *even though they had readily learned the symbol–phoneme relations in the final training session*. It appears that phonemic awareness by itself is not sufficient to produce alphabetic insights—it needs to be supplemented by direct letter–sound training. But learning the sounds that the letters represent is not sufficient either. It needs to be supplemented by appropriate insights into segment separability and segment identity. Phonemic awareness and letter–phoneme knowledge behave in a complementary fashion to generate an understanding of alphabetic orthography as children learn to read their first words.

Subsequent experiments (Byrne & Fielding-Barnsley, in press) have led us to favor instruction in phoneme identity as a vehicle for teaching phonemic awareness. For one thing, it is easier to teach than phoneme segmentation—that is, it is easier for children to reliably learn to notice that "sail" and "sun" start the same, or that "dog" and "jug" end the same, than to distort their speech to say "s...ail", "do...g", etc. Further, we have found that knowledge of phoneme identity is a firmer foundation for discovering the alphabetic principle than is segmentation ability. In one of our experiments, the correlation between identity score and subsequent transfer (our measure of alphabetic insight) was a statistically significant .49, whereas the segmentation-transfer correlation was only .20, nonsignificant statistically. We are encouraged in our view by the classroom success of an experimental program that had instruction in phoneme identity as the core activity (Bradley & Bryant, 1983). It is worth noting as well that Bradley and Bryant got their best results with children who not only learned about shared sounds in words but also how those sounds are represented by letters. It seems to be the same story—phonemic awareness combined with letter-sound knowledge forms a good basis for young children's progress in reading.

There are many gaps between the kind of research I have just outlined and good classroom practice. But experiments of this kind do help clarify the fine-grained structure of early reading acquisition, the transition from the initial state to mature reading. They suggest that whole-word-based curricula make assumptions about the deductive powers of young children that are unfounded and point to the wisdom of including both training in phonemic structure and in letter–phoneme relations in the teaching of reading.

ACKNOWLEDGMENTS

Much of the research reported in this chapter was funded by the Australian Research Council, with further financial help from the University of New England.

REFERENCES

Boder, M. (1973). Developmental dyslexia: A diagnostic approach based on three atypical reading–spelling patterns. *Developmental Medicine and Child Neurology, 15,* 663–687.

Bradley, L., & Bryant, P. E. (1983). Categorizing sounds and learning to read—a causal connection. *Nature, 301,* 419–421.

Byrne, B. (in preparation). Studies in the acquisition procedure for reading: Rationale, hypotheses, and data. In P. B. Gough, L. Ehri, & R. Treiman (Eds.), *Reading acquisition.* Hillsdale, NJ: Lawrence Erlbaum Associates.

Byrne, B., & Fielding-Barnsley, R. (1989). Phonemic awareness and letter knowledge in the child's acquisition of the alphabetic principle. *Journal of Educational Psychology, 81,* 313–321.

Byrne, B., & Fielding-Barnsley, R (in press). Acquiring the alphabetic principle: A case for teaching recognition of phoneme identity. *Journal of Educational Psychology.*

Gleitman, L. R., & Rozin, P. (1977). The structure and acquisition of reading I: Relations between orthographies and the structure of language. In A. S. Reber & D. L. Scarborough (Eds.), *Toward a psychology of reading: The proceedings of the CUNY conference.* Hillsdale, NJ: Lawrence Erlbaum Associates.

Johnston, P. H. (1985). Understanding reading disability. *Harvard Educational Review, 55,* 153–177.

Liberman, I. Y., Shankweiler, D., Fischer, F. W., & Carter, B. (1974). Explicit syllable and phoneme segmentation in the young child. *Journal of Experimental Child Psychology, 18,* 201–212.

Seymour, P. H. K., & Elder, L. (1986). Beginning reading without phonology. *Cognitive Neuropsychology, 3,* 1–36.

Snowling, M. (1980). The development of grapheme–phoneme correspondence in normal and dyslexic readers. *Journal of Experimental Child Psychology, 29,* 294–305.

Treiman, R., & Breaux, A. M. (1982). Common phoneme and overall similarity relations among spoken syllables: Their use by children and adults. *Journal of Psycholinguistic Research, 11,* 1982.

7 Individual Differences and Lexical Representations: How Five 6-Year-Old Children Search for and Copy Words

Laurence Rieben
Arianne Meyer
Christiane Perregaux
University of Geneva, Switzerland

INTRODUCTION

It is often difficult to judge the degree of real-world transferability of laboratory-based findings. This is as true in reading research as in any other research field and serves to highlight the importance of studies that investigate beginning reading in an everyday classroom situation. Indeed, fundamental research findings could be more directly useful to teachers when such findings have in part come from classroom research and demonstrate the application of basic research results to the school environment.

The exploratory research described in this chapter aims to study children's construction of lexical representations by observing how five beginning readers/writers looked for and copied words while producing a written text in classroom. It is a case study whose purposes are to underline, from a longitudinal perspective, the importance of individual differences in representational construction and to illustrate how a classroom study, even with its imperfections from a research methodology point of view, can be used to highlight the applications of research.

The Question of Lexical Representations

Reading and writing are sometimes described as using the resources of one or more memories containing representations of the meaning of words and visual and/or auditory images of the form of individual words. This lexical memory might contain, among other things, representations involving specific information about the individual letters comprising different words and might be consulted during both activities of reading and writing.

The question that arises is how do children construct these representations, and how are they modified as the child gains increasing mastery of the written language? Do there exist different ways of arriving at this construction, and does an individual child always refer to the same representations when moving from the role of reader to that of writer?

Ferreiro considers the observable stages in the production of writing as indicators reflecting the more general levels of conceptualization of the written language itself (Ferreiro, 1977; Ferreiro & Gomez Palacio, 1983; Ferreiro & Teberosky, 1982). In a first stage, to write would mean producing marks differing from an abstract design by several characteristics typical of writing, but the same sequence of letters might represent different words.

Next, the child would realize that different words must be written differently, that the order and number of graphemes play a role. Ferreiro considers these first two stages as being presyllabic because the child would not yet have established the correspondence between the graphic and the phonic elements. During the third stage the child would establish some correspondences at the syllabic level; a letter, arbitrary or conventional, would represent a syllable. Finally, at the fourth level, the child would become aware of the letter–phoneme system.

It is especially pertinent to pose the lexical representation question in relation to the last two stages, because children seem to progress from one to the other very gradually around the age of 6–7, and indeed the two stages can even coexist for an individual child. Berthoud-Papandropoulou (1980) has in fact shown that, at around 6 years of age, children talk spontaneously about letters when trying to define what words are. According to Perfetti (this volume), the acquisition of functional lexical representations would consist not only of the entries themselves (the number of words represented in the memory) but also in changes in the quality of the representations. There are two criteria to describe the qualitative changes: degree of precision and redundancy.

The beginning reader would have variable and incomplete representations, limited to certain graphical elements in certain positions; the missing elements can be considered as free, empty, or "floating" variables. The more advanced reader, on the other hand, will have more complete representations taking account of all the letters. For example, the beginning reader might have an imprecise representation of the word "mountain" with nonspecified letters representing the phonemes [ou], [n], [ei], and [n], that is to say a representation approaching the graphical image "m * t *" in which those parts of the word represented by asterisks would not be specified, either by the choice or number of letters involved.

As the representations become more and more precise, they progressively exhibit more and more redundancy. For the very beginning reader there would be little or no redundancy. In the example just given, the representation of the letter "m" for the word "mountain" would reflect the child's knowledge of the link between the grapheme "m" and the phoneme [m]. Later, the more complete representation of the group of letters "moun" could simultaneously reinforce the child's awareness of the correspondence between each of the phonemes [m], [ou], and [n] and their graphical forms "m," "ou," and "n" but could also reinforce the knowledge that "moun," as a whole, corresponds to [moun].

According to Perfetti these imprecise and low-redundancy representations would be characterized by their instability and amenability to change. Moreover, at some given point during the course of development the subject would use the same representations when reading as when writing.

This last hypothesis has not been very systematically tested. The links between reading and orthography have mainly been studied through correlational methods. In the model tested by Juel, Griffith, and Gough (1986), recognizing and writing words are tightly connected and appear to tap the same sources, code knowledge and specific lexical knowledge. Mann, Tobin, and Wilson (1987) show that the degree of precision in the grapheme/phoneme correspondence with which children of 5–6 years of age write words is highly predictive of reading ability 1 year later. In the same vein, Shanahan (1984) confirms the link between reading and orthography. But correlational studies such as these provide little information about the similarity of the processes or strategies involved in the acquisition of reading and writing skills.

There are a few studies that compare word recognition and writing strategies among learners (Ehri, 1980; Marsh, Friedman, Welch, & Desberg, 1980), and which reveal a parallelism in the acquisition of the two facets of the written language. On the other hand, taking into account examples of children able to write words they cannot read, Bryant and Bradley's results (1980) seem to indicate that, for learners, reading and writing are constructed on different representations. Nevertheless, it seems to us that any comparison between the ways in which children write under dictation or read the same words is not as direct as Bryant and Bradley suppose: In reading words the child must give attention to meaning, whereas during dictation this is predetermined. This distinction between the two situations could help explain why, on rare occasion, certain words can be written but not read, so that one cannot necessarily conclude anything about differences in their representations in memory.

It also seems to us possible to look for indicators concerning the lexical representations of beginning writers, for whom dictation is a difficult task, while observing copying activities. Some researchers have, in fact, studied how children copy expressions or isolated words (Fijalkow & Liva 1987; Prêteur & Telleria Jauregui, 1986; Rothkopf, 1980). In particular, the findings of Prêteur and colleagues demonstrate the tight relationship between reading ability and the strategies used for copying a sentence.

If the connections between the lexical representations of a beginning reader and beginning writer have been relatively little studied from a general standpoint, they have been even more rarely studied from the perspective of individual differences. The distinction between two reading styles, the "phoenicians" who rely more on the rules of grapheme/phoneme correspondence than on associations between particular words and their pronunciation, and the "chinese" who do the opposite (Baron & Strawson, 1976), has been found also in regard to writing (Treiman, 1984). However, this last study concerned children aged 9–10 years, and it remains an open question whether these styles of word recognition can be observed already in operation among beginning readers and writers. This is why we looked for a school-based activity that could provide evidence of qualitative indicators concerning the lexical representations of children asked alternately to find words in a text and then to write them.

THE RESEARCH

Method

The children concerned were observed during an activity suggested by Hébrard (1977) and Clesse (1977) that they called "activité d'énonciation écrite." Following this approach, during first grade (6–7 years), children are required to produce their own personal versions of a part of a story created by the class as a whole and put into written form by the teacher, piece by piece, with the participation of the children. The teacher's written version constitutes a reference text (RT) that, during the children's follow-up work, functions as a "dictionary" in which the children are more or less assured of finding any words they might need while writing their own stories.

The interesting feature of this situation is that, starting from a spontaneous writing project, the child here has access to meaning before searching for and copying each word. Moreover, we hypothesize that the analyses and syntheses that the child engages in during copying and that are put into short-term memory (isolated letter, letter groups, isolated word, word groups) form the foundation for the lexical representations that are entered into long-term memory. This situation must therefore allow a comparison between word representations at the time the words are searched for in a text and at the time they are copied.

Children were observed in the individual phase of written production, and the results analyzed here concern most particularly the sequences in which children search for words in the RT and then write them. Observations were made on four different occasions (October, November, January, February) under comparable but not identical conditions because the RT was different each time. The RT was hung on the classroom wall in the form of three posters each measuring 70cm by 50cm (a facsimile of the text used for the October observations is in the appendix), and the children left their places to consult it as they felt the need. The teacher replied to all their questions and helped them, as necessary, to find the words they were looking for. It is important to note at this point that the relevant grapheme/phoneme correspondences were not systematically taught either before or during the observation period (for a more detailed account of the classroom situation and the observation methods see Rieben, in press).[1]

A test battery covering different aspects of written language was administered in October before the first classroom observation session was undertaken, and again in May, 3 months after the last session of observation. It included these subtests: (a) a test of environmental word recognition (for example Stop, Sinalco) in which the child was asked to read 15 everyday words, preferably spontaneously but otherwise with the aid of picture matching (for example, a Stop sign, bottle of Sinalco); (b) a test of reading comprehension; (c) a writing test in which the child would be asked to write his/her name, two simple expressions (un vélo, trois vélos), and a brief sentence based on a picture of a bicycle; and finally (d) Ferreiro's task (Ferreiro, 1978), which assesses the ability of children to establish correspondences between the elements of a written sentence and those of the same sentence presented orally. The adult wrote a short sentence, read it aloud, and then asked the child, in random order, if each of the words were written and if so, where. The task also assesses the ability to indicate word separation correctly when copying an unsegmented written sentence after hearing it read by the researcher (for example, "l'oursmangedumiel," thebeareatshoney). Eighteen months after the second and final administration of the test battery, an oral reading and comprehension test was administered

---

[1]In fact, as in other Genevan classrooms, the observed children had been introduced to segmentation in oral language in kindergarten (5–6 years). On the other hand, in contrast with other classes, they had not been introduced to systematic presentation of single letters, digrammes, or trigrammes (such as "au," "eau," "in," "ain") during first grade.

and the reading grades awarded by the teacher of the third grade were retrieved.

Subjects

The case study concerns five first graders. A brief description of each child is given and the results of the first administration of the test battery simultaneously summarized.

Annia. (6;9 at the time of the preliminary testing; low socioeconomic level). Her native language is Portuguese, but she speaks French fluently having been educated in Geneva from the age of 4. At the time of preliminary testing she could read only 1 of the 15 environmental words, and she was only helped a little in this word recognition task by pictures. She does not respond to the written instructions given in a brief text. Under dictation she cannot write a short sentence but, in response to written words [un vélo] she writes [nuevo], and for [trois vélos] she writes [1 2 (number 3 in mirror image) nuevo], which can be taken as evidence of knowledge of some rules of grapheme/phoneme correspondence. She is not aware of the existence of plural indicators. Annia knows how to write her name. In Ferreiro's task she thinks that all the words in a sentence must be written and can identify almost all of them correctly (level A in the analysis system proposed by Ferreiro). On request, she correctly separates the words in the unsegmented sentence but was not spontaneously aware of the need for the segmentation.

Diane. (6;6, middle socioeconomic level, French mother tongue). In October she can read 6 of the 15 environmental words and another 3 after picture matching. Her reading comprehension is good, which allows her to carry out the instructions correctly. Diane knows how to write her name; under dictation she writes *un vélo* for *un vélo* and *troi véloe* for *trois vélos*. She says, referring to plural, that one must "put something at the end of the words" and thinks that it is an *e*. When asked to write a sentence about a bicycle, she writes *le m muz* for *Je m'amuse*. In Ferreiro's task she thinks that all the words must be written and recognizes them easily; she is spontaneously aware of the need to segment and does so correctly.

Frank. (6;5, middle socioeconomic level, French mother tongue). At the time of the preliminary testing he reads 5 of the 15 environmental words then 3 more using the picture clues. He cannot yet read text. He knows how to write his name; under dictation he writes *vo* for *un vélo* and writes *vo* three times, in a column, for *trois vélos*. He is not aware of plural indicators and claims to be incapable of writing a short sentence about the bicycle picture. In Ferreiro's task he thinks that all the words must be written but makes many errors when identifying them in writing (points to "repare" for "voiture," "demain" for "repare," "du miel" for "miel"). He is not surprised by the unsegmented sentence and cannot insert spaces between words when copying it.

Laura. (6;8, low socioeconomic level). She is of Spanish mother tongue and speaks French correctly. She doesn't read any of the 15 words but recognizes 6 after picture matching. She cannot read text. She knows how to write her name but produces an apparently random sequence of letters *VES-eAZPTXiLA*, with the exception perhaps of the initial *v* and *e*, to write *un vélo*. When trying to write *trois vélos*, she reproduces the same relatively random letter string as before but this time with a number 3 in front; she is not aware of the existence of plural indicators. She produces another apparently random sequence of letters, *LAVEZXX/VALITZA*, later in the session claiming to have written *Je m'amuse au parc et dans le jardin*. It is interesting to note that she inserts a vertical bar in the middle of the letter sequence "because there must be a space." In Ferreiro's task she thinks that all the words must be written but makes some errors identifying them ("lance" for "ballon," "ballon" for "lance"). She is spontaneously aware of the need for word separation but doesn't succeed in practice in the segmentation task ("Lour smange dumiel").

Marta. (6;10, low socioeconomic level). She has Spanish mother tongue and speaks French correctly. She can read only one of the 15 words but can identify another 9 using the picture cues. She cannot read continuous text. Marta knows how to write her name but writes *nu vlo* for *un vélo* and *3 vlo* for *trois vélos*. She thinks that something changes to plurals but doesn't know what. She claims not to be able to write a sentence about the bicycle picture. In Ferreiro's task Marta thinks that all the words must be written but does not recognize them all correctly ("man" for "mange," "ed" for "de"). She is not spontaneously aware of segmentation but admits that "it's better" when segmented. Her written version of the sentence presented to her in unsegmented form is not segmented completely correctly ("Lours mang edumiel").

In summary, it seems that prior to the first observation session four of the five children could be considered nonreaders, the exception being Diane who was already by that time a beginning reader. All the children, though, had at least some isolated pieces of knowledge about the rules of grapheme/phoneme correspondence.

Categorization of the Word-Searching and Copying Strategies

The main observations made of the children were strategies for searching for words and for copying them. Given that the child wished to find a specific word in the reference text, one of several strategies must be used. We distinguish among five of them here: (1) strategies oriented by the context (CON), i.e., that depend on previous knowledge and text comprehension; (2) strategies based on global visual similarity (VIS); (3) strategies depending on grapho–phonemic cues (GPH); (4) strategies relying on syllabic cues (SYL); and finally (5) nonmediated strategies (NME), for which there was insufficient information available to make a classification.[2] Table 7.1 provides definitions of these types of strategy, including examples of each.

Other types of word-search strategy were observed in practice, but these were less directly concerned with the problem of word recognition (for example, copying more or less blindly a part of the text or asking for help with some pairs) and are not discussed here (for details see Rieben, 1989). It should be noted that more than one strategy can in principle be used when searching for a single word in text, because an individual child can use several strategies simultaneously, and because the same word can be the subject of many search instances.

Three types of strategy were distinguished during word copying: strategies of copying letter by letter (LPL) strategies of copying in strings comprising at least two letters (GRL) and strategies of copying by whole-word transfer (TGM). Table 7.2 presents the copying strategy definitions with examples. Analysis was carried out separately for monosyllabic words and for plurisyllabic words. For these latter a more detailed analysis was undertaken aiming at characterizing the letter strings involved. Four types of letter string were thus identified based on criteria suggested by Catach (1977): phonic syllable—for example, when copying *froid* the child writes the string *froi*; graphic syllable—for example, the child copies *donne* in two strings *don* and *ne*; syllables simultaneously graphic and phonic— for example, the child copies *coucher* in two strings *cou* and *cher*; other—for example, the child copies *couche* in two strings *co* and *uche*.

RESULTS

For the five subjects and four texts there were 95 instances of search strategies being deployed. Average percentage frequencies of use for the different types were as follows: 30% CON, 20% VIS, 6% GPH, 10% SYL, and 34% NME. As to copying strategies for multisyllabic words (we do not consider the results for copying monosyllabic words because these are less interesting in this context), 99 instances of strategy deployment were observed and cat-

---

[2]It should be stressed that these strategies are considered nonmediated from the observer's point of view. As far as the subject is concerned, they are the automated outcome of progressive construction and are in no case considered "immediate."

TABLE 7.1

Categorization of Word-Searching Strategies

---

1. *Contextually-based Strategies Requiring Previous Knowledge and Text Comprehension (CON).*
  a) *Precise Localization (PLO)*
The child locates exactly the section of text containing the required word. He correctly locates the word or identifies an alternative one to five words before or after the one being searched. Where a word is located correctly, the child explicity describes the strategy used, saying for instance, "I must Look in this line" or "I know that I can find it in the title."

  b) *Vague Localization (VLO)*
The child again locates that part of the text containing the relevant word, but in a less precise manner. He identifies an incorrect word six to ten words before or after the word being searched, saying for example, "I know it's on this page."

2. *Global Visual Similarity Strategies (VIS)*
The child identifies a wrong word having the same length as, and, in the case of monosyllabic words, having one letter or, in the case of longer words, two letters in common with the correct word: for instance, the child searches for "maison" and points to "animaux" or looks for "le" and finds "et."

3. *Grapho–phonemic Strategies (GPH)*
The child uses alphabetic code knowledge to identify grapheme–phoneme correspondences; for example, when looking for the word "trouve" he says, "I'm looking for a word beginning with [t]."

4. *Syllabic Strategies (SYL)*
The child uses syllabic cues; for instance, looking for "ensuite" the child locates "enfant" and says it's appropiate because of the "en."

5. *Nonmedicated Recognition (NME)*
The child locates quickly and correctly the required word without showing any overt behaviors that would allow categorization of the strategy employed.

---

egorized (26% LPL, 43% GRL, 31% TGM). To highlight individual differences the results are presented in Fig. 7.1, for the combined observations from all four observation sessions; they take the form of percentage deviations from the average percentage frequency of use, for each child and each type of strategy (for example, Annia showed 13% greater use of the CON group of strategies and 6% less use of VIS strategies than the average).[3] This combined presentation does not, of course, allow us to note any changes that

---

[3]Computed on all five subjects only, the mean percentage frequency of use must not be taken too seriously. However, to the extent that discussion of the findings for individual children requires some kind of comparative reference, we have opted for this mode of presentation. It is clear that the size of any deviation from the mean should be interpreted in relation to the average percentage frequencies of use for each type of strategy as indicated in the text.

TABLE 7.2

Categorization of Word-Copying Strategies

---

1. *Letter–by–Letter Transfer   (LPL)*
After having located the relevant word in the RT, the child writes it letter by letter. The child returns to his place, writes a letter, looks again at the RT or even leaves his place again to have a closer look, copies another letter, and so on until the entire word is written (for example, having found "maison" the child writes [m], looks at the RT, writes [a], looks again at the RT and writes [i], and so on).

2. *Letter String Transfer   (GRL)*
After having located the relevant word in the RT, the child returns to his place and writes at least two letters without consulting the RT again. The rest of the word might be written letter by letter or in letter strings. The number of letter strings reproduced corresponds with the number of return visits to consult the RT. The letter strings might constitute a syllable in initial, intermediate, or final position; on the other hand it might equally be nonsyllabic (for example, after having found "piscine" the child writes [p], looks at the RT and writes [i], looks again at the RT and writes [s], looks again and writes [c], loks again and writes [ine]).

3. *Whole–Word Transfer   (TGM)*
After having located the required word, the child returns to his desk and reproduces the entire word without consulting the RT again (for example, after having found "hamster" the child returns to his place and writes [hanrster] without looking at the RT).

---

might have taken place over the period spanned by the four observation sessions (for more detailed results see Rieben, 1989); such changes are discussed, case by case, as the findings for each child are presented, if they illustrate some particularly important feature.

For word searching *Annia* essentially used context-dependent strategies (CON), more so than the other four children. She also frequently used those strategies based on grapheme–phoneme correspondence (GPH). On the other hand, she showed a negative deviation score for those strategies dependent on a syllabic treatment (in fact she never used a syllabic (SYL) strategy during any of the four observation sessions). When copying, she almost exclusively used whole-word transfer (TGM). Annia, then, appealed above all to those strategies dependent on a global word treatment, as much during word searching as during copying. Her whole-word copies were often perfect even when the words copied comprise eight or nine letters (for example, "maîtresse" or "piscine"), a surprising performance considering her results in the preliminary assessment. However, it is interesting to note that when she transferred letter strings rather than whole words, 70% of these strings are arbitrary groupings from a linguistic point of view (for example, [Marie-Laure] is dissected [Mari/e-Laure] and [Pauline] becomes [b/a/uline].

It is interesting to relate these findings to the results of the final assessment and the posttest. Annia could still only identify nine of the 15 environ-

Word–searching strategies
(% frequency of use)

Word–copying strategies
(% frequency of use)

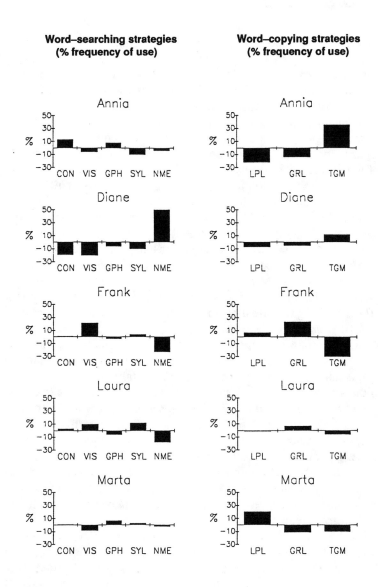

FIG 7.1

mental words (the poorest result of all five children). Her text-reading ability did not enable her to follow all the instructions. As to the writing of
words and sentences, one notes some confusion consistent with gaps in her
knowledge of the rules of grapheme–phoneme correspondence, even to the
extent of upper case/lower case confusion (for example, she wrote *je feu
Bouare du lai* for *Je veux boire du lait* or *Vitque* for *Victor*. Reading and
word-by-word segmentation of the unsegmented written sentence remained
difficult tasks for Annia ("Une/enfantest/sortie/del'eau"). She was still not
aware of the orthographic conventions for indicating noun plurals. One and
a half years later she was the poorest reader among the five children and,
relative to the demands of third-grade reading, she has reading problems.

Diane's results are very different. Having already begun to master reading
at the start of the observation study, her results illustrate the difficulty for the
researcher of finding evidence of the strategies being used when the relevant
skills are already, automated to a great extent. In fact we could record mostly
nonmediated strategies (NME). When copying words Diane essentially used
whole-word transfer strategies (TGM). When she broke words up into letter
strings (GRL), she gave attention to syllables simultaneously phonic and
graphic. So it seems that Diane already possessed completely specified representations of certain words, and that she could systematically cut words
into syllables that are equally relevant for written as for spoken language.
This last characteristic distinguishes her fundamentally from Annia.

As to the final assessment and posttest, Diane's results remained the best
of the five children. She could read the 15 words and follow the instructions
given in the text. Her writing of words and sentences testify to a good
knowledge of the rules of grapheme–phoneme correspondence and shows
that she uses graphic patterns (for example she writes *Victor mai une pantou-
fle dans sont lit*). She could without difficulty separate the words in the unsegmented written sentence and could apply the *s* rule for noun plurals.
Eighteen months later she remains the best reader among the five children
and her third-grade reading results were excellent.

For *Frank*, word searching was carried out using a variety of strategies.
He showed a clear change from the third observation session (January). In
fact, during the first two observation sessions Frank partially used global
visual similarity strategies (VIS), whereas syllabic strategies (SYL) made an
appearance from the third session. When copying words he never used
whole-word transfer (TGM) and dissected into strings which only rarely correspond with graphic and/or phonic syllables. It thus seems that he was more
systematically able as a reader to call on representations partially specified
in syllables than he was as a writer.

During the final assessment Frank could read the 15 words but could not
carry out all the instructions to be read in the text. While writing words and
sentences he appeared to master the grapheme–phoneme correspondence

and mainly exhibited orthographic errors (for example, he writes *Victor son a la port de la metson* for *Victor sonne à la porte de la maison*. The way in which he writes the word "maison" could illustrate the use of the specific representation of a word ("met" of the verb "mettre") or of a graphic pattern as an element of the representation of another word. Frank read with difficulty the unsegmented sentence, though he can segment it correctly. He knew that one must put an *s* for noun plurals and applied this rule. At the start of third grade his reading was still slow and syllabic, but correct. His comprehension was good and he knew how to use the text to find information. School assessments showed his performance as average for third grade.

In word searching, *Laura*, like Frank, mainly used VIS strategies in October and November and SYL strategies from January onwards. Her pattern also resembles Frank's in relation to word-copying strategies, with GRL strategies dominating (though her deviations from the mean are less marked). Among the GRL strategies more than half still involve arbitrary strings, which, again mirroring Frank, suggest that her call on syllabic representations is more systematic sending for than for copying. Laura differs from Frank, however, in the greater stability of her strategies; whereas Frank uses a variety of strategies during the same observation session, Laura demonstrates changes in strategy from one session to another.

During the final testing Laura read 13 of the 15 environmental words but only partially understood the text. For writing, her results were comparable with Frank's, including her use of graphic patterns (for example, she writes *Je boit du l'est* for *je boit du lait*. However, she experienced greater difficulty than Frank when faced with the unsegmented sentence, as much when reading it as when attempting to segment it ("Une/enfant/e/st/sortie/del'e/au"). By the start of third grade Laura read rapidly and with intonation, though still with a few hesitations and repetitions; her comprehension was good. Her school reading results were good too.

Marta's results are less complete, because she was absent from school during the third observation session. In regard to her word-searching strategies, she showed hardly any deviation from the average, other than a higher frequency of use of GPH strategies and a particularly low use of VIS strategies. Her word-searching and her writing strategies were almost the same. During word copying the letter-by-letter strategy (LPL) dominated (the highest percentage of use among all five children). Marta's lexical representations seemed very incomplete, because she often resorted to the use of an isolated grapheme. However, on the few occasions when Marta transferred letter strings, half of these correspond to syllables simultaneously graphic and phonic. This last result, which resembles that which we observed for Diane, could be a positive sign for predicting reading progress. But, and differing from the comments we made regarding Frank and Laura, her call on syllabic representations seems to work in parallel in word searching and word copying.

During the final administration of the test battery, Marta reads 14 of the 15 environmental words but did not fully understand the text. When writing the words and sentences she showed a good knowledge of grapheme–phoneme correspondence but still lacks reference to orthographic rules. For example, she writes *Je boi le lai* for *Je bois le lait*. She found difficulty reading the unsegmented sentence. Her word separation was incomplete in the sense that not all separations are indicated; those word separations she did indicate are correct and correspond among other things to the separation between the nominal group and the verbal group ("Unenfant/estsortie/de/ l'eau"). At the start of third grade Marta read quickly with many omissions, but her comprehension was good. Her school grades in reading are considered good.

Thus, although their levels of reading and code knowledge were almost similar at the start of the school year (with the exception of Diane), the five observed children differed in their use of the various word-search and word-copying strategies. Annia depended heavily on the use of context for word searching, and on the use of whole-word strategies when copying words. Frank and Laura resemble each other in their strategies. For word searching they mainly used global visual strategies until November, then syllabic strategies from January. Their dominant strategy for word copying remained the transfer of arbitrary (nonsyllabic) letter strings, suggesting a slightly later appearance of syllabic treatment in copying than in word searching. Finally, for Marta strategies based on graphic–phonic correspondence dominated in word-searching and letter-by-letter strategies in word copying. A call on syllabic representations rarely appeared simultaneously in copying and searching.

DISCUSSION

Despite the difficulties inherent in attempting to draw out general conclusions from the exploratory research just presented, the results of such a case study are nevertheless instructive. First, the findings support the dual hypothesis proposed by Perfetti (in preparation) according to which lexical representations will, at the start of learning, be both partially specified and similar in reading and writing. We have, in fact, observed that the children frequently proceed by processing fragments of words, attesting to the partial nature of their lexical representations. Moreover, one notes a quite close agreement between the strategies adopted for word searching and those used for copying, although for two of the five children an appeal to syllabic representations became evident sooner and also more systematically in word searching than in word copying. This slight decalage could be attributed to the fact that the children were still less accustomed to the activity of writing than to that of reading.

Second, the fact that the only child to experience difficulty in reading in third grade is Annia is consistent with the research that emphasizes the importance of code knowledge (Ehri; Byrne, this volume). For her, we did not observe a move away from contextually oriented and global visual similarity strategies towards those depending more on code. In an educational context, in which the code has not been systematically taught at the start of learning to read, Annia seems not to have been able to succeed in the way that Frank, Laura, and Marta did, that is to say to discover or deduce the rules of grapheme–phoneme correspondence from the proposed tasks. So one can suppose that, for Annia, systematic practice of these rules would be necessary whereas for the other children it would not. This surely confirms that it is essential to take individual differences into account if we are to avoid underestimating or, on the contrary, overestimating the role played by the discovery of grapheme–phoneme correspondence rules in the mastery of the written language by children.

Third, our findings suggest that some of the differences observed in the children's use of the various strategies must be attributable to differences in their stages of literacy development, but that others might be attributable rather to differences in the personal characteristics of the children as individuals. For example, we noted that Frank and Laura, who had at their disposal the same variety of strategies, differ in the degree of flexibility with which they moved from one type of strategy to another. We are currently following up our research to try to establish more clearly the distinction between inter individual and developmental sources of variation in the deployment of word-searching and word-copying strategies.

Finally, it remains to mention the positive, and in our view the most important, aspect of this work. It has shown that it is indeed possible to observe, in a classroom situation, behaviors that can, within the framework of available theoretical models, serve as indicators for analysis and interpretation of the processes of learning at play in the acquisition of written language. This level of psychoeducational research is an important link between fundamental research and individualized teaching.

ACKNOWLEDGMENT

The authors are grateful to Pierre Mounoud, Michèle Moynier, Anik de Ribaupierre, and Madelon Saada for their invaluable comments on earlier drafts of this chapter. We also thank the children of the Maison des Petits, a school attached to the Faculty of Psychology and Education in the University of Geneva, and their teacher, Martine Auvergne, for their cooperation. Finally, we thank Danielle Foglia and Francoise Hartmann for their help with the observations, and Sandra Johnson for translating the French version of this chapter into English.

REFERENCES

Baron, J., & Strawson, C. (1976). Use of orthographic and word-specific knowledge in reading words aloud. *Journal of Experimental Psychology: Human Perception and Performance, 2*, 386–393.

Berthoud-Papandropoulou, I. (1980). *La réflexion métalinguistique chez l'enfant.* Faculté de Psychologie et des Sciences de l'Education, Université de Genève: Thèse de doctorat.

Bryant, P., & Bradley, L. (1980). Why children sometimes write words which they do not read. In U. Frith (Ed.), *Cognitive processes in spelling* (pp. 355–370). New York: Academic Press.

Clesse, C. (1977). Apprendre à lire en parlant. Expérimentation dans un cours préparatoire. In L. Lentin (Ed.), *Du parler au lire* (pp. 91–152). Paris: ESF.

Ehri, L. (1980). The development of orthographic images. In U. Frith (Ed.), *Cognitive processes in spelling* (pp. 311–188). New York: Academic Press.

Ferreiro, E. (1977). Vers une théorie génétique de l'apprentissage de la lecture. *Revue suisse de psychologie pure et appliquée, 36*, 190–130.

Ferreiro, E. (1978). What is written in a written sentence? A developmental answer. *Journal of Education, 160, 4*, 25–39.

Ferreiro, E., & Teberosky, A. (1982). *Literacy before schooling.* Exeter: Heinemann Educational Books (translation).

Ferreiro, E., & Gomez Palacio, M. (1983). Analyse des difficultés rencontrées au cours du processus d'apprentissage de la lecture et de l'écriture. *Cahier du GCR/SSRE*, Neuchâtel, 7, 1–53 (translation).

Fijalkow, J., & Liva, A. (1987). *La copie de texte comme indicateur de l'apprentissage de la langue écrite chez l'enfant.* Paper presented at the 5th European Conference on Reading, Salamanca.

Hébrard, J. (1977). Rôle du parler dans l'apprentissage de l'écrit. In L. Lentin (Ed.), *Du parler au lire* (pp. 57–90). Paris: ESF.

Juel, C., Griffith, P., & Gough, P. (1986). Acquisition of literacy: A longitudinal study of children in first and second grade. *Journal of Educational Psychology, 78*, 243–255.

Mann, V., Tobin, P., & Wilson, R. (1987). Measuring phonological awareness through the invented spellings of kindergarten children. *Merrill-Palmer Quarterly, 33*, 339–355.

Marsh, G., Friedman, M., Welch, V., & Desberg, P. (1980). The development of strategies in spelling. In U. Frith (Ed.), *Cognitive processes in spelling* (pp. 335–370). New York: Academic Press.

Perfetti, C. (in preparation). The representation problem in reading acquisition. In P. Gough, L. Ehri, & R. Treiman (Eds.), *Reading acquisition.* Lawrence Erlbaum Associates.

Prêteur, Y., & Telleria Jauregui, B. (1986). L'empan de copie comme un des indicateurs de l'acquisition de la langue écrite chez des enfants de 5–8 ans (premiers résultats). *Psychologie Scolaire, 56*, 5–29.

Rieben, L. (in press). L'étude de l'apprenti-lecteur en situation de classe. *La lecture. Des pratiques pédagogiques à la neurobiologie.* Paris: L'Harmattan.

Rieben, L. (1989). Individual differences in word recognition: A path from an interactive model of reading to an interactive instructional setting. *European Journal of Psychology of Education, 4*, 329–347.

Rothkopf, E. (1980). Copying span as a measure of the information burden in written language. *Journal of Verbal Learning and Verbal Behavior, 19*, 562–572.

Shanahan, T., (1984). Nature of reading–writing relation: An exploratory multivariate analysis. *Journal of Educational Psychology, 76*, 466–477.

Treiman, R. (1984). Individual differences among children in spelling and reading styles. *Journal of Experimental Child Psychology, 37*, 463–477.

APPENDIX: FACSIMILE OF THE OCTOBER REFERENCE TEXT (RT).

Victor et le cadeau

Victor se fait tout beau pour aller à l'anniversaire de son copain Denis. Victor s'accroupit et prend sa veste sous son lit. Il boutonne sa veste parce qu'il fait froid dehors.
Avant de sortir, il prend le cadeau pour Denis.
Victor donne un baiser à sa soeur Pauline et à sa maman et il part.
Il se dépêche pour ne pas arriver en retard chez Denis. Il regarde à gauche

et à droite avant de traverser la rue dans le passage clouté. Il est presque arrivé chez Denis.
Denis attend Victor sur le trottoir. Il fait des grands signes à Victor pour qu'il vienne vite.
Denis accompagne Victor dans sa maison. Tous les copains les attendent dans la cuisine.
Victor enlève sa veste et la tient dans sa main. Il pose le cadeau par terre. Il dit bonjour aux copains. Victor donne le cadeau à Denis. Denis défait la ficelle

et déchire le papier. Il montre à ses copains le beau livre d'animaux que Victor lui a acheté. Denis pose le livre d'animaux sur la chaise.
Denis souffle les bougies qui sont sur le gâteau.
Il coupe le gâteau et il en donne à tous ses copains. Il leur donne aussi du jus d'orange.
Ensuite, ils vont lire le livre de Denis.

III Phonological Abilities

8 Phonological Awareness and Literacy Acquisition

William E. Tunmer
Massey University, New Zealand

INTRODUCTION

The acquisition of literacy has been defined by Juel, Griffith, and Gough (1986) as "acquiring the ability to both comprehend and produce written text" (p. 243). In developing a model of the literacy acquisition process, Juel et al. (1986) review research suggesting that the word-level skills of decoding and spelling are especially important in the early stages of learning to read and write. This evidence supports a major theoretical assumption of their model, which is that efficient word recognition and spelling are critical to the higher order cognitive processes of comprehension and composition. Stated simply, if children are having trouble reading and writing individual words, it is likely that they will also encounter difficulty in thinking about what they are reading and writing.

The Juel et al. (1986) model of literacy acquisition further proposes that an ability referred to as *phonological awareness* underlies the development of word recognition and spelling ability. In the sections that follow I examine the theoretical arguments and empirical evidence in support of this claim.

What is Phonological Awareness?

Phonological awareness is the ability to reflect on and manipulate the phonemic segments of speech. It is one of several general types of *metalinguistic ability*, a developmentally distinct kind of linguistic functioning that develops separately from and later than basic speaking and listening skills. As Shankweiler and Crain (1986) put it, "explicit conscious awareness of phonemic structure depends on metalinguistic abilities that do not come free with the acquisition of language" (p. 142). Evidence in support of this claim comes from studies that show that many kindergarten-aged children who appear to possess normal language-processing abilities are unable to perform such simple metalinguistic operations as counting the number of phonemes in spoken words, or deleting or adding individual consonants in words (see Tunmer, Pratt, & Herriman, 1984).

This conceptualization of phonological awareness provides an explanation for what at first seems rather paradoxical; namely, that young children can easily discriminate between speech sounds and use phonemic contrasts to signal meaning differences, but they encounter difficulty in segmenting spoken words into phonemes. The essential difference, however, is that using a phonemic contrast to signal a meaning difference, which is done intuitively and at a subconscious level, is not the same as the metalinguistic act of *realizing* that the relevant difference is a phonemic difference. Consciously reflecting on phonemic segments is much more difficult for children because there is no simple physical basis for recognizing phonemes in speech. Children must therefore develop an awareness of an entity that is inherently abstract. They must develop the ability to invoke control processing to perform mental operations on the products of the mental mechanism responsible for converting the speech signal into a sequence of phonemes.

Phonological Awareness and Reading

Three views of the relation of phonological awareness to reading acquisition have appeared in the literature. The first is that phonological awareness is causally related to reading acquisition; the second is that phonological awareness is a consequence of reading acquisition; and the third is that phonological awareness is both a cause and a consequence of learning to read, a phenomenon referred to as reciprocal causation.

According to the first view, the ability to segment spoken words into phonemes is necessary for children to be able to discover the systematic correspondences between the elements of spoken and written language. Letter–sound knowledge, in turn, is required to identify words not seen before and to gain the levels of practice necessary for developing speed and automaticity in recognizing words (Gough & Hillinger, 1980; Jorm & Share, 1983; Stanovich, 1986). Evidence in support of these claims comes from studies showing that letter–sound knowledge is intimately related to the acquisition of basic reading skills (Backman, Bruck, Hebert, & Seidenberg, 1984; Manis & Morrison, 1985), that training in phonemic segmentation skill produces significant experimental group advantages in reading achievement (Bradley & Bryant, 1983; Olofsson & Lundberg, 1985), and that phonological awareness influences reading comprehension indirectly through phonological recoding ability (the ability to apply the grapheme–phoneme correspondence rules, as measured by pseudoword decoding; Stanovich, Cunningham, & Feeman, 1984; Tunmer & Nesdale, 1985).

Proponents of the second view of the relation of phonological awareness to reading acquisition reject the claim that awareness of phonemes is a prerequisite for learning to read. This conclusion is based largely on the results of studies that show that, unlike normal adult readers, adult illiterates perform poorly on tests of phonological awareness (Byrne & Ledez, 1983; Morais, Cary, Alegria, & Bertelson, 1979). If phonological awareness develops spontaneously during childhood, illiterate but otherwise normal adults should show substantial levels of phonological awareness. Because they do not, it appears that phonological awareness is largely an effect of learning to read. Ehri (1984, 1987) goes a step further and argues that orthographic knowledge may be *necessary* for children to be able to manipulate phonological aspects of speech. Consistent with this suggestion are several studies conducted by Ehri (see Ehri, 1987, for a review of this work), which provide convincing evidence that orthographic knowledge influences children's performance on phonemic segmentation tasks. In light of these findings, Ehri (1987) recommends that children should be taught phonemic segmentation skills *while* they are learning to read, not beforehand.

In responding to these criticisms proponents of the first view have argued that the claim that phonological awareness is a prerequisite for learning to read is not inconsistent with the possibility that the process of learning to read itself may facilitate the development of phonological awareness. Some skills that are acquired or enhanced as a result of learning to read, such as the abilities to form and maintain a phonetic code in working memory and to generate orthographic images, may greatly improve performance of phonological awareness tasks.

Consider, for example, the phoneme reversal task (e.g., say *pat* backwards), which has been used as a measure of phonological awareness in adult illiterates (Byrne & Ledez, 1983). This task requires the subject not only to segment a word into its constituent phonemic elements but also to delete the initial (or final) phoneme, move this phoneme to the end (or beginning) of the sequence of phonemes, repeat the two preceding operations a second time, and then put the segments back together again to pronounce the word. The processing demands of this task are clearly much greater than those of a simple segmentation task, because five additional operations are required. These additional operations may place such a great strain on phonetic memory that the task can be performed successfully only if the subject is able to reduce the load on phonetic memory by generating orthographic images of the sounds.

Byrne and Ledez (1983) found that adult illiterates performed very poorly on the phoneme reversal task in comparison to normal adult readers and interpreted this result as supporting the claim that phonological awareness is largely a consequence of literacy acquisition. However, another possibility is that the phoneme reversal task and others like it, such as the phoneme deletion task, require high levels of ability in using a phonetic code in working memory and in generating orthographic images, in which case the poor performance of the adult illiterates would be expected, because both of these skills develop with increasing reading ability. Consistent with this suggestion, Byrne and Ledez found that, in addition to being the only subjects who performed well on the phoneme reversal task, the normal adult readers were also the only subjects who were susceptible to phonological confusability (an index of the use of phonemic-coding processes in working memory) in a continuous word recognition task that included words that rhymed with target words. This finding suggests that high levels of phonemic-coding processes in working memory may be required to perform the phoneme reversal task.

Direct evidence against the claim that phonological awareness is entirely a product of learning to read comes from studies that have shown that measures of phonological awareness obtained before formal reading instruction began predicted later reading achievement even when children showing any preschool reading ability were excluded (Bradley & Bryant, 1983; Tunmer, Herriman, & Nesdale, 1988), or when the influence of preschool reading ability was statistically partialled out (Vellutino & Scanlon, 1987). Controlling for initial reading ability is essential in predictive studies because, as noted before, the process of learning to read itself may produce spinoff skills that greatly facilitate children's performance of phonological awareness tasks. Consequently, children who possess some preschool reading ability may perform better on tests of phonological awareness than children with little or no preschool reading ability. This would make it difficult to rule out the possibility of having obtained a spurious predictive correlation between phonological awareness and later reading achievement, because preschool reading ability might have positively influenced the development of both.

It is possible, of course, that the two views of phonological awareness and reading that I have discussed so far are not mutually exclusive. Both views may be correct to some extent. In fact, the third view proposes just that; namely that phonological awareness is both a cause and a consequence of learning to read (and spell). According to this view, children must achieve at least some minimal level of explicit phonological awareness to acquire basic reading skills that, in turn, enable them to acquire the spinoff skills of reading that provide the basis for more advanced metalinguistic performances (Stanovich, 1986).

In support of the claim that some minimal level of explicit phonological awareness is necessary for being able to learn to read are the results of an earlier study that we conducted in which a scatterplot was presented display-ing the relationship between phonemic segmentation ability and pseudoword recognition, a measure of phonological recoding ability (Tunmer & Nesdale, 1985). The data suggested that explicit phonological awareness is a neces-sary, but not sufficient, condition for acquiring the grapheme–phoneme cor-respondence rules. Although there were many children who performed well on a phoneme segmentation task but poorly on pseudoword decoding, there were no children who performed poorly on phoneme segmentation but well on pseudoword decoding (see also Juel, Griffith, & Gough, 1986; Tunmer, Herriman, & Nesdale, 1988).

Shortly after children begin making progress in acquiring basic reading skills, the relationship between the development of phonological awareness and learning to read appears to become mutually supportive. Perfetti, Beck, Bell, and Hughes (1987) conducted a longitudinal study in which the phone-mic knowledge and reading ability of first-grade readers was assessed at four points throughout the year. The results of partial time-lag correlations suggested that the relationship between phonological awareness and reading acquisition was reciprocal in nature. Progress in reading appeared to result in progress in the ability to perform a phoneme deletion task that, in turn, appeared to bring about further gains in reading.

Phonological Awareness and Letter-name Knowledge

Another important aspect of phonological awareness is its relation to letter-name knowledge. Although letter-name knowledge is one of the best predic-tors of beginning reading achievement, it is not thought to be causally re-lated to reading achievement. Several studies have failed to demonstrate that children trained in letter names are better able to acquire reading skills than are controls. However, in a critique of these studies, Ehri (1983) pointed out that several factors were neglected, one of which was phonemic segmenta-tion skill. A possibility that was not considered in the earlier studies was that in addition to lacking letter-name knowledge, many poor and beginning readers may also lack phonemic segmentation skill. Letter-name knowledge should help beginning readers discover the grapheme–phoneme correspon-dences because the names of most letters contain the phoneme to which the letter normally refers. However, letter-name knowledge may interact with phonemic segmentation skill such that only children who can segment pho-nemes will benefit from letter-name knowledge. Whether children learn to associate the sound "buh" or the name "bee" or both with the letter *b*, they must still be able to segment the sound or name to make the connection be-tween the letter *b* and the phoneme /b/.

To investigate this issue further, we conducted two studies, the first of which was a training study in which an initial sample of 98 prereading kindergarten children was administered a letter-name test, the Peabody Picture Vocabulary Test, and a phonemic segmentation test (Tunmer & Lally, 1986). From this sample we formed four training groups and one control group. The four training groups, which were selected to be roughly equivalent in verbal intelligence, were as follows: low phonological awareness, low letter-name knowledge (LP–LL); low phonological awareness, high letter-name knowledge (LP–HL); high phonological awareness, low letter-name knowledge (HP–LL), and high phonological awareness, high letter-name knowledge (HP–HL). The children in the four training groups received four computer-monitored training sessions in which they were taught simple grapheme–phoneme correspondences. As expected, in a word recognition posttest of the generalization of the correspondence rules, the high letter-name knowledge, high phonological awareness group performed significantly better than any of the other groups.

The purpose of the second study, which was part of a larger longitudinal study (Tunmer, Herriman, & Nesdale, 1988), was to determine whether a similar pattern of results would occur in natural classroom settings. Included among the tests that we administered to 105 children when they were in first grade were tests of pseudoword decoding, letter-name knowledge, and phonological awareness. To test the hypothesis that the effects of letter-name knowledge on phonological recoding skill interact with phonological awareness, we performed a multiple regression analysis with pseudoword decoding at the end of first grade as the criterion variable. The results of the analysis indicated that the product of phonological awareness and letter identification accounted for a significantly greater amount of variance in pseudoword decoding than the linear combination of the two variables alone.

We then conducted a further analysis to determine whether the interaction was due to the tendency of children with high levels of letter-name knowledge *and* phonological awareness to be particularly advantaged in acquiring decoding skill, as predicted. Median splits of the distributions of the letter identification and phonological awareness scores provided the basis for assigning each child to one of four groups, as in the training study (i.e., LP–LL, LP–HL, HP–LL, and HP–HL). As expected, the high phonological awareness, high letter-name knowledge group performed better on the pseudoword decoding test than any other group. The means of the four aforementioned groups were 9.6, 21.9, 15.8, and 31.6, respectively. This pattern was even more marked when cut-off scores towards the ends of two distributions were used for group assignment rather than median splits. The means were 7.2, 10.4, 17.2, and 31.6 (the sample sizes of the latter groups were 12, 8, 5, and 32). Here the children with low phonological awareness scores performed poorly on the pseudoword decoding test regardless of their level of letter-name knowledge. These findings suggest that some minimal level of phonological awareness must be achieved by children before they can derive much benefit from letter-name knowledge.

Phonological Awareness and Spelling

Although there has been much research into the relationship between phonemic segmentation skill and learning to read, few studies have examined the role of phonemic segmentation skill in learning to spell. Evidence that the ability to access the phonological structure of words is important in the very beginning stages of spelling acquisition comes from analyses of the "invented" spellings of preliterate children (Read, 1971). The creation of such preconventional spellings as HKN for *chicken* and KLR for *color* suggests that beginning spellers are able to segment both letter names and spoken words into their constituent phonemic elements. In support of this interpretation of invented spellings are the results of a study by Liberman, Rubin, Duques, and Carlisle (1985), which showed that the phonological accuracy of invented spelling in kindergarten children was related to phonemic segmentation ability even when general intelligence was taken into account.

Phonological awareness also appears to be important in later stages of spelling development. From a longitudinal study of children during their first 2 years of formal schooling (Grades 1 and 2), Juel, Griffith, and Gough (1986) obtained data that suggest that phonological awareness influences the development of both spelling and word recognition indirectly through phonological recoding ability (or cipher knowledge, to use their terminology). This finding and the finding of a strong positive relationship between word recognition and spelling were interpreted by Juel et al. (1986) as support for a major assumption of their model of early literacy acquisition, which is that decoding and spelling share a common denominator in knowledge of the letter-sound rules of the language.

Some researchers, however, have concluded that phonological awareness is primarily related to spelling ability. Perin (1983) administered two phonological awareness tasks to subjects aged 14 and 15 years who were assigned to one of three groups: good reader–good speller, good reader–poor speller, and poor reader–poor speller. On the first task the subjects were asked to transpose the initial phonemes of the first and last names of pop stars, whereas on the second task the subjects were asked to indicate the number of phonemes in orally presented words of the following types: exception, regular, and pseudowords. Perin found that on both tasks the good reader–good speller group performed at a significantly higher level than both poor speller groups, who did not differ from each other. She concluded from these results that phonemic segmentation skill is more closely linked to spelling ability than to reading ability.

A major difficulty with Perin's interpretation of her findings, however, concerns the basis on which the subjects were responding to the tasks. To determine whether subjects were using orthographic knowledge in phonemic segmentation, Perin included three types of words in the materials for the second task: real words that had more letters than phonemes (Type 1); real words that had a one-to-one letter-phoneme match (Type 2); and pseudowords that were constructed on the basis of the Type 2 words. It was hypothesized that if spelling knowledge were used in phonemic segmentation, more errors should occur with the Type 1 words, because these words contained more letters than phonemes.

The results showed a clear effect of word type for all groups. Despite having been explicitly told not to think of the spelling of stimuli, the subjects made significantly fewer correct responses to the Type 1 words than to either the Type 2 words or the pseudowords, the number of correct responses to the last two categories being similar. The finding that both the good and poor spellers were using orthographic knowledge as a guide in their attempts to segment phonemically indicates that the subjects were not responding to the tasks intended. Because subjects were using spelling knowledge to respond to the items, it would be expected that the good spellers would perform better than the poor spellers. It therefore cannot be concluded from Perin's data that phonemic segmentation skill is more closely related to spelling ability than to reading ability.

In support of this interpretation are the results of two earlier studies that we conducted that examined the development of phonemic segmentation skill in children (Tunmer & Nesdale, 1982, 1985). By manipulating the presence of digraphs in both real and pseudowords, and by analyzing the pattern of overshoot errors in children's responses (i.e., errors in a phoneme counting task in which the response given exceeds the number of phonemes in the item), we obtained data that suggested that a test made up entirely of nondigraph pseudowords (i.e., pseudowords that contain a one-to-one letter–phoneme match) would provide the most unambiguous estimate of phonemic segmentation skill. Because pseudowords, by their very nature, have not been seen before, subjects would not be able to use stored orthographic images of words to segment on the basis of the number of letters in the word. An estimate of phonemic segmentation skill would still be obtained for those children who used their knowledge of phoneme–grapheme correspondences to generate graphemic representations of pseudowords and then counted the number of graphemes in them, because to apply the correspondence rules to spoken words not seen before, these children would first have to segment the words into phonemes.

A further criticism of the Perin (1983) study concerns the experimental design that was used. The problem in using designs in which good and poor spellers are matched on chronological or mental age is that it is difficult to determine whether any differences observed between the groups are causes or consequences of differential spelling ability. Although Perin found that poor spelling ability was associated with deficits in phonemic segmentation skill, it cannot be concluded that such deficits *cause* poor spelling. The good spellers differed from the poor spellers in their ability to recall accurately the orthographic images of words. Because the data suggest that all subjects were using orthographic knowledge to segment phonemically, it is equally likely that the superior phonemic segmentation ability of the good spellers was a *consequence* of their better spelling skill, not the cause of it.

To avoid this design problem, we used a spelling-age match design to test the hypothesis that deficits in phonologically related skills may be casually related to difficulties in acquiring basic spelling knowledge (Rohl & Tunmer, 1988). The major advantage of the spelling-age match design over the mental-age match design is that, because spelling levels are the same, it precludes the possibility that any differences that emerge between the normal and backward spellers are merely the product of spelling ability differences. Poor Grade-5 spellers, average Grade-3 spellers, and good Grade-2 spellers matched on a standardized spelling test, and a group of good Grade-5 spellers matched by chronological age with the poor Grade-5 spellers, were administered the Peabody Picture Vocabulary Test (PPVT), a phoneme segmentation test containing 20 nondigraph pseudowords (e.g. *ip, wob, slint*), and an experimental spelling test containing 72 words, 18 of each of the following four types: exception (e.g., *have, aching*), ambiguous (e.g., *town, teacher*), regular (e.g., *rush, himself*), and pseudowords. The words in each of the four groups were yoked according to the number of letters and syllables they contained, and, for the real words, according to their frequency of occurrence at the Grade-3 level.The results indicated that there were no significant differences between the groups in general intelligence (as measured by the PPVT). Consistent with the hypothesis, we found that the average spellers and two groups of good spellers each performed significantly better on the phoneme segmentation test than did the poor spellers. The means for the Grade-2 good spellers, the Grade-3 average spellers, the Grade-5 poor spellers, and the Grade-5 good spellers were 17.13, 15.80, 10.93, and 18.30, respectively.

Although the three spelling-matched groups performed at similar levels on the exceptional and ambiguous words of the experimental spelling test, the two groups of younger spellers each achieved significantly higher scores than the Grade-5 poor spellers on both the regular words and pseudowords, especially the latter. The scores for the Grade-2 good spellers, Grade-3 average spellers, and Grade-5 poor spellers were 13.73, 14.13, and 10.13 for the pseudowords, and 14.33, 14.27, and 12.53 for the regular words.

The difference in performance between the older poor spellers and the younger average and good spellers on the regular words was unexpected. A possible explanation of this finding is that the phonological problems that the poor spellers showed in both phonemic segmentation and the spelling of pseudowords were again evident in their poor spelling of regular words. The two younger groups of children, who had better phonemic segmentation skills than the poor spellers, would have been able to use either a visual or a phonological strategy to arrive at the correct spellings of the regular real words. On the other hand, the older poor spellers, with their limited phonemic segmentation skill, could well have made errors in the spelling of these words if they had attempted to use a phonological strategy.

In addition to quantitative analyses of the children's spellings, we also performed a qualitative analysis in which the children's real word spelling errors were classified as phonetic or nonphonetic and as orthographically legal or illegal. Misspellings were classified as phonetic if they could be pronounced to sound like the target words either by analogy to another word or by the application of spelling–sound rules (e.g., *seeze* for *seize, inuph* for *enough*). Misspellings were classified as orthographically legal if they did not violate any rules about the order in which letters can occur in words. Some misspellings that were judged to be illegal were *undlt, addld, bryy,* and *intd*.

For each child, percentages of phonetic errors to total errors and orthographically legal errors to total errors were calculated. The results revealed that when percentage of phonetic errors was the dependent variable, the two younger spelling-matched groups each made a significantly higher percentage of errors that were phonetically accurate than did the Grade-5 poor spellers. Once again the phonological problems of the Grade-5 poor spellers were evident, with less than 40% of their misspellings being phonetically accurate. However, when percentage of orthographically legal misspellings was the dependent variable, there were no significant differences between the three spelling-matched groups. All three groups performed well, suggesting that even the poor spellers were familiar with legal English letter sequences. Their errors, which were poor phonetic representations of the target words, conformed reasonably well to rules about how letters can be combined, thus emphasizing the specific phonological problems of these children.

Origins of Deficient Phonological Awareness

Relatively little is known about the origins of deficiencies in phonological awareness. A widely held view is that deficient phonological awareness is the reflection of a more general deficiency in the ability to hold and operate on verbal material in working memory (Liberman & Shankweiler, 1985). The evidence in support of this claim, however, is based almost entirely, if not exclusively, on studies comparing good and poor readers of similar age and intelligence (Bryant & Bradley, 1985). The problem with this type of research design is that it yields uninterpretable results when a difference in some reading-related ability is found. Good readers differ from poor readers in the amount of practice they receive in reading-related skills. It is possible that repeated occurrences of reflecting on spoken words and sentence structures to discover grapheme–phoneme correspondences improve children's ability to maintain a phonological code in memory (Tunmer, in preparation). Moreover, it has been found that "idea units" in written language are significantly longer and more syntactically complex than those of spoken language (Chafe, 1985). Because better readers are exposed to more written language than poor readers, they receive more practice in maintaining complex linguistic structures in working memory, a possible consequence of which is an improvement in their ability to make effective use of phonological representations in working memory. Differences in verbal working memory ability may therefore be a consequence of differences in reading ability rather than a cause of them.

Consistent with this suggestion are the results of studies that have shown that the phonological coding processes in working memory of older disabled readers are comparable to those of younger normal readers of similar reading ability (e.g., Bisanz, Das, & Mancini, 1984). Studies that have directly examined the relationship between verbal working memory ability and phonological awareness have either failed to find a significant correlation between the two abilities (Vellutino & Scanlon, 1987) or obtained a correlation that was weak and barely significant (Mann & Liberman, 1984).

Home background factors have also been considered as possible sources of individual differences in children's phonological awareness at school entry. Children of parents of higher social class and educational attainment may be exposed to activities in the home (such as learning nursery rhymes and playing various rhyming games) that foster growth in phonological awareness. This possibility was recently investigated in a longitudinal study by Maclean, Bryant, and Bradley (1987), who failed to find a convincing relationship between social background variables and the development of phonological awareness in preschool-age children. Maclean et al. (1987) did, however, find a significant relationship between knowledge of nursery rhymes at age 3 and subsequent development of phonological skills, a relationship that was highly specific because both general intelligence and social background had been statistically controlled. This finding suggests that the process of learning nursery rhymes helps children to become aware that words can be broken down into smaller units. Maclean et al. (1987) attribute the variation in young children's knowledge of nursery rhymes to differences in general intelligence.

Some researchers, however, have argued that deficits in phonological awareness are largely dissociated from other cognitive skills (Stanovich, 1986). This conclusion may have been based in part on the general finding that measures of *verbal* intelligence (typically the PPVT) are only weakly correlated with measures of phonological awareness or not at all (e.g., Tunmer & Nesdale, 1985). Verbal intelligence is the measure of general ability that has been most commonly used by researchers to investigate aspects of phonological awareness, perhaps because they assumed that phonological awareness is primarily a verbal skill. However, for reasons that I discuss next, it is possible that nonverbal and problem-solving measures of general ability are more closely related to phonological awareness than is general verbal ability. In support of this suggestion are the results of a study by Stanovich, Cunningham, and Feeman (1984), which showed that although two measures of phonological awareness did not correlate significantly with verbal intelligence they did correlate significantly with a measure of nonverbal intelligence.

Other researchers have suggested that metalinguistic skill may be linked to the Piagetian process of decentration (Lundberg, 1978; Tunmer, Herriman, & Nesdale, 1988). Metalinguistic performances such as separating a word from its referent, dissociating the meaning of a sentence from its form, and reflecting on the component elements of spoken words require the ability to decenter, to shift one's attention from message content to the properties of language used to convey content. An essential feature of both metalinguistic abilities and decentration is the ability to control the course of one's thought; that is, to invoke control processing. According to this view, then, poor phonemic segmentation skill is a reflection of a developmental lag in decentration processes.

This is not to suggest that high levels of metalinguistic ability emerge spontaneously in development. Rather, this view proposes that during middle childhood children develop the capacity for *becoming* metalinguistically aware when confronted with certain kinds of tasks, such as learning to read. Children may need first to reach a certain "threshold" level of decentration ability before they can perform the low-level metalinguistic operations necessary to acquire basic reading skills. This suggests that it is possible for children with little or no metalinguistic ability at school entry to learn to read normally provided that they posses the level of cognitive ability necessary for acquiring the requisite metalinguistic skills.

A major advantage of the decentration lag hypothesis is that it provides an explanation of why specific phonemic-analysis training is particularly effective for some children (see, for example, Williams, 1980), but unnecessary for most others who acquire basic reading skills without such training, despite the fact that some minimal level of explicit phonological awareness is necessary for learning to read. The decentration lag hypothesis proposes that by the time children begin formal schooling most will have developed the capacity for performing metalinguistic operations, even though they may never have encountered situations that required them to do so. However, as a result of naturally occurring differences in the rate of decentration development, the control processing abilities of some children may be such that they require, or at least would greatly benefit from, explicit training in phonemic segmentation.

In support of the decentration lag hypothesis are the results of a longitudinal study we conducted that showed that decentration (as measured by Piagetian tasks of concrete operativity) in preliterate children was strongly related to metalinguistic skills (including phonological awareness), both at school entry and at the end of the children's first year of formal schooling (Tunmer, Herriman, & Nesdale, 1988). These relationships remained highly significant even after general verbal ability, concepts about print, and letter-name knowledge had been entered into the regression equations. In contrast, general verbal ability failed to make an independent contribution to any of the metalinguistic measures either at school entry or at the end of Grade 1.

The results further showed that preliterate children with low levels of phonological awareness at school entry but above-average levels of decentration ability showed significantly greater improvement in phonological awareness during the school year than similar children with below-average levels of decentration ability at school entry (the mean phonological awareness score of the high-decentration ability group was above the mean of all children's phonological awareness scores at the end of the year, whereas the low-decentration ability group mean was one standard deviation below the overall mean). This finding suggests that many preliterate children with low levels of phonological awareness at school entry but high levels of decentration ability should do reasonably well in learning to read, even though their preliterate level of phonological awareness might suggest otherwise. However, the cognitive ability of some children may be such that they cannot readily perform the metalinguistic operations necessary for learning to read. These children may require explicit training in phonological awareness to derive maximum benefit from reading instruction.

REFERENCES

Backman, J., Bruck, M., Hebert, M., & Seidenberg, M. S. (1984). Acquisition and use of spelling–sound correspondences in reading. *Journal of Experimental Child Psychology, 38*, 114–133.

Bisanz, G. L., Das, J. P., & Mancini. G. (1984). Children's memory for phonemically confusable and nonconfusable letters: Changes with age and reading ability. *Child Development, 55*, 1845–1854.

Bradley, L., & Bryant, P. E. (1983). Categorizing sounds and learning to read—a causal connection. *Nature, 301*, 419–421.

Bryant, P., & Bradley, L. (1985). *Children's reading problems*. Oxford: Blackwell.

Byrne, B., & Ledez, J. (1983). Phonological awareness in reading-disabled adults. *Australian Journal of Psychology, 35*, 185–197.

Chafe, W. (1985). Linguistic differences produced by differences between speaking and writing. In D. Olson, N. Torrance, & A Hildyard (Eds.), *Literacy, language, and learning: the nature and consequences of reading and writing* (pp. 105–123). London: Cambridge University Press.

Ehri, L. C. (1983). A critique of five studies related to letter-name knowledge and learning to read. In L. M. Gentile, M. L. Kamil, & J. S. Blanchard (Eds.), *Reading research revisited* (pp. 143–151). Columbus, OH: Merrill.

Ehri, L. C. (1984). How orthography alters spoken language competencies in children learning to read and spell. In J. Downing & R. Valtin (Eds.), *Language awareness and learning to read*. New York: Springer-Verlag.

Ehri, L. C. (1987). Learning to read and spell words. *Journal of Reading Behavior, 19*, 5–31.

Gough, P. B., & Hillinger, M. L. (1980). Learning to read: An unnatural act. *Bulletin of the Orton Society, 30*, 179–196.

Jorm, A. F., & Share, D. L. (1983). Phonological recoding and reading acquisition. *Applied Psycholinguistics, 4*, 103–147.

Juel, C., Griffith, P. L., & Gough, P. B. (1986). Acquisition of literacy: A longitudinal study of children in first and second grade. *Journal of Educational Psychology, 78*, 243–255.

Liberman, I. Y., Rubin, H., Duques, S., & Carlisle, J. (1985). Linguistic abilities and spelling proficiency in kindergarten and adult poor spellers. In D. B. Gray & J. F Kavanagh (Eds.) *Biobehavioral measures of dyslexia* (pp. 163–176). Parkton, MD: New York Press.

Liberman, I. Y., & Shankweiler, D. P. (1985). Phonology and the problems of learning to read and write. *Remedial and Special Education, 6*, 8–17.

Lundberg, I. (1978). Aspects of linguistic awareness related to reading. In A. Sinclair, R. J. Jarvella, & W. J. M. Levelt (Eds.), *The child's conception of language*. Berlin: Springer-Verlag.

Maclean, M., Bryant, P., & Bradley, I. (1987). Rhymes, nursery rhymes, and reading in early childhood. *Merrill-Palmer Quarterly, 33*, 255–281.

Manis, F. R., & Morrison, F. J. (1985). Reading disability: A deficit in rule learning? In L. S. Siegel & F. J. Morrison (Eds.), *Cognitive development in atypical children* (pp. 1–26). New York: Springer-Verlag.

Mann, V., & Liberman, I. Y. (1984). Phonological awareness and verbal short-term memory. *Journal of Learning Disabilities, 17*, 592–599.

Morais, J., Cary, L., Alegria, J., & Bertelson, P. (1979). Does awareness of speech as a sequence of phones arise spontaneously? *Cognition, 7*, 323–331.

Olofsson, A., & Lundberg, I. (1985). Evaluation of long term effects of phonemic awareness training in kindergarten. *Scandinavian Journal of Psychology, 26*, 21–34.

Perfetti, C. A., Beck, I., Bell, L. C., & Hughes, C. (1987). Phonemic knowledge and learning to read are reciprocal: A longitudinal study of first-grade children. *Merrill-Palmer Quarterly, 33*, 283–319.

Perin, D. (1983). Phonemic segmentation and spelling. *British Journal of Psychology, 74*, 129–144.

Read, C. (1971). Preschool children's knowledge of English phonology. *Harvard Educational Review, 41*, 1–34.

Rohl, M., & Tunmer, W. (1988). Phonemic segmentation skill and spelling acquisition. *Applied Psycholinguistics, 9*, 335–350.

Shankweiler, D., & Crain, S. (1986). Language mechanisms and reading disorder: A modular approach. *Cognition, 24*, 139–168.

Stanovich, K. E. (1986). Matthew effects in reading: Some consequences of individual differences in the acquisition of literacy. *Reading Research Quarterly, 21*, 360–406.

Stanovich, K. E., Cunningham, A. E., & Feeman, D. J. (1984). Intelligence, cognitive skills, and early reading progress. *Reading Research Quarterly, 19*, 278–303.

Tunmer, W. E., (in preparation). Cognitive and linguistic factors in learning to read. In P. Gough, L. Ehri, & R. Treiman (Eds.), *Reading acquisition*. Hillsdale, NJ: Lawrence Erlbaum Associates.

Tunmer, W. E., Herriman, M. L., & Nesdale, A. R. (1988). Metalinguistic abilities and beginning reading. *Reading Research Quarterly, 23*, 134–158.

Tunmer, W., & Lally, M. (1986, July). *The Effects of Letter-name Knowledge and Phonological Awareness on Computer-based Instruction in decoding for Pre-readers.* Paper presented at the 12th Australian Reading Association Conference, Perth, Western Australia.

Tunmer, W. E., & Nesdale, A. R. (1982). The effects of digraphs and pseudowords on phonemic segmentation in young children. *Applied Psycholinguistics, 3*, 299–311.

Tunmer, W. E., & Nesdale, A. R. (1985). Phonemic segmentation skill and beginning reading. *Journal of Educational Psychology, 77*, 417–427.

Tunmer, W. E., Pratt, C., & Herriman, M. L. (1984). *Metalinguistic awareness in children: Theory, research and implications.* Berlin: Springer-Verlag.

Vellutino, F., & Scanlon, D. (1987). Phonological coding, phonological awareness, and reading ability: Evidence from a longitudinal and experimental study. *Merril-Palmer Quarterly, 33*, 321–363.

Williams, J. (1980). Teaching decoding with an emphasis on phoneme analysis and phoneme blending. *Journal of Educational Psychology, 72*, 1–15.

9 Phonological Abilities: Effective Predictors of Future Reading Ability

Virginia A. Mann
Department of Cognitive Sciences
University of California, Irvine

Consistent with the theoretical insight that writing systems are transcriptions of spoken language (see Liberman, Liberman, Mattingly, & Shankweiler, 1980), and the experimental evidence that certain spoken language skills mediate skilled reading (see for reviews Crowder, 1982; Mann, 1986a; Perfetti, 1985, or Stanovich, 1982a and 1982b), studies of American children are showing that spoken language skills can be strongly and significantly related to early reading skill (for recent reviews see, Liberman, 1982; Mann, 1986a; Mann & Brady, 1988; Stanovich, Cunningham, & Freeman, 1984; Wagner & Torgesen, 1987). Indeed, certain spoken language skills not only associate with reading ability; they may actually determine that ability. To illustrate this point, this chapter offers a brief review of the evidence that links spoken language skills to early reading ability and summarizes a longitudinal study that shows how those skills predicted the future reading ability of kindergarten-aged children. The focus is on phonological skills, those language skills that operate on the basic sound elements of language and the regular patterns among them. Phonological processing skills mediate all spoken language communication, and they are particularly important to beginning readers of alphabets because alphabets transcribe certain phonological elements referred to as phonemes.

PHONOLOGICAL SKILLS ASSOCIATE WITH EARLY READING ABILITY

The phonological skills that have been related to early reading ability fall within two basic areas. One concerns the explicit awareness of such phonological units as phonemes and syllables. The other concerns the ability to perceive, retrieve, and temporarily retain phonological information.

The explicit awareness of phonological structure is often referred to as "metalinguistic" awareness. From a theoretical perspective, children's awareness of the fact that words comprise sequences of phonemes is particularly critical to their realization of what the alphabet is "all about" because phonemes are more or less what the letters represent. This insight led many investigators to consider beginning readers' awareness of phonemes as evidenced in their reading behavior (Mann, 1984; Shankweiler & Liberman, 1972) and their spelling errors (Liberman, Rubin, Duques, & Carlisle, 1985; Mann, Tobin, & Wilson, 1987) as well as in their ability to count, delete, or otherwise manipulate phoneme-sized units in spoken words. All these diverse approaches have shown that insufficient awareness about phonemes is a common trait of poor beginning readers, whereas superior awareness about phonological structures associates with superior reading ability (for reviews, see Liberman, 1982; Mann, 1986a; or Perfetti, 1985 Stanovich, Cunningham, & Cramer, 1984; Treiman & Baron, 1981). The ability to manipulate syllables, a less abstract aspect of phonological structure, has also been linked to early reading ability and is lacking among many children who are poor readers (Katz, 1986; Mann & Liberman, 1984).

The second area of phonological skill that has been implicated in early reading concerns the processing of spoken language. Its importance is anticipated by findings that skilled readers retrieve and manipulate the phonological structure of printed material as they seek to comprehend and remember that material (see for reviews Crowder, 1982; Mann, 1986a, 1986b; Perfetti & McCutchen, 1982; Stanovich, 1982a, 1982b) and is confirmed by various comparisons of good and poor beginning readers. One realm of processing in which good and poor readers differ is in the retrieval and perception of phonological structures. Retrieval differences are evident from findings that poor readers make more errors than good readers when naming letters or pictures (Katz, 1986; Wolf & Goodglass, 1986). Perceptual differences are evident from such findings as Brady, Shankweiler, and Mann's (1983) observation that poor readers' perception of speech in noise tends to be inferior to that of good readers, although the two groups do not differ in audiometry and perform at more or less the same level when the test items are nonlinguistic sounds such as a cat meowing or a door slamming (Brady et al., 1983). Here, as in other cases (see Mann, 1986a), the problems of poor readers and the excellences of good readers are most consistently found in the linguistic domain.

Studies of short-term (working) memory (see, for example, Brady, 1986; Mann et al., 1980; Mann & Liberman, 1984) identify another aspect of phonological processing that is linked to early reading ability. These reveal that good readers surpass poor readers in the ability to recall sequences of letters, whether written or spoken (Shankweiler, Liberman, Mark, Fowler, & Fischer, 1979), in the ability to recall sequences of nameable pictures (Katz, Shankweiler, & Liberman, 1981), sequences of spoken words (Brady et al., 1983; Mann et al., 1980), and even in the ability to repeat meaningful sentence (Mann, Liberman, & Shankweiler, 1980). However, studies that have examined the recall of nonlinguistic material such as unfamiliar faces, nonsense drawings, or visual–spatial sequences on the Corsi block test reveal no differences between good and poor readers (see Liberman, Mann, Shankweiler, & Werfelman, 1982 and Katz et al., 1981, for example). Thus it is primarily those cases where the to-be-remembered material is either a spoken stimulus or nameable visual stimuli that distinguishes good and poor beginning readers. Further studies of the pattern of children's responses when they attempt to hold linguistic material in memory, along with studies of children's susceptibility to a manipulation of phonological structure (i.e., rhyme), offer an explanation of the poor readers' difficulty. These children may fail to recall linguistic material as well as good readers because they encounter some difficulty with using a speech code (phonetic representation) in working memory (see for a review Brady, 1986; Mann, 1986a). The impact of this working memory problem is quite far reaching. It can lead to problems in such "higher" levels of language use as sentence comprehension and even give the false impression that poor readers lack sufficient knowledge of grammar. Recent work has shown that, rather than reflecting some problem with grammar, the sentence comprehension problems of poor readers may best be viewed as the consequences of a processing limitation in working memory (Mann, Shankweiler & Smith, 1984; Shankweiler, & Crain 1986).

Thus there is substantial evidence that, in America, good and poor readers in the early elementary grades can be distinguished by their performance in two different areas of phonological skill. They tend to differ in the awareness of phonological structure and they differ in the ability to process phonological structures. The evidence stems from a variety of laboratories that have used a variety of paradigms and subject populations. It is quite consistent with what is known about the principle behind alphabetic writing systems and the spoken language skills involved in skilled reading.

CAN PHONOLOGICAL SKILLS PREDICT EARLY READING ABILITY?

Many studies have been concerned with early reading ability, but relatively few have concerned its antecedents. To do so requires longitudinal studies that examine children before and after they learn to read, and these tend to be time consuming and fraught with problems such as subject attrition. Yet longitudinal studies are both theoretically and practically important. They offer the only effective means of determining whether individual differences in phonological skills actually cause differences in reading ability, as opposed to being their consequence. They can also point the way towards effective preschool screening and the possibility of remediation and enrichment.

Although few in number, those longitudinal studies that appear in the literature are supporting the contention that phonological skills play a casual role in reading ability. Children who become poor readers in the first grade tend, as kindergarteners, to have been less aware of phonological structure (Blachman, 1983; Bradley & Bryant, 1985; Mann & Liberman, 1984; Stanovich, Cunningham, & Cramer 1984), less able to perform naming tasks (Mann, 1984, Wolf & Goodglass, 1986), and less able to repeat strings of words (Mann, 1984; Mann & Liberman, 1984). Children who become good readers tend to have excelled in each of these three areas and average readers fall somewhere between.

The promise of this research is aptly illustrated by a recent study (Mann & Ditunno, 1990), which is now described in some detail. That study has the virtue of having used several different tests to examine each area of phonological skill, and of having tested children both as kindergarteners and as first graders. It also compared children's performance on the various phonological tests to their performance on nonlinguistic tests, as a means of excluding demands on attention, logical deduction, graphomotor skill, etc. as confounding factors in previous research.

A STUDY OF PHONOLOGICAL SKILLS AS PREDICTORS OF READING ABILITY

The study began with 106 kindergarten children, of whom 70 were available as first graders. These children were divided into two equal groups, one tested in the fall of each year, the other in the spring. Each year all the children received a standardized reading test that required them to read words and phonologically plausible nonwords (i.e., the Word Identification and Word Attack subtests of Form A of the Woodcock Reading Mastery Tests; Woodcock, 1973). An IQ test (the vocabulary and block design subtests of the WPPSI) was given during kindergarten testing. A battery of experimental tests was also given each year of the study and it included five different phonological tests and five nonlinguistic control tests that made similar demands on attention, logic, motor skills, etc. without demanding linguistic skills, per se.

The Test Battery

The construction of the test items and the testing procedures have been described elsewhere (Mann & Ditunno, 1990) and are available on request. Two of the tests in the battery examined children's *awareness of phonological structure.* One was a test of syllable awareness that required children to deduce the rules of a language game that involved counting the number of syllables in spoken words (Liberman, Shankweiler, Fischer, Carter, 1974. This test had proven a successful predictor in the past (Mann & Liberman, 1984); in scoring it, the total number of correct responses is determined (ASC, Max. = 21). A pass/fail score is also computed; children "pass" the test if they have given at least five correct responses in a row on any part of the test (ASPF, Max. = 1). The other test in this area was an invented spelling test (Mann et al., 1987), which examined children's ability to create spellings for familiar words. This test scores children's responses (ISC, Max. = 56) according to their ability to capture the phonological structure of words. One point is given to a response that contains only the first letter of a word, up to three points are given for spelling "people" as "ppl" or "angry" as "ngre," and four points are given for conventionally correct spellings. One nonlinguistic control for these tests was a test of angle awareness (from Mann, 1986b), which was much like a "hidden figures" test. It's scores include the total number of correct responses (AAC, Max. = 21) and a pass/fail score (AAPF, Max. = 1). The other was the Goodenough Draw-a-Man test (Harris, 1963) in which the accuracy of a human figure drawing is scored according to standard protocol (DAM, Max. = 73).

Two other tests examined *retrieval and perception of the phonological structure of words.* One of these was a speeded naming test in which children had to name a randomized series of 25 letters as quickly as possible (from Mann, 1984). Scoring involves the total naming time (in seconds, LNT) and the number of incorrect responses (LNE, Max. = 21). The other test evaluated word perception in noise (as in Brady et al., 1983) and is scored according to the accuracy of children's responses (PWN, Max. = 36). The nonlinguistic control was a test of environmental sound perception in noise (also from Brady et al., 1983) scored according to the accuracy of children's responses (PSN, Max. = 36).

A final linguistic test examined the ability to make *use of phonetic representation in working memory.* This test, adapted from Mann (1984), required children to repeat six different sequences of four unrelated words. Responses are scored with (WSS, Max. = 24) and without (WSF, Max. = 24) respect to the order of the words in the original string. The control for this test was a test of memory for visual–spatial sequences on the Corsi blocks (as discussed in Mann & Liberman, 1984), also scored with (CBS, Max. =

TABLE 9.1

Mean Scores (and standard deviations) on Reading Tests and on the Experimental
Battery at Each Time of Testing

| | Kindergarten | | | | First Grade | | | |
	Fall		Spring		Fall		Spring	
Reading Ability:								
Word ID	1.55	(5.05)	8.11	(20.51)	17.86	(22.10)	71.89	(21.96)
Word Attack	0.00	(0.00)	0.00	(0.00)	6.60	(6.69)	24.96	(15.30)
Phonological Awareness:								
Counting tests								
Linguistic: ASC	7.28	(2.77)	8.11	(4.31)	10.27	(4.13)	12.49	(5.22)
ASPF	0.10	(0.30)	0.15	(0.36)	0.40	(0.50)	0.55	(0.50)
Control: AAC	7.90	(2.37)	7.56	(2.45)	7.80	(2.22)	7.53	(2.49)
AAPF	0.10	(0.30)	0.09	(0.29)	0.11	(0.32)	0.22	(0.42)
Phonological Awareness:								
Invented Spelling								
Linguistic: ISC	12.36	(7.67)	20.60	(12.04)	36.52	(9.78)	51.54	(4.72)
Control: DAM	15.61	(5.59)	20.44	(6.23)	16.20	(3.87)	20.58	(5.65)
Phonological retrieval:								
LNT	61.16	(42.65)	41.67	(28.49)	32.76	(22.67)	16.82	(4.20)
LNE	4.67	(4.67)	1.42	(1.42)	0.93	(1.20)	0.09	(0.29)
Phonological Perception:								
linguistic: PWN	16.39	(1.74)	15.86	(2.35)	16.13	(1.68)	19.84	(2.25)
control: PSN	9.80	(3.72)	6.36	(2.96)	10.56	(3.02)	10.33	(2.62)
Phonological Working Memory:								
linguistic: WSF	20.22	(4.50)	20.56	(4.86)	23.78	(2.98)	23.56	(3.44)
WSS	13.98	(7.71)	15.76	(8.29)	19.58	(5.83)	20.53	(0.83)
control: CBF	32.90	(2.01)	33.87	(2.13)	34.87	(1.27)	35.78	(1.12)
CBS	27.33	(4.53)	29.54	(4.80)	31.71	(3.21)	32.46	(2.64)
WPPSI subtests:								
vocabulary	16.98	(3.45)	18.84	(4.10)				
block design	12.22	(3.23)	14.93	(2.49)				
IQ	104.65	(8.34)	103.91	(6.40)				

36) and without (CBF, Max. = 36) respect to the order of items in the child's
response.

Table 9.1 gives the mean scores and the standard deviations that were
achieved by each group of children at each time of testing. The various test
scores are identified by the same codes that appeared in parentheses in the
preceding section. Inspection of that table reveals appreciable gains in reading ability over the course of the study. It also reveals improvements on

many of the tests within the experimental battery. The primary question to be asked is whether kindergarten performance on the phonological tests predicted first-grade reading ability. For an answer, we turn to time-lag correlations, partial correlations, and multiple regressions.

Results: Cross-lag and Partial Correlations

There are several ways to determine whether performance on a given test predicts future reading ability. One way involves the use of longitudinal *cross-lag correlations*, a form of analysis that asks whether kindergarten scores on the experimental battery bear a stronger relationship to first-grade reading ability (forward) than first-grade scores bear to kindergarten reading ability (backward). Table 9.2 gives the forward and backward correlations between each test and reading ability and indicates that, for seven of the eight linguistic tasks, the forward-directed "predictive" relation is indeed a higher value than the reverse-directed "control" relation. These tests include the two measures of syllable-counting performance (ASC and ASP), the invented spelling test of phonological awareness (ISC), the two measures of letter-naming ability (LNE and LNT, which is only greater in the case of the fall testing), and the two measures of word-string recall (WSS and WSF, which is only greater in the case of spring testing). In contrast, only one of the seven nonlinguistic control tests is more predictive of reading ability than vice versa (i.e., the order-strict Corsi block test, CB, and only for the spring-tested sample). For one nonlinguistic test (the Draw-a-Man test, DAM), the control relationship was actually stronger than the predictive one, and in all other cases the relations are either equivalent or nonsignificant.

A second, more stringent means of evaluating the predictive power of each test is to consider partial correlations. This is necessary because, although kindergarten performance on many of the tests within the experimental battery is related to first-grade reading ability (as was seen in Table 9.2), kindergarten reading ability is also related to first-grade reading ability and to kindergarten performance on many of the battery tests. Hence any correlations between the kindergarten scores on the test battery and first-grade reading ability could have been by-products of kindergarten reading ability, in which case phonological skills would be a consequence of reading ability rather than its cause. To control for this possibility we can set a criterion, following Perfetti (1985) and Wagner and Torgesen (1987), that any test that truly predicts reading ability should remain correlated with first-grade reading ability when partial correlations remove the contribution of kindergarten reading ability to each test and to first-grade reading ability. Many of the phonological tests in our battery pass this control, which we take as evidence

TABLE 9.2

Predictive Versus Control Correlations:

Relation Between the Experimental Test Battery and Reading Ability

| | Fall testing | | Spring testing | |
	Predictive	Control	Predictive	Control
Phonological Awareness:				
Counting tests				
Linguistic: ASC	.50	.06	.55	.31
ASPF	.47	.25	.59	.28
Control: AAC	.27	.07	.28	.13
AAPF	.22	.07	.16	.04
Phonological Awareness:				
Invented Spelling				
Linguistic: ISC	.71	.49	.41	.32
Control: DAM	.27	.42	.23	.46
Phonological Retrieval:				
Linguistic: LNT	−.39	-.10	−.25	−.38
LNE	−.41	.10	−.47	−.08
Control: DFTT	NA	.06	NA	.05
Phonological Perception:				
linguistic: PWN	.02	.04	.11	.27
control: PSN	−.11	.03	.04	.04
Phonological Working Memory				
linguistic: WSF	.36	.02	.52	.23
WSS	.16	.09	.54	.30
control: CBF	.09	.08	.09	.12
CBS	.26	.10	.35	.18
Reading ability	.56	.56	.51	.51
N	31	31	39	39
Significance levels				
$p < .05$	.31	.31	.27	.27
$p < .01$	.42	.42	.37	.37

that they are true predictors of future reading ability. Those tests that remain significantly correlated at p < .05 include the fall and spring testing of syllable awareness, invented spelling, letter-naming speed, and errors. The ordered word-string recall was significant for the spring-tested group and fell just short of significance for the fall one. As for the nonlinguistic tests, only the Corsi block-ordered score was significantly related to future reading ability (and only in the spring-tested group). The WPPSI vocabulary test was predictive in both fall and spring testing, but the block design test was not.[1]

The test of speech perception in noise is not significantly related to reading ability according to these correlational analyses, which suggests that speech perception skills may not be a very effective predictor of future reading ability. However, some of the other data reported by Mann and Ditunno (1990) suggests that speech perception in noise becomes a more appropriate predictor in the first grade, at which time scores become positively and significantly correlated with second-grade reading ability. This raises the possibility that the predictive power of a given test may depend on the age at which it is administered and the age at which reading ability is assessed.

Multiple Correlations

Multiple regressions offer another means of determining whether the phonological skills of kindergarteners predict their reading ability in the first grade. For both the fall-and spring-tested children, multiple regressions indicate that kindergarten performance on the phonological tests accounts for approximately 60% of the variance in first-grade reading ability. Among children tested in the fall, the multiple correlation coefficient is .78; among those tested in the spring, the multiple correlation coefficient is .76.

More specifically, for fall testing the invented spelling test score accounted for 51% of the variance in reading ability, syllable awareness (pass-fail score) accounted for an additional 7%, letter-naming speed accounted for an additional 1%, and word-string memory for an additional 2%. When these are accounted for, performance on the WPPSI vocabulary contributes less than 1% and kindergarten reading ability contributes an additional 15%. In the spring group, performance on the angle counting test (pass–fail score) account for 35% of the variance and performance on the invented spelling test accounts for an additional 4%. Memory for the word strings accounts for an additional 13%, errors in letter naming for an additional 4%, and speed of letter naming for an additional 2%. When the contri-

---

[1]For fall testing, the actual correlations are: for ASC r =.41, t(28) = 2.3 for ASPF, r =.37, t(28) = 2.11, for ISP, r =.59, t(28) = 3.86, for LNT, r = -.36, t(28) = 2.12, for LNE, r = -.40, t(28) = 2.12). WSS fell just short of significance r =.29, t(28) = 1.6. For spring testing, the actual correlations are: for ASP, r =.51, t(36) = 3.28, for ASPF, r =.51, t(36) = 2.62, for ISC, r =.34, t(36) = 2.17, for LNT, r = -.41, t(36) = 2.84, for WSS, r =.40 (36) = 2.88, for CBS, r =.35, t(36) = 2.24. The WPPSI vocabulary test was also predictive in both fall, r =.25, t(28) = 2.76, and spring t(36) =, r =.33, 2.18 testing, but not the block design test.

bution of the phonological tests is accounted for, performance on the Corsi block test contributes an additional 11%, WPPSI vocabulary contributes 2%, and kindergarten reading ability contributes 2%.

CONCLUDING REMARKS

One of the more important conclusions that can be drawn from longitudinal research is that phonological abilities do indeed predict children's ability to learn to read. In this chapter we have seen how use of cross-lag correlations reveals that phonological abilities predict future reading ability more successfully than present reading ability predicts future phonological abilities. Even in the case of letter naming, a skill where one might expect reading experience to have a strong effect, the ability to name letters rapidly is a better predictor of reading ability than vice versa. Moreover, when kindergarten reading ability is taken into account, phonological skills remain effective predictors of first-grade reading ability. This confirms that phonological skills are not merely concomitants or by-products of reading ability; they are true antecedents that may account for up to 60% of the variance in children's reading ability.

Another conclusion concerns the fact that measures of phonological abilities appear to be more consistent and effective predictors of future reading problems than measures of comparable nonlinguistic abilities. In studies such as Mann and Ditunno (1990) and Mann and Liberman (1984), nonlinguistic tests did not predict reading ability as well as linguistic ones, even when they were designed to make analagous demands on attention, memory, etc. Some tests such as the Draw-A-Man test and the Corsi block test bear an elusive and inconsistent relation to reading ability (for example, compare Mann & Liberman, 1984 with Mann & Ditunno, 1990). Full-scale IQ is also a factor that has been related to reading ability; however, Stanovich, Cunningham, and Freeman (1984) have successfully shown that phonological awareness is a more important factor in early reading ability than general IQ. Also, as seen in the data of Mann and Ditunno, those measures of IQ that most successfully predict reading ability tend to be verbal tests that recruit both perception and retrieval of phonological structures.

It is interesting to note that the importance of language skills to early reading ability is consistent with a recent biological model of developmental dyslexia that was proposed by Geschwind and Galaburda (1985). According to their model, dyslexia arises out of an imbalance of hemispheric development that hinders left-hemisphere development while favoring the development of the right hemisphere. As a consequence, dyslexics possess deficiencies in left-hemisphere processing and superiorities in right-hemisphere processing. The data of Mann and Ditunno are particularly supportive of this view in showing that poor readers who lack phonological skills may show surprisingly high performance on tests of such right-hemisphere skills as environmental sound perception.

Whatever biological or experiential variables underline individual differences in phonological skills, it is becoming clearer and clearer that those differences can be harbingers of individual differences in early reading ability. Thus far, most of the evidence has been garnered from studies conducted in America and other English-speaking countries (see for example Bradley & Bryant, 1985; Share, Jorm, MacLean, & Matthews, 1984) However, if these findings about beginning readers of English reflect the fundamental importance of phonological skills to all language communication and the special role of phonological structure in alphabetic transcription, then they should generalize to beginning readers of other alphabetic systems. Some very interesting studies in Sweden (Lundberg, Oloffson, & Wall, 1980; Torneus, 1984) and in Belgium (Morais, Cluytens, & Alegria, 1984) have already confirmed this possibility, and research in other countries is now in progress.

As we come closer and closer to isolating the substrate of early reading ability, it behooves us to also consider the practical applications of this valuable information. Ultimately, it will not be sufficient to merely determine which children are ready to learn to read and which children are at "risk" for reading failure. We should also strive to develop more effective prereading programs and remedial exercises that will make learning to read a less problematic task. Training procedures that can facilitate phonological awareness have been of interest in recent research (Bradley & Bryant, 1985), and the results are quite promising (see Bradley & Bryant, 1985, for example). The time is ripe for consideration of training methods that can improve other phonological skills, as well.

ACKNOWLEDGMENTS

The longitudinal study reported in this chapter was conducted at Bryn Mawr College, supported by NICHD grant HD211–82–01. Preparation of the manuscript and much of the research herein described was supported by NICHD grant HDO1994 to Haskins Laboratories, Inc. The same data and many of the same points appear in Mann and Ditunno (1990).

REFERENCES

Blachman, B. A. (1983) Are we assessing the linguistic factors critical in early reading. *Annals of Dyslexia, 33*, 91–109.

Bradley, L., & Bryant, P. (1985). *Rhyme and reason in reading and spelling.* Ann Arbor: University of Michigan.

Brady, S. (1986) Short-term memory, phonological processing and reading ability. *Annals of Dyslexia, 36*, 138–153.

Brady, S. Shankweiler, D., & Mann, V. (1983), Speech perception and memory coding in relation to reading ability. *Journal of Experimental Child Psychology, 35*, 345–367.

Crowder, R. (1982) *The psychology of reading*, New York: Academic Press.

Geschwind, N., & Galaburda, A. (1985) Left-handedness: Association with immune disease, migraine and developmental learning disorder. *Archives of Neurology, 42*, Nos. 5–7.

Harris, D. B. (1963) *Children's drawings as measures of intellectual maturity.* New York: Harcourt, Brace, & Jovanovich.

Katz, R. B., (1986) Phonological deficiencies in children with reading disability: Evidence from an object naming task. *Cognition, 22*, 225–257.

Katz, R. B., Shankweiler, D., & Liberman, I. Y. (1981) Memory for item order and phonetic recoding in the beginning reader. *Journal of Experimental Child Psychology, 32*, 474–484.

Liberman, I. Y., Liberman (1982) A language-oriented view of reading and its disabilities. In H. Mykelbust (Ed.), *Progress in learning disabilities* (Vol. 5). New York: Grune & Stratton.

Liberman, I. Y., Liberman, A. M., Mattingly, I. G., & Shankweiler, D. (1980). Orthography and the beginning reader. In J. Kavanaugh & R. Venezsky (Eds.), *Orthography, reading and dyslexia* (pp. 137–154). Baltimore: University Park Press.

Liberman, I. Y., Mann, V. A., Shankweiler, D., & Werfelman, M. (1982) Children's memory for recurring linguistic and non-linguistic material in relation to reading ability. *Cortex, 18*, 367–375.

Liberman, I. Y., Rubin, H. Duques, S., & Carlisle, J. (1985) Linguistic abilities and Spelling proficiency in kindergarteners and adult poor spellers. In D. B. Gray & J. F. Kavanagh (Eds.), *Biobehavioral measures of dyslexia.* Parkton, MD: York Press.

Liberman, I. Y., Shankweiler, D., Fischer, F. W., & Carter, B. (1974). Explicit syllable and phoneme segmentation in the young child. *Journal of Experimental Child Psychology, 18*, 201–212.

Lundberg, I., Oloffson, A., & Wall, S. (1980). Reading and spelling skills in the first school years predicated from phoneme awareness skills in kindegarten. *Scandinavian Journal of Psychology, 21* 159–173.

Mann, V. A. (1984) Longitudinal prediction and prevention of reading difficulty. *Annals of Dyslexia, 34*, 117–137.

Mann, V. A. (1986a) Why some children encounter reading problems: The contribution of difficulties with language processing and linguistic sophistication to early reading disability. In J. K. Torgesen & B. Y. Wong (Eds.), *Psychological and educational perspectives on learning disabilities* (pp.133–159). New York: Academic Press.

Mann, V. A. (1986b) Phonological awareness: The role of reading experience. *Cognition, 21*, 65–92.

Mann, V. A., & Brady, S. (1988). Reading disability: The role of language deficiencies. *Journal of Consulting and Clinical Psychology, 56*, 811–816.

Mann, V. A., & Ditunno, P. (1990) *Phonological deficiencies: Effective predictors of future reading problems.* In G. Pavlides (Ed.), *Perspectives on dyslexia; Vol. 2: Cognition, language and treatment.* Chichester England: J. Willy & Sons.

Mann, V. A., & Liberman, I. Y. (1984) Phonological awareness and verbal short-term memory. *Journal of Learning Disabilities, 17*, 592–598.

Mann, V. A., Liberman, I. Y., & Shankweiler, D. (1980). Children's memory for sentences and words in relation to reading ability. *Memory & Cognition, 8*, 329–335.

Mann, V. A., Shankweiler, D., & Smith, S. T. (1984) The association between comprehension of spoken sentences and early reading ability: The role of phonetic representation. *Journal of Child Language, 11*, 627–643.

Mann, V. A., Tobin, P., & Wilson, R. (1987) Measuring phonological awareness through the invented spellings of kindergarten children. *Merrill–Palmer Quarterly, 33*, 365–392.

Morais, J. Cluytens, M., & Alegria, J. (1984) Segmentation abilities of dyslexic and normal readers. *Perceptual and Motor Skills, 58*, 221–222.

Perfetti, C. A., (1985) *Reading ability.* New York: Oxford University Press.

Perfetti, C. A., & McCutchen, D. (1982) Speech processes in reading. *Speech and Language: Advances in Basic Research and Practice, 7*, 237–269.

Shankweiler, D., & Crain, S. (1986) Language mechanisms and reading disorders: A modular approach. *Cognition, 21*, 139–168.

Shankweiler, D., & Liberman, I. Y. (1972) Misreading: A search for the causes. In J. F. Kavanaugh & I. G. Mattingly (Eds.), *Language by ear and by eye: The relationships between speech and reading.* Cambridge, MA: MIT Press.

Shankweiler, D., Liberman, I. Y., Mark, L. S., Fowler, C. A., & Fischer, F. W. (1979). The speech code and learning to read. *Journal of Experimental Psychology: Human Perception & Performance, 5*, 531–545.

Share, D. L., Jorm, A. F., MacLean, R., & Matthews, R. (1984) Sources of individual differences in reading acquisition. *Journal of Educational Psychology, 76*, 1309–1324.

Stanovich, K. E. (1982a) Individual differences in the cognitive processes of reading: I. Word decoding. *Journal of Learning Disabilities, 15*, 485–493.

Stanovich, K. E. (1982b) Individual differences in the cognitive processes of reading: II. Text-level processes. *Journal of Learning Disabilities, 15*, 549–554.

Stanovich, K. E., Cunningham, A. E., & Cramer, B. B. (1984) Assessing phonological awareness in kindergarten children: Issues of task comparability. *Journal of Experimental Child Psychology, 38*, 175–190.

Stanovich, K. E., Cunningham, A. E., & Freeman, D. J. (1984) Intelligence, cognitive skills and early reading progress. *Reading Research Quarterly, 14*, 278–303.

Torneus, M. (1984) Phonological awareness and reading: A chicken and egg problem? *Journal of Educational Psychology, 76*, 1346–1358.

Treiman, R., & Baron, J. (1981) Segmental analysis ability: Development and relation to reading ability. In T. G. Waller & G. E. Mackinnon (Eds.), *Reading research: Advances in theory and practice* (Vol. 3). New York: Academic Press.

Wagner, R. K., & Torgesen, J. K. (1987) The nature of phonological processing and its causal role in the acquisition of reading skills. *Psychological Review, 101*, 192–212.

Wolf, M., & Goodglass, H. (1986) Dyslexia, dysnomia and lexical retrieval: A longitudinal investigation. *Brain and Language, 28*, 159–168.

Woodcock, R. W. (1973) *Woodcock Reading Mastery Tests.* Circle Pines, MN: American Guidance Services.

10 Segmental Analysis and Reading Acquisition

Jesus Alegria
José Morais
Université libre de Bruxelles

INTRODUCTION: THE DEVELOPMENT OF READING MECHANISMS

Learning to read is essentially the acquisition of a new path to linguistic knowledge, one based on the written representation of language. The challenge to psychological research is to describe and explain the mechanisms that allow the learner to connect writing to linguistic abilities that previously had been used only for understanding and producing speech.

Research devoted to the study of reading mechanisms in the advanced reader has focused on word identification. One reason for this choice is theoretical. It can be argued that, when a word has been identified, the subsequent processes of comprehension do not depend on whether the access route was auditory or visual. These processes are common to spoken and written understanding. Thus, one can assume that specific reading difficulties, as well as problems in reading acquisition, are mainly related to written word processing. Besides these theoretical considerations, a great mass of empirical work shows that word identification is indeed critical in the analysis of reading difficulties. Thus it is proper that the study of literacy acquisition be considered the development of written word identification.

Recent work agrees in distinguishing three identification mechanisms for written words, namely logographic, alphabetic, and orthographic. These are considered by certain authors as characteristics of three successive stages in reading acquisition (cf. notably Frith, 1985; Seymour & Mc Gregor, 1984). Logographic identification is the recognition of a visual pattern whose signification has been learned "by heart" by the child. This procedure does not require the analysis of the written word into its letters or groups of letters. For instance, a logographic process that leads to the recognition of the written word "two" is the same process that leads to the recognition of the number "2."

A number of recent studies have been concerned with the characteristics of logographic reading in children (Ehri & Wilce, 1985; Masonheimer, Drum, & Ehri, 1984). These studies suggest that certain changes made in the graphic composition of a word have no effect on readers who use a logographic process. For example, when the first P in PEPSI is replaced with an X, while respecting the global appearance of the word (calligraphy, color, etc...), the child who uses a logographic process continues to identify it as PEPSI. Even when attention is drawn to the place where the substitution has been made, he or she will claim that nothing has changed.

Seymour and Elder (1986), in a study of the reading mechanisms used by a group of children during their first year of formal training in a school practicing a strict whole-word method, found a considerable effect of word familiarity: Only words that had been learned at school could be identified correctly by the child. The phonological mediation was totally absent from the process of word identification. For example, the child produced no neologisms or nonwords that would have resulted from the erroneous application of grapheme/phoneme rules. On the other hand, the reading errors demonstrated the global clues the child used to read words that he or she did not know. Thus the child would read "smaller" (known) for "yellow" (unknown), as well as "black" for "like," "cat" for "big" (via dog), etc.

In general, such research indicates that during the logographic stage the child develops internal representations of words characterized by visual features such as word length, and the presence and location of vertical segments (the "ll" in "smaller" or the "k" in "black"). The process of word identification for such children consists in searching the mental lexicon for an item visually related to the word that has to be identified. The total lack of reference to speech at the submorphemic level is a basic characteristic of this search process. The idea of a link between the orthographic version of the word and the constituents of its phonological version is not present either in the internal representation of the words or in the access process.

The relationships between the written word and its meaning are strictly arbitrary in a logographic-type reading system. In a phonographic writing system, however, it is possible to eliminate this arbitrariness. One must take into account the existence of systematic relationships between the orthographic characters, letters and/or groups of letters, and their corresponding phonological identity. This leads to the elaboration of a system of generative rules that allows the reader to assemble the phonological representation of a word from its orthographic version. The word can be identified because the reader possesses a phonological representation of the word that corresponds to the assembled phonology.

Note, however, that a phonological translation does not need to be a process in which each letter is transformed into a phoneme. The advanced reader follows more complex ways of conversion that take the intralexical context into account. The conversion system will also adopt analogical procedures that encode an unknown word by exploiting its orthographic similarity with known words (see Content, Morais, Alegria, & Bertelson, 1986; Glushko, 1981; Goswami, 1987; Patterson & Morton, 1985). The use of context and analogical procedures contributes to developing phonological conversion rules that apply to letter sequences. It must be added that the advanced reader's phonological encoding procedures operate automatically. A distinction must be made between these procedures and the deliberate and laborious decoding performed by the novice reader.

The progressive working-out of a generative system of rules for the phonological conversion of orthography plays a dynamic part in reading acquisition. Jorm and Share (1983) have suggested a mechanism that accounts for this phenomenon. When the reader, expert as well as novice, comes up against an unknown word, the only certain way to identify it is to elaborate the corresponding phonological code through the translation procedures currently available. If the process is successful, two types of long-term effects will take place. The first effect is to reinforce and improve the conversion system by making it more and more automatic and sophisticated. The second one is to help establish a direct access code for this particular word, the orthographic code. Thus, the subsequent identification of this word can be mediated by this orthographic code rather than by phonological processing. The phonological decoding procedure is therefore a self-teaching mechanism. One may characterize the competent reader by the ability to recognize most of the words he meets through a direct access procedure based on a large vocabulary of orthographic representations. In parallel, the phonological assembling system generates phonology from writing and contributes to the identification of those words for which the reader still lacks an orthographic representation.

On the assumption that this description of changes in reading mechanisms is correct, the basic question is what permits the child to give up the logographic strategy and enter into a phonological one that brings him to progressively build up orthographic codes. We argue that the most significant element of this evolution is the awakening of speech segmental structure, which is a necessary condition for understanding the alphabetic code. Thanks to this code, the written representation of words loses its arbitrary nature, and the self-teaching process can begin.

Although we acknowledge the importance of distinguishing among logographic, phonological, and orthographic reading strategies, we think the idea that reading acquisition necessarily goes through three successive stages, each characterized by a particular reading procedure, may be wrong. Two aspects of the acquisition process are especially worth discussing.

First, the notion of a logographic stage refers to the period during which the child has only rote-learned representations of the visual characteristics of words. However, these representations may remain available for a number of words, even in the expert reader. Thus, the adoption of a more advanced reading procedure does not imply the giving up of the logographic mechanism but only a loss in its relative importance compared to the number of words that are read this way.

Second, the initial contact of the novice reader with most words takes place in the context of learning the alphabetic code. Therefore, for the vast majority of words, no logographic stage would take place before the phonological stage. Moreover, for many children the two mechanisms probably occur simultaneously at the beginning of the reading acquisition process. This happens for children who live in an environment rich in written resources and incentives to read as well as for children whose environment is poorer. It is true that children from privileged homes are often exposed from an early age to written words, thus probably allowing the development of a relatively large logographic vocabulary. Most of them, however, also receive early information about the phonological values of letters. As far as the underprivileged children are concerned, it is known that they have a far smaller knowledge of the written word when they arrive to formal reading instruction. In short, the logographic–phonological sequence only applies to a small part of the lexicon in a small number of novice readers. In the same vein, as soon as some command of the alphabetic code is reached, the phonological and the orthographic reading process may co-occur: Some words must be identified through phonological decoding, whereas other words are identified through the orthographic representations created by previously successful phonological decoding.

The distinction between logographic and orthographic reading also deserves some comments. This distinction allows for either a minimal hypothesis or a stronger one, according to the characteristics of the representations implied in these two types of reading. According to the stronger hypothesis, phonological decoding plays a more significant role in accessing the representation. The orthographic representation would not only associate pronunciation with the visual pattern—this is also the case in the logographic representation—but would also systematically associate parts of the visual pattern with the corresponding phonological units (syllabic or subsyllabic). These parts of the orthographic representation would be used in the process of word recognition. The minimal hypothesis assumes phonological decoding plays little role accessing a representation. Some cases of good readers having serious difficulties in reading pseudowords, as the subject described by Campbell and Butterworth (1985), could be considered within the scope of the minimal hypothesis. Such readers might be assumed to have elaborated many orthographic representations without previous phonological decoding. But the great majority of good readers may read according to the mechanism implied by the stronger hypothesis.

The Acquisition of the Alphabetic Code

To acquire the alphabetic code, the child has to mentally isolate the different elements of speech to which letters correspond. These elements are, at first approximation, segments (for our purpose a segment is every single phonetic or phonemic unit). The operation that permits the isolation of segments involves conscious awareness and must be distinguished from the one that governs the understanding of a spoken message. The process implied in speech perception actually performs analytical operations in which segments are probably taken into consideration, but in an automatic way and without conscious awareness. The only way to understand the alphabetic principle involves carrying out segmental analysis at a conscious level.

The reader acquainted with the alphabetic code knows that all three items, RAT, CAT, and BAT, are composed of three segments and that they differ only in the first one. Because this is so obvious to the skilled reader, it may be difficult for him to realize that the prealphabetic child has problems at making such analysis. At this stage, indeed, the child makes a clear distinction between words like RAT and CAT, but this is the result of the unconscious and automatic activity of the speech-processing system. The conscious analysis of the items RAT and CAT into three segments is of no use in speech production and understanding. The important point, as far as reading acquisition is concerned, is that this phonemic awareness is essential to the understanding of the alphabetic code.

The investigation of segmental awareness abilities has used tasks requiring explicit operation on segments such as counting, suppressing, adding, inverting, substituting, etc. The pioneering work by researchers from the Haskins Laboratories, Liberman, Shankweiler, Fisher, and Carter (1974), required 4-, 5-, and 6-year-old children to count either the number of syllables or the number of segments included in a word pronounced by the experimenter. Under the segmental condition, for instance, the child had to answer 1 for /a/, 2 for /ba/, and 3 for /bat/. To provide the answer, the child is assumed to isolate the segments mentally and to count them. Children under 6 were able to count only syllables and not segments: Half the children succeeded under the syllabic condition, whereas only one-sixth of them succeeded under the segmental condition. Six-year-old children, who were the only ones to have started formal training in reading, performed better than the younger ones in the segment counting task: More than two-thirds among them reached the desired level. These results confirm other ones obtained with different tasks in various languages (Calfee, Chapman, & Venezky,

1972; Leroy-Boussion & Martinez, 1972; Rosner & Simon, 1971; Zhurova, 1973). (See Content, 1984 and 1985, for a well-documented review of the question.)

The difference in difficulty between syllabic and segmental analysis is probably due to the fact that syllables roughly correspond to articulatory units and, therefore, can be easily separated. For the segments, the situation is quite different insofar as no simple physical correlate of these units might be highlighted. Furthermore, the fact that syllables represent speech units devoid of meaning is significant in the present context. Because young children can perform operations on syllables, and not on segments, we cannot interpret this last result in terms of difficulty in manipulating meaningless units.

Writing systems in which the syllable is the basic unit, such as Japanese Kana, appear to be easily accessible for children in comparison with alphabetic systems. According to Japanese authors (Makita, 1968; Sakamoto, 1980; Sakamoto & Makita, 1973), Japanese children manage to learn Katakana before starting school and without any previous systematic training. In addition, these authors point out that reading disabilities seldom arise in Japan. This is potentially a telling point concerning the causes of reading disabilities, although it must be considered cautiously. As far as reading acquisition and reading disabilities are concerned, comparisons between different countries are difficult (for a discussion, see Stevenson, Stigler, Lucker, & Lee, 1982; see also a critical analysis concerning the implications of this work in Gleitman, 1985).

It is significant, both from a theoretical and a pedagogical point of view, that young children cannot spontaneously isolate the segmental units of speech. In the study of Liberman et al. (1974) previously discussed, the sudden increase in performance observed between the age of 5 and 6 could well be the result of exposure to the alphabetic code through learning to read. But a different interpretation was possible: The increase in performance might also be the result of a psychological maturation process taking place around 6, making this an adequate age to start reading instruction. The rest of this section examines the arguments concerning these possibilities.

The first argument emerges from the comparison of segmental and syllabic manipulation abilities in 6-year-old children whose reading instruction was in a strict whole-word setting with children taught by a phonics method. During a first experiment (Alegria, Pignot, & Morais, 1982), children were tested in December, 4 months after they started reading training. For phonics-taught children, the instructional program emphasized the alphabetic code. For children in the whole-word setting, reading instruction consisted in the memorization of an increasing number of words, which were to be subsequently identified without relying on segmental analysis. The experimental task required the child to invert either a pair of segments or a pair of syllables. For instance, in the segmental condition, the experimenter said /os/ and the child had to answer /so/; in the syllabic condition /radi/ would invert to /dira/. In the segmental task, phonics-trained children and whole-word-trained children responded correctly on 58% and 15% of the test trials, respectively. In the syllabic condition, the performance approached 70% for both groups, with a small nonsignificant difference between them. A recent experiment using a similar procedure confirm and extend these results (Alegria, Morais, & D'Alimonte, submitted). In this experiment, children educated in the whole-word setting were studied during the first year of their training. One of the segmental tasks required the deletion of the initial segment. For instance, when the experimenter said /po/, the child had to answer /o/. In agreement with the results of the previous experiment, children's performance in this task was rather weak at the beginning of the year. Furthermore, the children made little progress during the year: 6% correct answers at the beginning of the year to 18% by the end of the year.

The detailed examination of the individual results demonstrates that the vast majority of children (34 out of 39) do not make any progress at all in the segmental task. The five remaining children achieve scores of above 50% by the end of the year. Thus, for most of the children, exposure to orthographic material, even in the context of reading instruction, is not enough to develop segmental awareness sufficient to allow segmental manipulations such as segmental inversion or initial segment deletion. The small group (5 out of 39) who did make progress in the segmental suppression task confronted us with a problem. It was not known whether their progress resulted from extracurricular learning or from exposure to orthographic material within the whole-word setting. An additional study, aimed at answering this question, suggests that the extracurricular hypothesis is the right one: All the children who showed high segmental abilities have indeed received specific training at their homes.

A number of experiments carried out with illiterate adults provide additional evidence on the significant part played in segmental awareness by reading acquisition. The starting point of this work is the following: If segmental awareness and consequent abilities in explicit segmental analysis develop outside reading training, illiterate adults might show these segmental abilities. The results of these experiments have been reported in detail elsewhere (Morais, Cary, Alegria, & Bertelson, 1979; Morais, Bertelson, Cary, & Alegria, 1986). They demonstrate that illiterates prove to be extremely weak in tasks that require the manipulation of the initial segment of an utterance. Their performance increases significantly when they have to manipulate syllables, to make a rhyme decision (Morais et al., 1979, 1986), or to estimate the length of an expression (Kolinsky, Cary, & Morais, 1987).

Read, Zhang, Nie, and Ding (1986) have recently carried out an experiment identical to the one of Morais et al. (1979), focusing on alphabetized and nonalphabetized Chinese readers. The former had been educated in the traditional Chinese logographic system and, in addition, had learned "pin-yin," which is an alphabetic representation of Chinese that aids in the pro-nunciation of characters. The nonalphabetized group consisted of traditional Chinese readers who were educated in logographic system only and had never been confronted with a segmental analysis task in their own language. The results were that only alphabetized readers were able to perform the seg-mental task. The performance of nonalphabetized readers were similar to those of illiterates.

In a recent experiment, Mann (1986) considered the same question in Jap-anese children educated in Kana and Kanji (Kanji is the logographic system borrowed from the Chinese and used by Japanese in combination with Kana, the syllabary system). These children have no formal exposure to an alpha-betic system. Children from first to fourth grade of primary school were pre-sented with different speech analysis tasks. Consistent with the hypothesis that alphabetic literacy is important in phonemic awareness, children from the first grade proved to be significantly weaker in segmental analysis than the control group of American children. Most of the children from this group were incapable of segmenting. Their performance was similar to that of the nonalphabetized populations considered earlier—illiterates, Chinese tradi-tional readers, and children educated in a whole-word setting. Japanese chil-dren in the fourth grade, however, performed well in the segmental task. Such a result was not expected because, according to the hypothesis, seg-mental awareness depends on learning to read in an alphabetic system. The-ory and observations can however be reconciled if one takes into account certain characteristics of Kana. For example, a number of segments such as vowels and the nasal /n/ possess separate graphic representations. Moreover, Kana includes diacritic marks that distinguish between voiced and voiceless stops. Such features might help the child in acquiring segmental awareness. The way in which the kana syllabary is represented in schoolbooks consti-tutes another clue. It is displayed in a table of five lines, one per vowel, and 15 columns. The first column contains only the five Japanese vowels, and the successive columns mention the vowels in the same order preceded by a different consonant. Thus, the child can identify what is common between the different elements in the same column, taking an important step toward acquiring awareness of Japanese segments. However, this route to the seg-mental structure of speech is presumably more laborious than the explicit instruction of the alphabetic code.

In summary, subjects who acquire reading in an alphabetic system gener-ally develop an ability to manipulate segments: suppression, counting, etc. In all the other conditions considered, the ability either does not develop, or it develops more slowly. We assume that segmental awareness and segmen-tal analysis ability develop conjointly in interaction (for a survey of the question, see Morais, Alegria, & Content, 1987a, 1987b). Thus, claims about the conditions of emergence of segmental analysis ability can be also applied to segmental awareness. This form of awareness does not seem to be acquired through just any kind of reading training, but rather through confrontation with the alphabetic code and, perhaps, through explicit instruction concerning this code.

Reading Difficulties

In the reading acquisition model outlined so far, segmental awareness is of the utmost importance. Such awareness gives the child an understanding of the alphabetic code and thereby permits identification of words encountered for the first time as well as the progressive-elaboration of orthographic codes for an ever- increasing number of words. According to this theory, children who have difficulty in bringing to mind precise segments (i.e., speech elements that correspond more or less to letters) will face reading acquisition difficulties. This prediction has been confirmed by a number of studies, a few of which we use to illustrate our thesis.

Morais, Cluytens, and Alegria (1984) found that a group of dyslexic children (mean age 8;0) was extremely weak in segmental tasks. In a task of initial phoneme deletion, subjects performed correctly on only 13.7% of the items. The control group, composed of average readers from the first grade of primary school, attained a score of 71.3%. The difficulty for the dyslexic children was specific to the segmental task. When they were asked to delete an initial syllable (/abyr//byr/), their performance was by far better (68.3%). When they had to delete the first note in a series of notes played on a xylophone, no significant difference between the dyslexics and average readers was found 28.8% to 16.6%, respectively). The better performance by dyslexic children in this task probably reflects the fact that these children were older than children in the control group. These results suggest that the difficulties of dyslexic children stem from their inability, even with explicit training on the alphabetic code, to view speech as composed of a sequence of segments. This conclusion is consistent with the demonstration of Rozin, Poritsky, and Sotsky (1971), that second-grade children with serious difficulties in reading could easily read sentences written in Chinese characters. For these children, logographic reading is possible, even easy. It seems reasonable to conclude that their difficulties take place at the level of understanding the alphabetic code.

The results discussed so far can be summarized in two points. First, segmental awareness appears only when the individual has been introduced to the alphabetic code. Second, children who find it difficult to perform segmental tasks, although they have received their reading training in an alphabetic context, also encounter reading difficulties. Thus the relationship between segmental analysis and reading has a very strong empirical basis. Nevertheless, this relationship, strong though it is, is not necessarily a causal one. A third factor, causally related to each of the previous ones, might be responsible for the close correlation. It is important, theoretically as well as pedagogically, to establish that segmental analysis is a causal factor of success in reading. The only way to establish such a relationship is to carry out longitudinal experiments in which a group of subjects is trained on the variable supposed to be the cause and tested afterwards on the variable supposed to be the effect. All things being equal (a difficult condition to respect in longitudinal work), if the performance of the group in this test proves to be superior to that of the control group who did not benefit from training with the putative cause, one can conclude that the link between the variables is truly a causal one (Bradley & Bryant, 1983; Bryant & Alegria, 1988).

From this viewpoint, two large-scale longitudinal experiments have been attempted. Bryant and his collaborators from Oxford University, and Lundberg's research team in Umea, Sweden, obtained results that, on the whole, confirm the existence of a correlation between segmental analysis and reading acquisition. Bradley and Bryant (1983) trained children of low reading skill in rhyme and alliteration manipulation. Following training, they performed better in reading than children from a control group who were trained for the same period in semantic classification (Bryant & Bradley, 1985). The work carried out by the Swedish team focused on preschoolers who were trained in segmental, syllabic, and rhyme manipulation tasks. The trained group turned out to be superior to a control group on certain reading tests and, particularly, on spelling tests used in the first and second grades of primary school. However, the differences were not dramatic, partly because of inadequate matching between experimental and control groups before testing (Lundberg, Olofsson, & Wall, 1980; Olofsson & Lundberg, 1983, 1985). More recent work carried out by the same research team has demonstrated the effectiveness of "metaphonological" training in preschools on reading and spelling during the first grade (Lundberg, Frost, & Petersen, reported by Lundberg, 1987).

CONCLUSION

Our survey has reached an apparently circular conclusion: Reading acquisition requires the discovery of the alphabetic principal, which implies segmental awareness; however, such awareness does not develop except through learning to read in an alphabetic system. Segmental awareness seems to be at the same time the cause and the consequence of reading acquisition.

The circularity is only apparent. Two major points must be taken into account to understand the link between the two variables. First, learning to read is a complex task that requires the integration of an entirely new type of information, contained in the orthographic system, to the preexisting system for understanding and producing speech. Failure at learning to read can, therefore, arise from a number of reasons related to the complexity of the learning task. The difficulty of segmental analysis is one of the most important of these, but not the only one. It is helpful to view the relationship between segmental analysis and reading acquisition as "part" to "whole." To acquire the whole (learning how to read), each constituent part has to be acquired. Any difficulty encountered with the constituent parts will obviously create problems with the "whole." This is why children who have difficulty with segmental analysis also have problems in reading.

The second point is that segmental awareness does not appear outside learning to read in the alphabetic system because no other ability used in "ordinary life" requires such awareness. Illiterates, pure logographic Chinese readers, and children who learn to read in a strict whole-word setting have no segmental awareness of speech because none of them has been confronted with a situation requiring such awareness. Such an ability, because it had no opportunity for use, has never been developed. Our view, explained in detail in Morais, Alegria, and Content (1987a, 1987b), is definitely an interactive one.

Part of our account is that the use of grapheme–phoneme transformation rules in reading depend on the development of explicit segmental analysis as "part" of reading. An objection could be made to this account on the grounds that it is possible to acquire these rules in an implicit way. Their use in reading, therefore, would not rely on segmental awareness. In fact, such awareness would be an epiphenomenon of reading acquisition, without any causal role. An experimental analysis of this alternative point of view would address three questions: First, is it possible, not only in exceptional cases but in general, to learn grapheme–phoneme correspondence rules outside the explicit knowledge of segmental structure of the speech? Second, if so, does this explicit knowledge nevertheless have a favorable effect on the acquisition of grapheme–phoneme correspondence rules? Finally, if so, what is the mechanism or instructional intervention that is responsible?

Available data in the literature fail to provide a clear answer to these questions. We are convinced, as far as the third point is concerned, that segmental awareness has a causal effect on reading acquisition via the development of grapheme–phoneme correspondence rules. Our conviction is rooted in the substantial differences found between children who learn to read by phonics methods and those who learn to read in a whole-word setting, both for the use of such rules and for explicit segmental tasks. We cannot however conclusively eliminate the possibility that the crucial factor that characterizes phonics-trained children is not the understanding of the alphabetic code but an implicit learning of the grapheme–phoneme correspondence rules produced by the training exercises typically given to those children. Experimental studies that attempt to establish the effect of such exercises on reading, while making sure that segmental awareness is still absent, have just been undertaken (Byrne, 1987; also this volume).

Generally speaking, children who are good readers prove both that they are good at phonological decoding (reading pseudowords, for example) and that they posses segmental awareness. One question is whether children who can use phonological decoding to some extent also develop a significant segmental ability. Conversely, is it true that all children who cannot decode also lack segmental ability? Answers to these questions shed light on the basic issue of whether phonological decoding is critically dependent on the conscious knowledge of segments. They would also address the possibility that phonological decoding requires automaticity in segmental analysis that goes well beyond the capacity to represent segments consciously. It is also important, in such research, to consider children who are poor at reading, looking at the relationships between their reading mechanisms and their segmental awareness. It is possible that deficits in some particular aspects of the segmental ability are responsible for poor phonological decoding that leads to poor reading. By assessing those aspects we might perhaps improve our understanding of how phonological decoding constrains the acquisition of orthographic representations.

In considering research that could allow progress in the understanding of reading acquisition mechanisms, one is certainly concerned with the causal role of segmental awareness in reading acquisition. Our guess at present brings us toward a research strategy of relating individual data obtained in segmental analysis tasks with information concerning the reading mechanisms in the novice reader.

ACKNOWLEDGMENTS

This work has been supported by the Belgian Fonds de la Recherche Scientifique Fondamentale Collective d'Initiative Ministérielle (convention: "Evaluation des effets des méthodes d'enseignement sur les mécanismes cognitifs de la lecture et de l'écriture," the Belgian Ministry of Scientific Policy (A.R.C.: "Mécanismes cognitifs dans la lecture"), and the Belgian Fonds de la Recherche Scientifique Médicale (convention n° 3.4526.89).

REFERENCES

Alegria, J., Morais, J., & D'Alimonte, G. (submitted). *The development of speech segmentation and reading acquisition in a whole word setting.*

Alegria, J., Pignot, E., & Morais, J. (1982). Phonetic analysis of speech and memory codes in beginning readers. *Memory and Cognition, 10,* 451–456.

Bradley, L., & Bryant, P. E. (1983). Categorizing sounds and learning to read: A causal connection. *Nature, 301,* 419–421.

Bryant, P. E., & Alegria, J. (1988). The transition from spoken to written language. In A. de Ribaupierre (Ed.), *Transition mechanisms in child development: The longitudinal perspective.* Cambridge: Cambridge University Press.

Bryant, P. E., & Bradley, L. (1985). *Rhyme and reason in reading and spelling.* Ann Arbor: The University of Michigan Press.

Byrne, B. (1987). Is the interactive view premature? *Cahiers de Psychologie Cognitive, 7,* 444–450.

Calfee, R. C., Chapman, R., & Venezky, R. (1972). How a child needs to think to learn to read. In L. W. Gregg (Ed.), *Cognition in learning and memory* (pp. 139–182). New York: Wiley.

Campbell, R., & Butterworth, B. (1985). Phonological dyslexia and dysgraphia in a highly literate subject: A developmental case with associated deficits of phonemic processing and awareness. *Quarterly Journal of Experimental Psychology, 37A,* 435–476.

Content, A. (1984). L'analyse phonetique explicite de lat parole et l'acquisition de la lecture. *L'Annee Psychologique, 84.* 555–572.

Content, A. (1985). Le developpement de l'habilete d'analyse phonetique de la parole. *L'Annee Psychologique, 85,* 73–99.

Content, A., Morais, J., Alegria, J., & Bertelson, P. (1986). Acquisition de la lecture et analyse segmental de la parole. *Psychologica Belgica, 26,* 1–15.

Ehri, L. C., & Wilce, L. S. (1985). Movement into reading: Is the first stage of printed word learning visual or phonetic? *Reading Research Quarterly, 20,* 163–179.

Frith, U. (1985). Beneath the surface of developmental dyslexia. In K. E. Patterson, J. C. Marshall, & M. Coltheart (Eds.), *Surface dyslexia* (pp. 301–370). London: Lawrence Erlbaum Associates.

Gleitman, L. R. (1985). Orthographic resources affect reading acquisition—if they are used. *RASE Remedial and Special Education, 6,* 24–36.

Glushko, R. J. (1981). Principles for pronouncing print: The psychology of phonography. In A. M. Lesgold & C. A. Perfetti (Eds.), *Interactive processes in reading* (pp. 61–83). Hillsdale, NJ: Lawrence Erlbaum Associates.

Goswami, U. (1987). Orthographic analogies and reading development. *Quarterly Journal of Experimental Psychology.*

Jorm, A. F., & Share, D. L. (1983). Phonological recoding and reading acquisition. *Applied Psycholinguistics, 4,* 103–147.

Kolinsky, R., Cary, L., & Morais, J. (1987). Awareness of words as phonological entities: The role of literacy. *Applied Psycholinguistics, 8,* 223–232.

Leroy-Boussion, A., & Martinez, F. (1972). Un pre-requis auditivo-phonetique pour l'apprentissage du langage ecrit: L'analyse syllabique. *Enfance, 8,* 111–130.

Liberman, I. Y., Shankweiler, D., Fisher, W. F., & Carter, B. (1974). Explicit syllable and phoneme segmentation in the young child. *Journal of Experimental Child Psychology, 18,* 201–212.

Lundberg, I. (1987). Are letters necessary for the development of phonemic awareness? *Cahiers de Psychologie Cognitive, 7,* 472–475.

Lundberg, I., Frost, J., & Petersen, O. P. (1987). *Effects of an extensive program for stimulating phonological awareness in preschool children. Reading Research Quarterly, 23,* 263–284.

Lunberg, I., Olofsson, A., & Wall, S. (1980). Reading and spelling skills in the first school years predicted from phonemic awareness skills in kindergarten. *Scandinavian Journal of Psychology, 21,* 159–173.

Makita, K. (1968). Rarity of reading disability in Japanese children. *American Journal of Orthopsychiatry, 38,* 599–614.

Mann, V. (1986). Phonological awareness: The role of reading experience. *Cognition, 24*, 65–92.

Masonheimer, P. E., Drum, P. A., & Ehri, L. C. (1984). Does environmental print identification lead children into word reading? *Journal of Reading Behaviour, 16*, 257–271.

Morais, J., Alegria, J., & Content, A. (1987a). The relationships between semental analysis and alphabetic literacy: An interactive view. *Cahiers de Psychologie Cognitive, 7*, 415–438.

Morais, J., Alegria, J., & Content, A. (1987b). Segmental awareness: Respectable, useful, and almost always necessary. *Cahiers de Psychologie Cognitive, 7*, 415–438.

Morais, J., Bertelson, P., Cary, L., & Alegria, J. (1986). Literacy training and speech segmentation. *Cognition, 24*, 45–64.

Morais, J., Cary, L., Alegria, J., & Bertelson, P. (1979). Does awareness of speech as a sequency of phones arise spontaneously? *Cognition, 7*, 323–331.

Morais, J., Cluytens, M., & Alegria, J. (1984). Segmentation abilities of dyslexics and normal readers. *Perceptual and Motor Skills, 58*, 221–222.

Olfosson, A., & Lundberg, I. (1983). Can phonemic awareness be trained in kindergarten? *Scandinavian Journal of Psychology, 24*, 35–44.

Olofsson, A., & Lundberg I. (1985). Evaluation of long-term effects of phonemic awareness training in kindergarten: Illustration of some methodological problems in evaluation research. *Scandinavian Journal of Psychology, 26*, 21–34.

Patterson, K. E., & Morton, J. (1985). From orthography to phonology: An attempt at an old interpretation. In K. E. Patterson, J. C. Marshall, & M. Coltheart (Eds.), *Surface dyslexia*. London: Lawrence Erlbaum Associates.

Read, C., Zhang, Y., Nie, H., & Ding, B. (1986). The ability to manipulate speech sounds depends on knowing alphabetic reading. *Cognition, 24*, 31–44.

Rosner, J., & Simon, D. P. (1971). The auditory analysis test: An initial report. *Journal of Learning Disabilities, 4*, 384–392.

Rozin, P., Poritsky, S., & Sotsky, P. (1971). American children with reading problems can easily learn to read English represented by Chinese characters. *Science, 171*, 1264–1267.

Sakamoto, T. (1980). Reading of Hiragana. In J. F. Kavanagh & R. L. Venezky (Eds.), *Orthography, reading and dyslexia*. Baltimore: University Park Press.

Sakamoto, T., & Makita, K. (1973). Japan. In J. Downing (Ed.), *Comparative reading: Cross national studies of behavior and processes in reading and writing*. New York: MacMillan.

Seymour, P. H. K., & Elder, L. (1986). Beginning reading without phonology. *Cognitive Neuropsychology, 1*, 1–36.

Seymour, P. H. K., & MacGregor, C. J. (1984). Developmental dyslexia: A cognitive experimental analysis of phonological, morphemic and visual impairments. *Cognitive Neuropsychology*, 43–82.

Stevenson, H. W., Stigler, J. W., Lucker, W., & Lee, S. (1982). Reading disabilities: The case of Chinese, Japanese and English. *Child Development, 53*, 1164–1181.

Zhurova, L. Y. (1973). The development of analysis of words into their sounds by preschool children. In C. A. Ferguson & D. I. Slobin (Eds.), *Studies in child development*. New York: Hold, Rinehart, & Winston.

11

The Role of Intrasyllabic Units in Learning to Read

Rebecca Treiman
Wayne State University

INTRODUCTION

As many investigators (e.g., Gough & Hillinger, 1980; Liberman, 1982) have pointed out, children's knowledge of spoken language plays an important role in their acquisition of written language. Because writing systems reflect spoken language, studies of language structure provide an important foundation for studies of how children learn to read. This chapter focuses on one specific aspect of spoken language structure—phonological units that are intermediate in size between syllables and phonemes. After reviewing the linguistic status of these intrasyllabic units, I discuss their role in the development of phonological awareness and the learning of reading. Implications for reading instruction are also considered.

LINGUISTIC VIEWS OF SYLLABLE STRUCTURE

Until relatively recently, the syllable was little discussed within linguistics. Some linguists mentioned the syllable only to ignore it; others asserted that the syllable played no role in phonological organization. Recently, however, there has been increased attention to syllables and their structure. In one view (e.g., Hooper, 1972), the syllable is a linear string of phonemes. There are no levels of structure intermediate between the syllable and the phoneme. Another view (e.g., Fudge, 1969; Hockett, 1967/1973; Selkirk, 1982) holds that the phonemes within a syllable are organized hierarchically. There exist phonological units that are intermediate in size between syllables and phonemes. The linguists just cited postulate two major subunits of the syllable, the *onset* and the *rime*. The onset, or initial consonantal portion of the syllable, is a single consonant or consonant cluster. The rime is the vowel and any following consonants. Thus, the word *blast* has the onset /bl/ and the rime /æst/.

Much of the evidence for onset and rime units comes from English. For English, there are several converging lines of evidence, including constraints on the distributions of phonemes within syllables, errors in the production of speech, natural and experimental word games, and errors in short-term memory for spoken syllables. This evidence is reviewed by Treiman (1988). The examples in this chapter are confined to English. Further research is needed to determine whether the findings generalize to other languages.

SYLLABLE STRUCTURE AND PHONOLOGICAL AWARENESS

Many researchers have investigated children's awareness of the phonological units of spoken language. These studies are based on the idea that language awareness plays an important role in learning to read (see Gough & Hillinger, 1980; Liberman, 1982; Rozin & Gleitman, 1977; Tunmer & Bowey, 1984). For alphabetic writing systems, awareness of phonemes is thought to be especially critical. For example, if a child is not aware that the syllables /blæst/ and /bæg/ begin with the same phoneme, the child will not understand why their written versions begin with the same letter.

Most research on phonological awareness has implicitly assumed that syllables are linear strings of phonemes, that there are no units intermediate between syllables and phonemes. Consequently, studies have examined children's awareness of syllables and of phonemes but have not considered their awareness of intrasyllabic units. A number of researchers (Fox & Routh, 1975; Hardy, Stennett, & Smythe, 1973; Leong & Haines, 1978; Liberman, Shankweiler, Fischer, & Carter, 1974; Treiman & Baron, 1981) report that children achieve an awareness of syllables earlier than they achieve an awareness of phonemes. For example, in the study of Liberman et al. (1974), about half the preschool and kindergarten children could learn a task that required them to tap once for each syllable in a spoken word (e.g., one tap for *but*, two taps for *butter*, three taps for *butterfly*). Few preschoolers and kindergartners could master the analogous task with phonemes (e.g., one tap for *oo*, two for *boo*, three for *boot*). It was not until first grade that a majority of children succeeded in the phoneme counting task.

The idea that syllables have an internal structure suggests that previous studies may have overlooked some important steps in the development of phonological awareness. There may be a point at which children are good at analyzing spoken syllables into onsets and rimes but have difficulty analyzing onsets and rimes into their component phonemes. For some syllables, of course, an onset/rime analysis is equivalent to a phonemic analysis. For example, /bo/ contains the onset /b/ and the rime /o/; the onset and rime are single phonemes. For more complex syllables, however, an onset/rime analysis is not identical to an analysis into phonemes. For example, a child who could not go beyond an onset/rime analysis would be aware that /blæst/ begins with /bl/ but would be unable to analyze the /bl/ unit as a /b/ phoneme followed by an /l/ phoneme. This child would also lack awareness of the internal structure of the rime.

Research evidence is consistent with the hypothesis that awareness of intrasyllabic units is easier than and developmentally prior to awareness of phonemes. For example, a study by Barton, Miller, and Macken (1980) suggests that children have difficulty dividing initial consonant clusters into their component phonemes at a time when they *can* separate single initial consonants from the remainder of the syllable. In this study, children between 4 and 5 years old were taught to give the "first sound" of words like *mouse*. For these words, the onset is a single phoneme. The children could perform this task with only a small amount of training. The children were then asked for the "first sound" of words like *swing* and *train*. Some children (about a third of those tested) consistently produced the first singleton sound of the cluster. Others (about 20% to 40% of those tested, depending on the cluster), consistently produced the entire cluster. For example, these children said that *swing* began with /sw/ rather than /s/. The remaining children gave a combination of singleton and cluster responses.

Barton et al.'s (1980) results indicate that some children prefer to keep the onset of a syllable intact. It does not tell us whether these children are *able* to divide the onset into phonemes when asked to do so. A study by Treiman (1985) tested children's ability to perform such a division. Children about 5 1/2 years old were asked whether spoken syllables like /spa/, /sap/, /sa/, and /nik/ began with /s/. If a child can analyze two-phoneme onsets into their component phonemes, he or she should respond "yes" to the first three syllables and "no" to the last. If a child can analyze /spa/ into /sp/ and /a/ but has difficulty dividing /sp/ into /s/ and /p/, a relatively high rate of erroneous "no" responses to /spa/ would be expected. The task was presented with the help of a puppet, who was said to like all "words" that began with the target sound. After a series of practice trials, the child heard a tape-recorded list of test syllables and was asked whether the puppet liked each one. Children more often failed to recognize the initial consonant in syllables like /spa/ (28% error rate) than in syllables like /sap/ (14% error rate) and /sa/ (12% error rate). The subjects did fairly well at rejecting the syllables that began with other phonemes (13% erroneous "yes" responses). Apparently, young children have difficulty recognizing an initial phoneme within a cluster onset.

The studies just described suggest that there is a point in the development of phonological awareness when children are fairly good at dividing syllables into onsets and rimes but have difficulty dividing onsets into phonemes. Other evidence suggests that rimes, too, are difficult to analyze. Several studies (Marsh & Mineo, 1977; Stanovich, Cunningham, & Cramer, 1984) have found tasks that require children to focus on syllable-final consonants to be harder than tasks that require them to focus on syllable-initial consonants. This difference is consistent with the notion that single initial consonants are units on their own (onsets), whereas final consonants are part of a larger unit (the rime). It is easier to divide the onset from the rime (which permits success in the initial consonant task) than to divide the rime into phonemes (which is necessary for the final consonant task).

To summarize, onsets and rimes seem to be cohesive units for children. Children have difficulty analyzing these constituents of the syllable into individual phonemes. Although phonemes may play a tacit role in speech production and perception, they appear to be less accessible to conscious awareness than are larger units of the syllable. The awareness of intrasyllabic units such as onsets and rimes may be developmentally intermediate between the awareness of syllables and the awareness of phonemes.

Because of the role of phonological awareness in the acquisition of literacy, our views of phonological awareness and its development influence our views of reading. Behind traditional views of reading is the notion that there are two levels of phonological awareness—awareness of syllables and awareness of phonemes. The present view—that the awareness of intrasyllabic units is easier than and developmentally prior to the awareness of phonemes—leads us to take a fresh look at how children read words.

SYLLABLE STRUCTURE AND CHILDREN'S READING

An important skill that must be mastered in learning to read is decoding— the mapping of unfamiliar strings of letters onto familiar spoken words. Many previous discussions of this process (e.g., Coltheart, 1978) have emphasized two levels at which the mapping may take place. The first level involves rules that link letters or groups of letters to single phonemes. For example, the reader can use a correspondence between the printed letter *b* and the phoneme /b/ or a correspondence between the printed letters *sh* and the phoneme /š/. Such mappings are often referred to as spelling–sound rules. Spelling–sound rules in this sense can involve units larger than a single letter only if they correspond to a single phoneme, as does *sh*. In addition to letter–phoneme mappings, researchers have emphasized the use of memorized associations between whole printed words and whole spoken words. These have been called word-specific associations. Because many of the earliest learned printed words are monosyllabic, word-specific associations often link printed words to spoken syllables. The distinction between spelling–sound rules and word-specific associations forms the core of dual process models of reading.

Dual-process models imply that a printed word like *blast* can be read in one of two ways. A child can use the correspondences *b* to /b/, *l* to /l/, *a* to /æ/, *s* to /s/, and *t* to /t/, or the child can memorize that the letter string *blast* corresponds to the spoken syllable /blæst/. The idea that children use correspondences either at the level of phonemes or at the level of syllables assumes that the syllable is a linear string of phonemes, that there are no phonological units intermediate in size between the syllable and the phoneme. If syllables and phonemes are the only available phonological units, the child must either treat the printed syllable as a whole or must parse it into units that correspond to phonemes.

The notion of phonological units intermediate in size between syllables and phonemes raises the possibility of correspondences between print and sound that are based on these intermediate units. For example, a child could use links between *bl* and /bl/ and *ast* and /æst/ to pronounce the word *blast*. In this view, a child may not derive the correspondence between *bl* and /bl/ from knowledge of correspondences between *b* and /b/ and *l* and /l/. Instead, the child may store the *bl*–/bl/ correspondence separately and use it whenever he or she encounters *bl* at the beginning of a word.

The preceding considerations suggest that dual-process models of reading, with their emphasis on spelling–sound rules and word-specific associations and their neglect of other possibilities, are oversimplified. This criticism is not new. Other investigators (e.g., Baron, 1977; Glushko, 1979; Patterson & Morton, 1985; Shallice, Warrington, & McCarthy, 1983) have also proposed that groups of letters that correspond to more than a single phoneme play a role in reading. However, without a theory specifying which multiletter sequences are most useful, there is no principled justification for picking some units over others. I propose that linguistic theories of syllable structure can suggest which types of multiletter units are most likely to be used by readers. Readers may be less likely to use a unit like *bla* than a unit like *bl* because *bla* does not correspond to a natural constituent of the syllable whereas *bl* does.

Only a few studies have directly compared children's use of different multiletter units. Santa (1976–1977) worked with second and fifth graders as well as adults. Subjects were first given practice at naming words and pictures. During the practice phase, the words were printed in lower case letters with normal spacing between letters. (The reading practice was omitted for the adult subjects.) Then, pairs of words and pictures were presented simultaneously in a tachistoscope. Subjects had to judge as quickly as possible whether the picture illustrated the word. The words were presented in one of five forms. They could be intact, as in the practice phase (*blast*), or they could have two spaces after the first letter (*b last*), second letter (*bl ast*), third letter (*bla st*), or fourth letter (*blas t*). Fifth graders and adults responded quickly in all conditions. For them, the task may be insensitive due to ceiling effects. When the second graders' data were analyzed alone, a significant effect of spacing emerged. The children responded faster when the words were divided after the second letter than when they were divided elsewhere. In fact, the second graders responded as quickly to words divided after the second letter—a form to which they had presumably not been exposed before the experiment—as to the intact words with which they had practiced. These results are consistent with the idea that children use vowel plus final consonant (or cluster) units in reading. These units seem to be more natural than initial consonant (or cluster) plus vowel units.

A study by Goswami (1986) makes a similar point. Goswami showed children a real-word "clue" and then asked them to try to use this clue to read related items and control items. In the real-word condition, the related and control items were real words. For example, the clue word might be *beak*. Half the related words shared the initial consonant and vowel of the clue word; half shared the vowel and final consonant. For example, *bean* and *peak* might occur with the clue word *beak*. Controls included words like *lake* and *rain*. In the nonsense-word condition, the clue word *beak* was paired with nonsense words like *beal* (initial CV shared), *neak* (final VC shared), and *pake* (control item). Beginning readers about 7 years old benefited from the presence of the clue word. They were able to read more related items when a clue word was present than when no clue was given. Importantly, this benefit was greater for items that shared the V and final C with the clue than for items that shared the initial C and V with the clue. The pattern of results was the same in the real-word condition and the nonsense-word condition. Thus, the clue *beak* was more helpful in reading *peak* and *neak* than in reading *bean* and *beal*.

A group of 5-year-olds who could not yet read any words on a standardized test of reading achievement also participated in Goswami's (1986) experiment. As might be expected, these children were able to read related items only rarely, even when a clue word was provided. However, they succeeded more often on related items that shared a final VC with the clue (7.4% correct responses) than on related items that shared an initial CV with the clue (0.9% correct responses). Goswami's (1986) results suggest that children derive more benefit from multiletter units that correspond to the rime portion of the syllable than from units that correspond to an initial CV.

I have implied that children use letter groups like *b* and *eak* and *bl* and *ast* because these groups correspond to natural phonological units of the syllable. Before learning how to read, a child may be aware that the spoken syllable /blæst/ is divisible into the onset /bl/ and the rime /æst/. When confronted with the printed word *blast*, the child is therefore predisposed to use units that correspond to the spoken language units, namely *bl* and *ast*. There is, however, a somewhat different explanation of why readers parse printed words into an initial consonant (or cluster) unit and a vowel plus final consonant (or cluster) unit. These units may be preferred because of the nature of English orthography. In English (see Venezky, 1970), consideration of the consonant that follows a vowel can help specify the vowel's pronunciation. For example, *a* is pronounced differently before *ll* than before other consonants (e.g., *tall* vs. *tact*). Only rarely does a preceding consonant influence the pronunciation of a vowel (e.g., *wad* vs. *bad*). Readers may parse printed words into an initial consonant unit and a vowel-final consonant unit because they know that the final consonant can modify the pronunciation of the vowel, not because these units correspond to the onsets and rimes of spoken syllables. However, this argument does not explain why Goswami's (1986) nonreaders benefited from shared VC's but not from shared CV's. Because these children could not yet read, they did not know that final consonants may modify vowel pronunciations in English.

The idea that readers use units that correspond to onsets and rimes applies to both children and adults. Dual-process models of reading, which neglect these units, may therefore be oversimplified for all readers. I argue, however, that these models are particularly inappropriate for children. This argument is based on the notion that many beginning readers are aware of onset and rime units of the syllable but have difficulty analyzing these units into their component phonemes. A child who can analyze a spoken word like /blæst/ into /bl/ and /æst/, but who is not aware that /bl/ is composed of /b/ plus /l/ and that /æst/ is composed of /æ/, /s/, and /t/, may be unable to learn individual letter–phoneme mappings. However, this child *may* be able to learn the correspondence between *bl* and /bl/ and *ast* and /æst/. Thus, lack of ability to fully analyze spoken syllables into phonemes may cause children to treat printed words in terms of intrasyllabic units. It does *not* necessarily force them to read via a "sight word" method.

IMPLICATIONS FOR READING INSTRUCTION

A number of investigators (e.g., Gough & Hillinger, 1980; Liberman, 1982) have suggested that children must be able to explicitly analyze spoken words into phonemes in order to master an alphabetic writing system. In their view, children who are equipped with phonemic analysis skills can learn links from letters to phonemes and vice versa. Without these skills, children have no recourse but to read words (or syllables) as wholes. Supporting these views, phonemic analysis skill correlates with and predicts reading success (e.g., Lundberg, Olofsson, & Wall, 1980; Stanovich et al., 1984; Treiman & Baron, 1981). In addition, instruction in phonemic analysis seems to help children learn correspondences between printed and spoken words (e.g., Bradley & Bryant, 1983; Fox & Routh, 1984; Treiman & Baron, 1983). If the goal of initial reading instruction is to teach correspondences at the level of single phonemes, and if these correspondences cannot be learned until children are able to analyze spoken syllables into phonemes, training in phonemic analysis should precede instruction in spelling–sound relationships. Reading instruction should begin when pupils can analyze syllables into phonemes and should focus on correspondences between letters (or letter groups like *sh*) and phonemes. Williams' (1980) program exemplifies this approach. After learning to analyze spoken words into syllables, children proceed to the analysis of syllables into phonemes. When children can analyze spoken syllables like /bæt/ into phonemes, letters are introduced. The child learns the pronunciations of a small number of letters, including *b, a,* and *t*. Next, the child learns to decode words and nonwords like *bat* and *ab* that are made up of these letters. Later, additional letters and more complex items are introduced.

An advantage of the preceding approach is that it teaches children tools with which to read large numbers of unfamiliar words. A disadvantage, however, may lie in the assumption that the only such tools are rules that link letters and phonemes. Even if we grant that children must *eventually* learn correspondences between print and speech at the level of phonemes, instruction need not begin at the phoneme level. As I have argued, children's difficulty in analyzing syllables into phonemes makes it hard for them to learn and use letter–phoneme correspondences. The fundamental notion that print represents speech might be more easily understood if it were introduced by reference to a larger, more accessible unit of sound.

Rozin and Gleitman (1977) propose to teach children that spoken words and written words are related by beginning at the syllable level rather than at the phoneme level. In their view, children can begin to learn about the relationship between print and speech *before* they are able to divide spoken words into phonemes. Once pupils in Rozin and Gleitman's program are able to segment familiar multisyllabic words into syllables, they are introduced to the notion that spoken syllables can be represented visually. For example, /sænd/ is represented by a picture of sand; /wɪč/ is represented by a picture of a witch. These two pictures are combined to stand for the spoken word /sændwɪč/. This phase of Rozin and Gleitman's program is intended to teach that written symbols stand for sounds and that these symbols can be concatenated to represent words and sentences. Children grasp these concepts more easily, Rozin and Gleitman maintain, when they are introduced at the level of the syllable than when they are introduced at the level of the phoneme. Only when children have achieved success at the syllable level does instruction in letter–phoneme relationships begin.

Rozin and Gleitman's use of higher level units—in their case, syllables—to introduce the concept that written words stand for sounds seems to be helpful. It appears that pupils from low-achieving populations learn this concept relatively easily, achieving fair success with the syllabary system. Although the idea of beginning with higher level units may be good, the syllable may not be the ideal choice for languages that have many different syllables. A child who memorizes symbols for only a small number of syllables has the tools to decode only a limited number of words. This child will be unable to decode new polysyllabic words that are composed of unfamiliar syllables. More seriously, the child will also be unable to decode new monosyllables.

Rozin and Gleitman (1977), by concentrating on relationships between print and sound at the level of syllables, may have chosen a level that is too high. Their program may give children the idea that print and speech are related, but may not give them the tools to read a large number of words. Williams (1980), by beginning at the level of single phonemes, may be using a level that is too low. Although her program teaches skills that can be used to read many new words, correspondences at the phoneme level may be difficult for many young children to master at first. The level of onsets and rimes, I suggest, may be a suitable introduction to English orthography.

An onset/rime approach to reading instruction would begin by teaching children to analyze spoken words into syllables. Next, pupils learn to analyze syllables into onsets and rimes. At this point, correspondences between print and speech at the level of onsets and rimes are introduced. For example, children learn that *bl* corresponds to /bl/ and that *ast* corresponds to /æst/. They join these units to read *blast*. In such a program, children memorize that *bl* stands for /bl/ in the same way that they memorize that *sh* stands for /š/. They are not expected to derive for themselves the correspondence between *bl* and /bl/.

Once children have achieved a certain degree of success at the onset/rime level, correspondences between print and speech at the level of phonemes are introduced. Children first receive training in segmenting onsets and rimes of spoken syllables into phonemes. Then, children begin to learn correspondences between phonemes and letters. Children already know, for example, that initial *bl* is pronounced as /bl/ and that initial *br* is pronounced as /br/. Their attention is now drawn to the fact that the both letter groups contain *b*. Because children have been trained to analyze the onsets /bl/ and /br/, they can notice that both groups of phonemes contain a /b/. In this way, children learn the relationship between the grapheme *b* and the phoneme /b/.

The proposed approach shares an advantage with Williams' (1980) program in that it gives children tools that can be used to read a relatively large number of unfamiliar words. For example, if a child at the onset/rime stage of the program can read *men* and *bat*, the child can deduce the pronunciations of *mat* and *Ben*. Because these deductions are based on onsets and rimes, they may be easier than those that are based on phonemes.

The proposed approach shares an advantage with Rozin and Gleitman's (1977) program in that the concept that printed words correspond to spoken words is introduced by reference a level that is more accessible than is the phoneme. However, by focusing on correspondences at the level of onsets and rimes rather than at the level of syllables, the proposed program may avoid one disadvantage of Rozin and Gleitman's approach—that relatively few new words can be read by a child who knows correspondences between a limited number of syllables and their pronunciations. The child who knows correspondences between a limited number of onsets and rimes and their pronunciations *could*, if the onsets and rimes were carefully selected, read a fair number of new monosyllabic words. Even if the child had difficulty in progressing to the level of the phoneme, he or she would experience some success with unfamiliar words.

An onset/rime approach to reading instruction is not a completely novel idea. It is consistent with the common practice of teaching "word families" like *bat*, *cat*, and *hat* and with the teaching of "blends" like *bl* as units. Theories of syllable structure provide a theoretical rationale for these practices and suggest that they should be followed more consistently.

CONCLUSIONS

Many investigators have assumed that because alphabetic writing systems *can* be described, used, and learned at the level of phonemes, they *must* be described, used, and learned at this level. I have suggested that this assumption is not necessarily correct, that levels larger than the phoneme and smaller than the syllable ought also to be considered. Although children must *eventually* learn rules at the level of phonemes, such rules are not easy or natural in early stages of learning to read. Children may more readily learn links between groups of letters and groups of phonemes that are natural units of the syllable. Instruction that begins with such correspondences may be more successful than instruction that initially focuses on the phoneme level.

ACKNOWLEDGMENTS

Thanks to Steve Lapointe, Kathy Straub, and Andrea Zukowski for their assistance. Preparation of this chapter was supported by a Research Career Development Award from NICHD (HD00769).

REFERENCES

Baron, J. (1977). Mechanisms for pronouncing printed words: Use and acquisition. In D. LaBerge & S. J. Samuels (Eds.), *Basic processes in reading: Perception and comprehension.* Hillsdale, NJ: Lawrence Erlbaum Associates.

Barton, D., Miller, R., & Macken, M. A. (1980). Do children treat clusters as one unit or two? *Papers and Reports on Child Language Development, 18*, 93–137.

Bradley, L., & Bryant, P. E. (1983). Categorizing sounds and learning to read—a casual connection. *Nature, 301*, 419–421.

Coltheart, M. (1978). Lexical access in simple reading tasks. In G. Underwood (Ed.), *Strategies of information processing.* London: Academic Press.

Fox, B., & Routh, D. K. (1975). Analyzing spoken language into words, syllables, and phonemes: A developmental study. *Journal of Psycholinguistic Research, 4*, 331–342.

Fox, B., & Routh, D. K. (1984). Phonemic analysis and synthesis as word attack skills: Revisited. *Journal of Educational Psychology, 76*, 1059–1064.

Fudge, E. C. (1969). Syllables. *Journal of Linguistics, 5*, 253–286.

Glushko, R. (1979). The organization and synthesis of orthographic knowledge in reading aloud. *Journal of Experimental Psychology: Human Perception and Performance, 5*, 674–691.

Goswami, U. C. (1986). Children's use of analogy in learning to read: A developmental study. *Journal of Experimental Child Psychology, 42*, 73–83.

Gough, P. B., & Hillinger, M. L. (1980). Learning to read: An unnatural act. *Bulletin of the Orton Society, 30*, 179–196.

Hardy, M., Stennett, R. G., & Smythe, P. C. (1973). Auditory segmentation and auditory blending in relation to beginning reading. *Alberta Journal of Educational Research, 19*, 144–158.

Hockett, C. F. (1973). Where the tongue slips, there slip I. In V. Fromkin (Ed.), *Speech errors as linguistic evidence.* The Hague: Mouton. (Originally published 1967).

Hooper, J. B. (1972). The syllable in phonological theory. *Language, 48*, 525–540.

Leong, C. K., & Haines, C. F. (1978). Beginning readers' analysis of words and sentences. *Journal of Reading Behavior, 10*, 393–407.

Liberman, I. Y. (1982). A language-oriented view of reading and its disabilities. In H. Myklebust (Ed.), *Progress in learning disabilities* (Vol. 5). New York: Grune & Stratton.

Liberman, I. Y., Shankweiler, D., Fischer, F. W., & Carter, B. (1974). Explicit syllable and phoneme segmentation in the young child. *Journal of Experimental Child Psychology, 18*, 201–212.

Lundberg, I., Olofsson, A., & Wall, S. (1980). Reading and spelling skills in the first school years predicted from phonemic awareness skills in kindergarten. *Scandinavian Journal of Psychology, 21*, 159–173.

Marsh, G., & Mineo, R. J. (1977). Training preschool children to recognize phonemes in words. *Journal of Educational Psychology, 69*, 748–753.

Patterson, K., & Morton, J. (1985). From orthography to phonology: An attempt at an old interpretation. In K. Patterson, J. C. Marshall, & M. Coltheart (Eds.), *Surface dyslexia.* London: Lawrence Erlbaum Associates.

Rozin, P., & Gleitman, L. R. (1977). The structure and acquisition of reading II: The reading process and the acquisition of the alphabetic principle. In A. S. Reber & D. L. Scarborough (Eds.), *Toward a psychology of reading: The proceedings of the CUNY conferences.* Hillsdale, NJ: Lawrence Erlbaum Associates.

Santa, C. M. (1976–1977). Spelling patterns and the development of flexible word recognition strategies. *Reading Research Quarterly, 12*, 125–144.

Selkirk, E. O. (1982). The syllable. In H. Van der Hulst & N. Smith (Eds.), *The structure of phonological representations* (Part II). Dordrecht, Netherlands: Foris.

Shallice, T., Warrington, E. K., & McCarthy, R. (1983). Reading without semantics. *Quarterly Journal of Experimental Psychology, 35A*, 111–138.

Stanovich, K. E., Cunningham, A. E., & Cramer, B. (1984). Assessing phonological awareness in kindergarten children: Issues of task comparability. *Journal of Experimental Child Psychology, 38*, 175–190.

Treiman, R. (1985). Onsets and rimes as units of spoken syllables: Evidence from children. *Journal of Experimental Child Psychology, 39*, 161–181.

Treiman, R. (1988). The internal structure of the syllable. In G. Carlson & M. Tanenhaus (Eds.), *Linguistic structure in language processing.* Dordrecht, Netherlands: Kluwer.

Treiman, R., & Baron, J. (1981). Segmental analysis ability: Development and relation to reading ability. In G. E. MacKinnon & T. G. Waller (Eds.), *Reading research: Advances in theory and practice* (Vol. 3). New York: Academic Press.

Treiman, R., & Baron, J. (1983). Phonemic-analysis training helps children benefit from spelling–sound rules. *Memory and Cognition, 11*, 382–389.

Tunmer, W. E., & Bowey, J. A. (1984). Metalinguistic awareness and reading acquisition. In W. E. Tunmer, C. Pratt, & M. L. Herriman (Eds.), *Metalinguistic awareness in children.* Berlin: Springer-Verlag.

Venezky, R. L. (1970). *The structure of English orthography.* The Hague: Mouton.

Williams, J. P. (1980) Teaching decoding with an emphasis on phoneme analysis and phoneme blending. *Journal of Educational Psychology, 72*, 1–15.

IV Reading Skill and Reading Problems

12

Learning (and Not Learning) To Read: A Developmental Framework

Frederick J. Morrison
Department of Psychology
University of North Carolina, Greensboro

The psychological investigation of normal and abnormal reading acquisition followed distinct paths for many years. Research on normal acquisition focused on word decoding and comprehension processes underlying reading activity, using sophisticated information—processing methodology (Perfetti, 1985). In contrast until recently, scientific study of reading disorders (especially developmental dyslexia) suffered from a lack of coherence in working definitions, theoretical framework, and methodology (Vellutino, 1979). During the last decade, an important convergence of perspective and approach between the two fields has been growing. For the first time the possibility is emerging of a common, integrative effort to understand how children learn (or do not learn) how to read.

This chapter begins with a discussion of recent themes and issues in the study of developmental dyslexia (or specific reading disability, as it is alternatively called). A number of unresolved issues are identified, and it is argued that future progress would benefit from a developmental perspective. The chapter follows with a description of a working model of reading acquisition, which attempts to provide a common framework for understanding normal and abnormal reading and, in addition, to circumvent some of the conceptual and methodological problems in the field of dyslexia.

UNDERSTANDING READING DISABILITY: CURRENT ISSUES

Three interlocking questions have dominated the study of reading disability in recent years. First, who is the reading-disabled child? Moving beyond standard definitional criteria, researchers have searched for additional correlates and discriminators whereby dyslexic children may be more reliably separated from other poor learners (Jorm, Share, Maclean, & Matthews, 1986b; Rutter & Yule, 1975). Second, is reading disability a heterogeneous disorder? Specifically, do different groups of reading-disabled children suffer from qualitatively different underlying cognitive deficits (Rourke, 1975)? Third, depending on the answer to question 2, what is (are) the underlying cognitive problem(s) that prevent disabled readers from making normal reading progress?

In recent years, most research and controversy has centered on the second and third questions. Some investigators have emphasized the homogeneous nature of the dyslexic's difficulty by demonstrating major reliable and arguably exclusive deficits in phonological decoding in disabled readers (Siegel, 1986; Stanovich, 1986; Vellutino, 1979).

Others have argued equally forcefully that the problems exhibited by disabled readers are not uniform and that sensitive long-term clinical assessments, buttressed by factor-analytic studies, consistently reveal two or more fundamentally distinct subtypes of specific reading disability. With some exceptions, the subtype most often proposed apart from a phonological subtype is a visual or visuospatial subtype (Boder, 1973).

Yet progress in documenting the heterogeneity of reading disability as well as in specifying "the underlying cognitive disorder(s)" has been modest at best. Several empirical and logical problems have hampered progress in these areas. First, despite recent methodological advances, subject selection procedures in current work continue to suffer from serious methodological and conceptual shortcomings, leaving open the possibility that the great majority of studies of "reading-disabled children" routinely have included other groups of poor learners. Second, claims about heterogeneity of the disorder have not systematically entertained or tested the simpler hypothesis that differences among identifiable subgroups of disabled readers represent a simple continuum of severity, primarily because research has not been cast in a developmental framework. Finally and related to the preceding problem is the persistent focus on elementary process deficits. Results of the last 10 years of work on elementary processes like visual discrimination, serial ordering, or short-term memory have made little progress in uncovering the underlying cognitive difficulties of disabled readers, primarily because of their inherent inability to separate cause from effect, again lacking a developmental framework. A more profitable avenue, I argue, would be to focus on the skills of reading itself and how they change with experience and development.

Who is the Disabled Reader? The Problem of Subject Selection

To successfully address the questions of heterogeneity and the underlying cognitive disorder, one must be reasonably confident that the sample of subjects selected for study is not seriously contaminated by other kinds of poor learners. It is precisely this assumption that recent work casts in serious doubt. Despite advances in the methodological rigor with which research on reading disabilities has been conducted, subjects continue to be selected in ways that risk inclusion of several different groups of children with separate learning disorders. Four major criteria bear closest scrutiny.

1. *IQ* Typically, disabled readers in scientific articles are described as possessing "normal IQ's." Recent years have witnessed an increase in using real test scores (as opposed to teacher ratings) to assess IQ. Less common is equating subjects on IQ, leaving open the possibility that reader group differences in performance are in part caused by IQ differences (Wolford, 1985). More crucial, however, is the practice of including children with IQ scores of 80 and even below. A recent notable example is a study by Stevenson and his colleagues (Stevenson, Stigler, Tucker, Lee, Hsu, & Kitamara, 1982) that included subjects with IQ's above 70! This is not an isolated case. Significant numbers of studies continue to include poor readers with IQ scores hovering in the low 80s. What is the significance of this practice? A growing body of research has documented major differences between groups of poor learners differing in IQ. Over 10 years ago Rutter and Yule (1975) found that a group of normal IQ poor readers (mean IQ of 98.4) reading below expected level differed from lower IQ readers (mean IQ 85.6) in sex distribution, in incidence of hard and soft neurological signs, in presence of motor disorders as well as language disorders, in the tendency to come from disadvantaged homes, and in mathematics achievement. More recently Jorm and his colleagues (Jorm et al., 1986b; Jorm, Share, Matthews, & Maclean, 1986a) confirmed Rutter and Yule's findings and discovered that low IQ poor readers were deficient in a broad range of cognitive skills, assessing both visual and auditory processing, whereas normal IQ poor readers showed deficits on a more limited range of language-related tasks.

The implication of these findings is clear. Selecting poor readers with IQ scores below around 90 or 95 runs the serious risk of including children with qualitatively different problems than higher IQ disabled readers. The direct impact of such selection procedures is to contaminate the sample of truly disabled readers with children who have other neurological, social, visual, and motor deficits. As a result, any conclusion about the heterogeneity of reading disability or of the underlying cognitive problems of disabled readers must be viewed with skepticism.

Beyond the question of IQ cut-off point lies the equally important issue of which aspects of IQ to utilize in matching disabled with normal readers—verbal IQ, nonverbal (performance) IQ, or both. Although full consideration of this complex issue is beyond the present scope, it seems clear that controlling for verbal IQ poses the most serious risks for research purposes. Because experience with and progress in reading can reasonably be expected to enhance performance on IQ subscales measuring verbal IQ, the verbal IQ's of disabled readers could routinely be underestimated in standardized testing situations, invalidating any matching efforts.

2. *Reading Skill.* A separate concern has been raised about the skills used in selecting subjects as reading disabled. As Siegel (1985) recently noted, most studies of reading disability utilize a reading "comprehension" test to assess degree of reading skill. In other instances a composite score, comprised of both decoding and comprehension, is utilized. Nevertheless, decoding and comprehension tests measure different skills; whereas decoding tests typically assess phonics skills, comprehension tests involve memory processes, reading speed, inferencing, and other general intellectual skills. Consequently, relying on composite reading scores or purely on comprehension scores increases the probability of including in the reading-disabled sample children with a wide variety of cognitive or even social/emotional problems. By implication, an appreciable decrease in the heterogeneity of the sample of "disabled readers" could be achieved by ensuring that subjects exhibited major deficits in word decoding. Such an assessment does not deny the existence of a separate "reading comprehension" disability—on the contrary, it provides a direct test of the hypothesis—but it does caution against lumping together two potentially distinct deficits in the same sample of children.

3. *Mathematics Achievement.* A potentially important, yet relatively unexplored, question is the meaning of differential achievement in mathematics versus reading in reading-disabled children. Somewhat counterintuitively, almost no investigations take mathematics achievement into consideration in selecting specific disabled readers. Yet, scattered evidence suggests that math-reading discrepancies may prove to be a sensitive discriminator of different groups of poor readers. For instance, one of the most striking findings emerging from Rutter and Yule's (1975) analysis of differences between lower IQ and higher IQ poor readers was differential achievement in mathematics. Higher IQ poor readers performed closer to grade level in math, whereas lower IQ poor readers lagged behind equally in math and reading. Further, Hall and his associates (Hall, Wilson, Humphreys, Tinzmann, & Bowyer, 1983) examined phonological coding and short-term

memory in two groups of poor readers differing in math achievement. Poor readers achieving well in mathematics outperformed students with low achievement in both subjects and showed a different pattern of phonological coding deficits.

Taken together, these findings raise the possibility that poor readers who continue to make progress in mathematics may constitute a different group of children than those who lag behind more generally.

4. *Social-Emotional Problems.* Finally a related issue that has surfaced recently is the possible inclusion in reading-disabled samples of children whose primary problem is social or emotional in origin. Although the standard definition of reading disability requires that a child be free of "primary emotional disturbance" (Rourke, 1975), almost never do cognitive studies directly assess emotional functioning, relying primarily on teacher reports. Whereas teacher reports may be reasonably accurate for very severe emotional disturbance, their assessments of less severe social or family problems are less reliable. In a recent study, we interviewed teachers about the family life and behavior problems of two groups of children: *low achieving* (i.e., equally behind in reading and math) and *specific reading disabled* (behind only in reading). Our classification of the children was unknown to the teachers—they referred to all the children simply as "reading-" or more commonly "learning-disabled." For 8 of the 10 low-achieving children, the teachers described some degree of social-emotional problem (e.g., an alcoholic or abusive parent, continued absenteeism or truancy). Comparable problems were reported for only one of the specific reading-disabled children. Although clearly anecdotal, these reports suggested that at least some of the low-achieving children may have been experiencing significant family or emotional stress, though not enough to produce the kind of serious emotional disturbance required for exclusion from most studies. Such findings at least raise the suspicion that the reason some normal IQ children are doing generally poorly in school is linked directly to family or social problems. A recent study by Jorm et al. (1986a) confirmed this suspicion in comparisons of lower IQ poor readers with generally low achievement (Grade 1 IQ of 84.7) with higher IQ poor readers (IQ of 101) exhibiting primarily a reading disorder. Responses to the Children's Behavior Questionnaire revealed that the low-achieving poor readers had a significantly higher incidence of behavior problems (including attentional deficits) than either specific reading-disabled children or normal readers, who did not differ from each other. These findings suggest that without independent assessment children with significant though nontraumatic emotional problems could easily be included in samples of children selected for studies of reading disability.

As the foregoing section implies, there are legitimate reasons to suspect that the majority of studies of reading disability have included significant numbers of children whose primary problem may be related to general intellectual, social, or emotional problems. Further, as Siegel (1986) recently concluded in an extensive review of the subtyping literature, those studies employing the most careful and logically consistent definitions of reading disability reliably have failed to discover significant heterogeneity in the reading-disabled sample. One might argue that more stringent definitions of reading disability will obviously produce less heterogeneity in the sample of poor readers. Yet the empirical evidence just reviewed argues persuasively that greater delimitation of the reading-disabled sample is more than a futile exercise in "semantics" or "operationalism" (Kagan, 1989). The variables identified are linked in theoretically and clinically meaningful ways to very different etiologies for reading and other learning disorders. In any case, sufficient empirical data have accumulated to warrant systematic examination of the impact of IQ, decoding versus comprehension problems, differential math achievement, and social-emotional problems on traditional subtyping schemes.

Is Reading Disability a Heterogeneous Disorder: Subtypes or Severity?

An equally complex problem centers on the difficulty in the subtyping and clinical literatures of distinguishing between *heterogeneity of the underlying disorder* and *heterogeneity of the symptoms* different children manifest. The latter is routinely and illogically induced as the former. Hence, if one child in a special class is obviously highly distractible whereas another sits quietly and mixes up the order of letters in words, the first child is presumed to suffer a fundamental problem with attention whereas the second might have a basic sequencing disorder. Although reasonable, such conclusions fail to see the two disorders as possible points on a continuum of severity or as different coping strategies. One reason for this failure is the relative lack of a theoretical and developmental perspective on reading acquisition in the current subtyping literature. Without some clearer idea of what the act of reading (or at least word decoding) is and how it changes with age and experience, conclusions about subtypes must forever be mired in ambiguity.

What is the Underlying Disorder?

A similar shortcoming exists in the continued focus on elementary process deficits in disabled readers. For almost a century disabled readers have been presumed to suffer from some fundamental problem in elementary cognitive processes like perception, attention, memory, serial ordering, and visuospatial coding. Regardless of whether a unitary or subtype view was favored, this enterprise carried the assumption that the cognitive system consists of a set of stable, individual processes whose nature and functioning can be isolated from the rest of the system and examined experimentally. Yet three fundamental problems have arisen with this view in recent years. First, an impressive corpus of data has failed to uncover major process differences between normal and disabled readers (Morrison & Manis, 1982; Vellutino, 1979). Second, those differences in processing that have been unearthed are more easily explained as a result rather than a cause of the reading problem (Morrison & Manis, 1982). Third, and most critically, it has become increasingly apparent in cognitive development research that basic information-processing skills are heavily (if not primarily) dependent on knowledge about a given domain (Chi, 1978; Keil, 1986; Ornstein & Naus, 1978). All these findings seriously undermine a research strategy that focuses on supposedly isolable elementary information processes. For example, if working memory processes in reading are heavily dependent on one's knowledge of symbol–sound correspondence rules as well as on the degree of unitization or automaticity in word decoding, then focusing one's inquiry on short-term memory is fundamentally misdirected—rather like opting to study the flickering shadows on the wall of Plato's cave. The more fruitful focus, I argue, is the process of reading acquisition itself. Not only does it represent a more direct assault on the problem, but it may afford a clearer perspective for examining the heterogeneity issue. If, finally, one adds to this analysis the emerging realization that selected skills (like word decoding) may constitute special-purpose, encapsulated modules, the ultimate answer to the disabled reader's problem may lie in a highly specialized domain-specific skill, having little to do with general information processing.

A DEVELOPMENT FRAMEWORK

As the foregoing discussion indicates, there are two central foci that need to be incorporated in a full account of the nature of reading disability. First is a systematic examination of the impact of different selection criteria on the nature and range of the problems exhibited by disabled readers. Second is development of a model of early reading acquisition within which to address the question of heterogeneity and the underlying cognitive deficit. Whereas a fully developed model of reading acquisition has not previously been elaborated, recent work by several researchers (including Perfetti, Stanovich, Olson, and Bruck) provides the elements of a working model of early reading acquisition, focusing predominantly on mastery of elementary word-decoding operations.

For simplicity of exposition, the acquisition process is divided into three phases (early, middle, late), without implying any stage-like characteristics.

Approximate North American grade-level designations are provided, although recognizing the importance of individual variation.

Early Phase (Grades 1–2).   During the initial stages of reading acquisition, most children focus primarily on learning grapheme–phoneme correspondence rules (Ehri, 1987), together with some limited sight-word learning. Throughout this period decoding is effortful (Morrison & Manis, 1982) and the size of the orthographic unit used to parse words is relatively small (1–2 letters, Olson, 1985). Beginning and ending letter positions dominate decoding attempts and at this stage surrounding letters do not constrain word attack skills to the extent they will in the next phase.

Middle Phase (Grades 3–4).   With experience and instruction, the size of the orthographic unit increases such that medial vowels and word stems become a more important parsing unit (because greater phonological regularities exist at the higher unit level; Olson, 1985; Santa, 1976–1977; Seidenberg, Waters, Barnes, & Tanenhaus, 1984). At this point, decoding of new or less familiar words begins to include analogy or rhyming strategies to a greater extent than in the earlier phase. For the most part decoding is still effortful, but some whole-word codes are becoming unitized in long-term visual memory, especially high-frequency words (Waters Seidenberg, & Bruck, 1984). As a consequence comprehension skills begin to show sharp improvement. At this point individual differences in reading strategies may emerge. Some children may continue to rely predominantly on lower level grapheme–phoneme correspondence (GPC) rules, albeit increasingly sophisticated ones. Other children may jump sharply to an exclusively whole-word or analogy strategy (obviously a mixture of the two is also possible).

Late Phase (Grades 5–6).   Ultimately, however, for most normal readers, on the majority of words attention is focused increasingly on larger orthographic units (stems and whole words). Visual and phonological neighborhoods become firmly established in long-term memory (Glushko, 1979). Direct visual access to the lexicon may come to dominate skilled word decoding (Coltheart, 1978; Seidenberg, et al., 1984), though some automatic phonological activation may occur (Van Orden, 1987). Now when confronted with unfamiliar words, the more experienced reader utilizes a flexible repertoire of strategies or word attack skills to deal with the novel letter string. Comprehension, as a consequence, continues to improve.

The preceding conceptualization captures the essential elements of a working model of early reading acquisition, up to mastery of word decoding. Further, the framework is eminently testable utilizing currently available experimental manipulations (including comparisons of pronunciation of words vs. pseudowords, regular vs. irregular words, high-vs. low-frequency words, as well as others). Most important, such a developmental framework can help to address some currently unresolved issues in the study of developmental dyslexia.

Two Examples

Consider first the question of subtypes versus severity, using as an illustrative case Boder's (1973) distinction between "dysphonetic" (primarily phonologically impaired) and "dyseidetic" (primarily visually/orthographically impaired). Olson (1985) has developed a set of tests aimed at revealing relatively specific deficits in phonological versus orthographic processing. To assess how well children decode words phonologically, he asks them which of two visually presented pseudowords (e.g., *sope* and *bape*) sounds like a real word. Performance on this task, according to Olson, requires phonological processing. Conversely, in assessing orthographic processing children decide which of two indentically pronounced letter strings (e.g., *sail* vs. *sayle*) is spelled correctly. In this task phonological processing alone isn't sufficient for correct responding; children must know the correct orthographic pattern.

To the extent that Boder's two subtypes of dyslexics exist, they should perform differently on the phonological processing versus orthographic processing tasks adapted from Olson (1985). Specifically dyslexics suffering primarily a phonological problem should equal reading-level (perhaps even age-level) matched normal readers on the orthographic task, whereas the dyseidetic groups should manifest the opposite pattern. Therefore, these tasks could be utilized initially to attempt to subtype the two groups of dyslexics.

If successful, a converging pattern of findings would be predicted across tasks and across time. For example, the younger phonologically impaired dyslexics should perform below reading-level matched children on pronunciation of pseudowords and on pronunciation of regular/consistent versus irregular/inconsistent words. On converging orthographic processing tasks (e.g., Santa 1976–1977), they are expected to be equal to or better than reading-level matched normal readers.

Over time, they would make less progress in phonological processing than in orthographic processing. In particular, they should continue to perform below reading-level matches on pronunciation of regular/consistent versus irregular/inconsistent words, whereas they could be expected to develop whole-word visual codes assessed in orthographic matching tasks (Santa, 1976–1977). Such a pattern of findings would reveal that phonologically impaired dyslexics were learning to read predominantly by visual–verbal paired-associate learning (or whole-word learning), abandoning symbol–sound correspondence rules, and analogies and other phonological strategies.

A contrasting picture would be drawn for the orthographically impaired dyslexics. They should perform at expected reading levels on phonological tasks but lag behind reading-level matched normal readers on orthographic tasks. Over time, they would be expected to get better and faster on pseudoword pronunciation, and on pronunciation of regular/consistent versus irregular/inconsistent words but continue to show a regularity effect for high-and low-frequency words. Such results would confirm that they suffer a fundamental deficit in constructing orthographic codes in memory. Obviously, they should not manifest representations for whole-word visual codes in orthographic matching tasks.

To the extent that most dyslexics show a reasonably common pattern of deficits over tasks and time, differences among children would most reasonably emerge on a continuum of severity. In fact, Olson (1985) recently obtained evidence favoring a "continuum-of-severity" interpretation for orthographic problems, with all dyslexics manifesting severe phonological deficits.

The developmental framework can also be used to address the underlying nature of the disorder. Two recent hypotheses can be contrasted, namely the "phonological decoding deficit" and the "correspondence rule-learning deficit" views. A number of investigators have hypothesized that the fundamental disorder in developmental dyslexia is poor and/or slow phonological decoding (Olson, 1985; Stanovich, 1988). In contrast, Morrison and Manis (1982) proposed that disabled readers may suffer a more fundamental problem in learning the complex irregular symbol–sound correspondences in English, thereby preventing them from decoding words adequately. These two views make somewhat contrasting predictions about the pattern and development of early reading skills. The "phonological decoding deficit" view would predict a reasonably global pattern of deficits across all aspects of the phonological decoding tasks. In contrast, the "rule learning deficit" view predicts that pronunciation of regular/consistent words should equal that of reading-level matched children but he significantly lower on irregular/inconsistent words. Correspondingly, the growth of phonological and orthographic processing skills for regular/consistent words should reliably exceed that of irregular/inconsistent words over time. Hence, disabled readers should begin to manifest whole-word visual codes (comparable to reading-level matches) for regular/consistent words on orthographic processing tasks. Their accuracy and speed of pronunciation of regular/consistent words should equal reading-level matches, whereas they should fall further behind on irregular/inconsistent words.

Whatever the research outcomes of these two examples, they illustrate how a developmental framework may help to more adequately address the difficult problems facing researchers attempting to understand childhood reading disorders.

OVERVIEW AND CONCLUSIONS

As the foregoing analysis implies, problems in understanding the nature of reading disorders in children stem in part from failure to provide an interpretive framework incorporating solid theoretical and developmental perspectives. Recent advances in theory and method have made possible an integration of work on normal and abnormal patterns of reading acquisition. This chapter represents an attempt to provide a unifying conceptualization that simultaneously may help to address some of the thorny, unresolved questions in the study of children's reading problems.

REFERENCES

Boder, E. (1973). Developmental dyslexia: A diagnostic approach based on three atypical reading–spelling patterns. *Developmental Medicine and Child Neurology, 15*, 663–687.

Bruck, M. (1987 April). *Paper presented at Symposium on The development of word recognition processes in normal and disabled readers.* Biennial meeting of S.R.C.D., Baltimore.

Chi, M. T. H. (1978). Knowledge structures and memory development. In R. S. Sieger (Ed.), *Children's thinking: What develops (pp. 73–96?* Hillsdale, NJ: Lawrence Erlbaum Association.

Coltheart, M. (1978). Lexical access in simple reading tasks. In G. Underwood (Ed.), *Strategies in information processing* (pp. 151–216). London: Academic Press.

Ehri, L. C. (1987). How orthography alters spoken language competencies in children. In J. Downing & R. Valtin (Eds.), *Language awareness and learning to read.* New York: Springer-Verlag.

Gilmore, J. V., & Gilmore, E. C. (1968). *Gilmore Oral Reading Test.* New York: Harcourt, Brace, Jovanovich.

Gluskho, R. (1979). The organization and activation of orthographic knowledge in reading aloud. *Journal of Experimental Psychology: Human Perception and Performance, 5*, 647–691.

Hall, J., Wilson, K., Humphreys, M., Tinzmann, M., & Bowyer, P. (1983). Phonemic similarity effects in good vs. poor readers. *Memory and Cognition, 11*(5), 520–527.

Jorm, A. F., Share, D. L., Maclean, R., & Matthews, R. (1986b). Cognitive factors at school entry predictive of specific reading retardation and general reading backwardness: A research note. *Journal of Child Psychology and Psychiatry, 27*(1), 45–54.

Jorm, A. F., Share, D. L., Matthews, R., & Maclean, R. (1986a). Behaviour problems in specific reading retarded and general reading backward children: A longitudinal study. *Journal of Child Psychology and Psychiatry, 27*(1), 33–43.

Kagan, J. (1989). Meaning and procedure. In F. J. Morrison, C. Lord, & D. P. Keating (Eds.), *Applied developmental psychology,* (Vol. 3, pp. 9–39). New York: Academic Press.

Keil, F. C. (1986). Conceptual domains and the acquisition of metaphor. *Cognitive Development, 1*(1), 73–96.

Morrison, F. J., & Manis, F. R. (1982). Cognitive processes and reading disability: A critique and proposal. In C. J. Brainerd & M. I. Pressley (Eds.), *Progress in cognitive development research* (Vol. 2). New York: Springer-Verlag.

Olson, R. (1985). Disabled reading processes and cognitive profiles. In D. Gray & J. Kavanaugh (Eds.), *Behavioral measures of dyslexia.* Parkton, MD: York Press.

Ornstein, P. A., & Naus, M. J. (1978). Rehearsal processes in children's memory. In P. A. Ornstein (Ed.), *Memory development in children* (pp. 69–100). Hillsdale, NJ: Lawrence Erlbaum Association.

Perfetti, C-A. (1985). *Reading ability.* New York: Oxford University Press.

Rourke, B. (1975) Brain-behaviour relationships in children with learning disabilities: A research program. *American Psychologist, 30*, 911–920.

Rutter, M., & Yule, W. (1975). The concept of specific reading retardation. *Journal of Child Psychology and Psychiatry, 8*, 1–11.

Santa, C. (1976–77). Spelling patterns and the development of flexible word recognition strategies. *Reading Research Quarterly, 2*, 125–144.

Seidenberg, M. S., Waters, G. S., Barnes, M., & Tanenhaus, M. K. (1984). When does irregular spelling or pronunciation influence word recognition? *Journal of Verbal Learning and Verbal Behavior, 23*, 383–404.

Siegel, L. S. (1985, April). *Phonological deficits in children with reading disabilities.* Paper presented at the biennial meetings of S.R.C.D., Toronto.

Siegel, L. S. (1986). Subtypes of dyslexia: Do they exist? In F. J. Morrison, C. Lord, & D. P. Keating (Eds.), *Applied developmental psychology* (pp. 170–190). New York: Academic Press.

Siegel, L. S. (in press). Issues in defining learning disabilities. In F. J. Morrison (Ed.), *Child development: When things go wrong. Canadian Journal of Psychology.*

Stanovich, K. E. (1988). Explaining the difference between the dyslexic and the garden-variety poor reader: The phonological-core variable-disprence model. *Journal of Learning Disabilities, 21*, 590–612.

Stanovich, K. E., & Bauer, D. W. (1978). Experiments on the spelling-to-sound regularity effect in word recognition. *Memory and Cognition, 6*, 410–415.

Stevenson, H. W., Stigler, J. W., Tucker, G. W., Lee, S., Hsu, C., & Kitamura, S. (1982). Reading disabilities: The case of Chinese, Japanese and English. *Child Development, 53*, 1164–1181.

Van Orden, G. C. (1987). A *ROWS* is a *ROSE*: Spelling, sound and reading. *Memory and Cognition, 15*(3), 181–198.

Vellutino, F. R. (1979). *Dyslexia: Theory and research.* Cambridge: MIT Press.

Waters, G. S., Seidenberg, M. S., & Bruck, M. (1984). Children's and adults' use of spelling–sound information in three reading tasks. *Memory and Cognition, 5*, 427–451.

Wolford, G. (1985). Information processing approaches to reading disability. In L. S. Siegel & F. J. Morrison (Eds.), *Cognitive development in atypical children* (pp. 27–44). New York: Springer-Verlag.

13 Word-Identification Strategies in a Picture Context: Comparisons between "Good" and "Poor" Readers

Liliane Sprenger-Charolles
INRP and CNRS, Paris

Central to current discussions concerning reading and its acquisition are three related questions: What strategies are used by readers to identify words? How do these strategies develop? What is the role of context at this level?

For the questions of word-identification strategies and their development, Coltheart (1978) and Harris and Coltheart's (1986) theories offer one clear approach. Given an alphabetic writing system, competent readers follow two distinct strategies: (1) "direct," in which written letter strings contact lexical forms in memory; and (2) "indirect," in which rules of correspondence between graphemes and phonemes (CGP) are applied. These different modes of processing must gradually become automatic. First, according to Harris and Coltheart's (1986) model, before they learn true reading, children use a direct procedure to read a small set of words (the "sight-vocabulary" phase). Around age 5–6, at the "discrimination-net" stage, children rely more heavily on partial clues such as the length of items, the form of the letters, etc. in order to find a partial match in memory. This strategy, however, does not permit them to read new words, so the "phonological-recoding" phase (CGP), the third stage, takes over and is dominant until around the age of 8 years. However, many orthographic systems do not provide direct one-to-one mapping between graphemes and phonemes. In these "mixed" writing systems, which include both English and French (cf. Catach, 1979, concerning French), the simple use of CGP strategies is insufficient. In reading in these mixed systems, an "orthographic" phase will slowly, although not completely, replace the CGP strategy.

The distinction between a CGP strategy and a later orthographic strategy is assumed to be evidenced by differences in children's responses in sensibility judgments that involve homophones (e.g., "tell me wear/where he went"). Younger subjects (age 6) make a number of errors on this type of test as they regularly recode the written chains phonologically (cf. Doctor & Coltheart, 1980).

Turning now to the role that context plays in the identification of words, evidence suggests that "good" readers are less dependent on context than "poor" ones (cf. Perfetti, 1985; Perfetti & Roth, 1981; Stanovich, 1980). An interactive-compensatory hypothesis (cf. Stanovich, 1980, 1986) accounts for this difference by noting the tradeoff between facilitating effects of context and the reader's competence in word identification. According to Stanovich (1986, p. 369) this tradeoff results from the "fact that the information processing system is arranged in such a way that when the bottom-up processes that result in word recognition are deficient, the system compensates by relying more heavily on another knowledge source (e.g., contextual information)." Perfetti and Roth (1981) provide a similar explanation.

Following Posner and Snyder (1975) this hypothesis led Stanovich (1981) and Perfetti (1985) to differentiate "automatic" processes from "attentional" ones. The former are rapid and efficient and are not sensitive to the effects of contextual inhibition. In contrast, attentional strategies are slower and much more sensitive to the effect of context and, more specifically, to the effect of inhibition in the case in incongruency between the context and the target word.

Explanations based on this processing distinction do account for the differences that have been observed between younger and less competent readers' use of context and that of older and more skilled readers. For the former, the procedures of word identification are not totally automatic, thus encouraging the use of attentional strategies guided by context. This would also explain the slowness of the reading. The implementation of attentional strategies, however, implies extra processing and thus less skilled readers have fewer resources available for other aspects of reading comprehension.

Goodman's (1976) results, which showed that good readers rely heavily on context, might be thought to contradict the accounts of Stanovich and Perfetti. However, Goodman does not differentiate between the role played by context in word recognition and its role in comprehension. "Good" readers indeed use context more efficiently (and without any rigidity; cf. Perfetti, Goldman, & Hogaboam 1979), at global levels than do "poor" readers, but they appear not to use it for word identification.

The experiment reported next concerns these questions of context, word identification, and skill. It examines the types of strategies that are brought into play for word identification by more and less competent readers, and more specifically by a group of "good" readers and one of "poor" readers having chronic difficulties in learning to read.

THE EXPERIMENT

To observe the type of strategies that are spontaneously used by children, we chose a task developed by Khomsi (1985) in which a single word was to be read in the context of a picture. (Other possibilities were considered to be too likely to bias particular strategies. For example, reading aloud might encourage a decoding strategy and reading a long text might encourage an anticipation strategy and would also be punishing for poor readers.)

The task required subjects to judge the correctness of a name given to an object or animal in a picture. Two types of errors were introduced into the picture names:

First, spelling errors were created by changing a single letter in a word, thus creating what we have called " pseudononsense words" (PN = 15 items) (e.g., "pantalin" instead of "pantalon" [pants]). They were so called because the created nonwords were all very similar to real French words. Although the nonwords were not homophonic to real words, some were created from closely related phonemes (i.e., f/v as in "falise" instead of "valise" [suitcase]).

Second, some words were semantic errors, given the picture context. In such cases, the picture was given a name related to the correct name but not synonymous with it (e.g., the word "limace" [slug]) written under a picture of a snail. These modifications were called "pseudosynonyms" (PS). So as not to favor those strategies that poor readers tend to opt for, there were only three examples of this type of item.

The three types of items, PN, PS, and the correctly named objects or animals were randomly presented in sets of 5, each having 3 PN's, O or 1 PS's, and 1 or 2 correct names.

The children were individually presented with cards that had a picture and its name. They were to "look at" the cards and say whether what was written under the picture was the "correct word." A "no" answer was followed by a request to explain why it was not correct. For subjects giving a high proportion of "yes" responses, the experimenter turned the card over and asked them to say the word written on the card. This helped to encourage attention to the task demands.

The subjects were "good" and "poor" readers of the same age. The "poor" readers included 21 children whose average age was 10;1. These subjects showed no clinical pathological signs. Their operating level was normal and their IQ was equal to or higher than 85 on one of the WISC-R scale (average verbal IQ of 88, average performance IQ of 101).[1] Their best reading level was equivalent to that of children having finished half of first grade (age 6–7).

The population of "good" readers included 21 subjects of about the same age as the population of "poor" readers (average age:9;4) who had shown no particular difficulties in learning to read and were considered by their teachers to be good readers. The children from both groups were from non-deprived (middle-class) socioeconomic backgrounds with schooling in French from the time they entered kindergarten.

Before reporting the results of the experiment, take note of what kinds of results might be expected from current theories of reading. According to Stanovich (1979, 1980), poor readers identify words by anticipating meaning from context. They should use the context offered by the picture to respond and would check only globally to see if context and word fit together. Thus, poor readers would detect semantic errors (pseudosynonyms) through their use of strategies of global word recognition. On the other hand, graphic errors (pseudononsense words) might not be readily detected by these subjects. Poor readers would also be expected to show a certain amount of behavioral rigidity (cf. Perfetti, Goldman, & Hogaboam, 1979).

Moreover, if it is hypothesized that even during silent reading the phonetic representation of a word plays a role in its identification, especially at certain stages of the learning process (cf. Doctor & Coltheart, 1980), readers would be expected to make a number of errors in the detection of pseudononsense words that are phonetically similar to the expected word.

General Results of the Experiment

The number of pseudononsense words (PN) and pseudosynonyms (PS) rejected by the children, as well as the reasons they gave for the rejection, were calculated for both groups. In the case of PN's, correct reasons were those that referred to the word's spelling and corrected the error. Corrections that retained spelling errors or added them were accepted as long as they were phonetically equivalent to the correct word. When the children refused PN's by referring to some other word altogether, their semantic justifications were scored as "incorrect" (e.g., the rejection of "aupomobile" because the written word was not "voiture" [car]). When children answered that the item

---

[1] It should be noted that "poor readers have, in particular, a low verbal IQ, certainly related to their inability to learn to read, whereas their performance IQ is average (cf. Kossanyi, Netchine, & Waiche, for an analysis of the IQ of this population).

was indeed a correct word, the experimenter turned over the card and asked them to tell what word was written on it. In this manner, cases of semantic paralexia could be brought out (i.e., cases in which a related word was used as the basis for a response that referred to spelling). For example, the response to the pseudononsense word "binyclette" (similar to the French word "bicyclette" [bicycle]) was scored as paralexic when the child said "it is written "velo" (bike).

The important results, as shown in Table 13.1, were as follows:

1. There was a large difference in how well poor readers detected PN errors (37%) and PS errors (81%).

2. On the other hand, good readers rejected virtually all the PN errors (97%) and nearly all the PS errors (79%).

3. Good readers, but not poor readers, correctly justified almost all correct "no" responses. Poor readers, in fact, correctly justified only 12% of their correct "no" responses.

4. There was considerable semantic paralexia (10%) among poor readers. Thus, altogether 25% of the justifications given by poor readers for PN were incorrect.

5. Both semantic paralexias and incorrect semantic justifications were virtually nonexistent in the population of good readers.

The results thus generally indicate that poor readers detected spelling er-

TABLE 13.1

General Results

Types of Responses	Pseudo-Nonsense Words		Pseudo-Synonymes	
	Poor Readers	Good Readers	Poor Readers	Good Readers
correct responses	37 % <-**->	97 %	81 % <-*->	79 %
correct justifications	12 % <-**->	96 %	38 % <-*->	79 %
incorrect semantic just.	15 % <-**->	0.6%	—	—
nonresponses (& others)	10 %	0.3%	43 %	0 %
semantic paralexias	10 %	0.3%	8 %	0 %

Note: F significant at .01 <-**-> or at .05 <-*->.

rors in the written word only rarely. On the other hand, they did notice semantic errors. Good readers, by contrast, detected almost all the graphic errors and only slightly fewer errors in the words used to name a pictured object.

We can further understand the patterns of differences between good and poor readers by examining some of the individual subject responses, starting with the poor readers.

For pseudononsense words (PN), some poor readers rejected or accepted some of the PN merely as a function of their global image. For example, Nicolas accepted "montage" (an incorrect substitution of "montagne"—mountain) by saying that he knew this word "by heart." François explained his rejection of "aupomobile" by saying that the word "voiture" (car) that he had "already seen" was "not that long." Both children seemed to be checking a global perception of the written item against a global image of an expected word. Checking against expectations can also be done by picking out various graphic clues from the written words, and this is what almost all the poor readers did. Most often it was the first letter of the written item that was used. For example, the PN's "binyclette" and "aupomobile" were frequently rejected because they did not begin by /v/, the first letter of "vélo" (bike) and "voiture" (car). On the other hand, the /lam/ in "lampasaire" (instead of "lampadaire" = pole-lamp) and /tam/ in "tampourin" (instead of "tambourin" = tambourine) permitted poor readers to judge each of these PN's as a "correct word," as if the word were "lampe" (lamp) or even "lumière" (light) and "tambour" (drum). In other cases, although more rarely, the graphic clues that were used to justify either a rejection or an acceptation were in the middle of the word or at the end.

Nicolas's responses are a good example of these types of problems. Like other poor readers, Nicolas was not able to use CGP strategies even when he read the words aloud (contrary to the instructions), although his careful pronunciation of each syllable might lead to the opposite conclusion. Thus for "péléphone," Nicolas read "/té/lé/fo/ne" and judged the written item to be correct. On the other hand, he systematically rejected the items, "binyclette" and "aupomobile," by saying "their writing is too long...it's not car" (*voiture*) (or bike).

The rejection of PN's by poor readers was characterized by the priority given to contextual expectations. They almost always rejected the written item when it did not correspond to the expected word, reflecting an absence of flexibility that is often found in poor readers. This rigidity is also seen in the absence of any change in the poor readers responses from the beginning to the end of the testing situation. Table 13.2 shows poor readers' responses to PN's over three testing points. As can be seen in the table, there was actually a decrease in the number of correct answers from almost 50% at the beginning of the test to less than 30% at the end. Although there also seems

TABLE 13.2

Changes in Responses by Poor Readers

PN Position	Error Detections	Justifications			Non Detections
		CJ	ISJ	OR	
initial	49.5%	12.5%	24%	13%	50.5%
middle	31.5%	12.5%	10.5%	8.5%	68.5%
end	29.5%	11.5%	9.5%	8.5%	70.5%

Note: PN = pseudononsense words; CJ = correct justifications;
ISJ = incorrect semantic justifications; OR = other responses.

to be a slight change over time in the type of strategy being used (fewer semantic errors by the end), this mainly reflects the decrease in the number of correctly detected PN's. There is no increase in correct justifications.

These results seem to indicate that poor readers have difficulty both in knowing whether an item is written correctly and being certain that it correctly corresponds to what is drawn in the picture. It also seems that poor readers at least partially give up their attempts to find an adaptive strategy for the task.

It is interesting that poor readers detected pseudosynonyms better than they do pseudononsense words. 81% of the PS's were correctly detected, and 38% of these detections were correctly justified with responses of the type, "It's not correct; it says "slug," but it's a picture of a snail." There is thus a high degree of correspondence between correct responses and correct justifications; more than 1/3 of the subjects correctly justified all their rejections of PS's, whereas only 1/10 of these children produced the same number of correct responses and correct justifications in the case of PN's.

An analysis of Denis' responses illustrates this difference and suggests an explanation for it. When he was shown a picture of a snail with the word "limace" (slug) underneath it, he gave a relatively quick response, rejecting it ("it's not right...it doesn't say snail...it's slug"). However at the end of the test, when he was shown just the written word "limace" without the picture, it took him a long time to pronounce the French word /li:mas/ incorrectly as /li://mak/. One way to interpret this difference is that the expectation induced by the picture (i.e., the word "snail") activates lexical knowledge concerning "slug" and thus requires less information from print for its identification.

The results for good readers were of course quite different. Good readers were capable of using reading strategies that permitted them to detect virtually all the PN's and to give pertinent justifications for their responses. For example, Aurélien said " 'lampasaire' is wrongly written, you need a /d/ instead of an /s/." In the case of PS's, good readers differ from poor readers in that they often offered a number of synonyms. Thus, Mathilde suggested replacing "boot," "which doesn't go" with "shoe" or "slipper" or even, "as Mommy says," with "heels." This type of response, which shows a certain amount of lexical comparison ("it would be better to say" or "as so-and-so says") was often given by good readers.

The fact that good readers detected semantic errors (PS) somewhat less well than graphic errors (PN) seems to reflect their adaptation to task demands. They were able to figure out quite rapidly what was expected of them: They were to find the writing mistakes. The picture is pointless for a subject who has correctly mastered word-identification strategies. Only when the good readers realize that there are also errors in the correspondence between the picture and the word written under it do they begin to systematically check this correspondence as well as the spelling of the written word. In support of this is the fact that good readers failed to detect semantic errors mainly in the first part of the test. They made almost no errors toward the end of the test.

There thus seems to be a general adaptability of good readers. They found strategies that worked well in the task and they quickly generalized their use, but without any rigidity. They also are flexible enough to summon up a number of vocabulary items (i.e., to offer several lexical replacements when the word written on the card did not correspond to the picture).

Error Analysis

To further understand the poor readers' word-identification processes in this task, we examined their responses to the pseudononsense words to answer two questions: (1) Which words produced the most semantic mistakes (i.e., incorrect justifications and paralexias); (2) which graphic errors were the most difficult for the poor readers to detect?

Incorrect semantic justifications were given on three items in particular: "binyclette," "aupomobile," and "voilie" (similar to "voilier" = sailingship). These PN's were rejected because, on the whole, they did not correspond to the word the subjects expected: respectively, "vélo" (bike), "voiture" (car), "bateau" (boat). Similar results were found for "lampasaire" and "locobotive," where the expected words were "lampe" (lamp) and "train" (train) or "wagon" (train-car).

The PN's "tampourin" and "lampasaire," with the addition of "télérision," brought about the greatest number of semantic paralexias. This appears due to the graphic similarities between the written word and the expected one, respectively: "tambour" (drum), "lampe" (lamp) or "lumiére" (light), and "télé" (TV).

These different errors seem to be due to the fact that children rarely use the words (pseudowords) printed on the cards to talk about the objects shown in the pictures. They normally use more frequent synonyms. These errors might indicate some rigidity by the poor readers, who, unlike the good readers, are either unable or unwilling to come up with alternatives to name an object.

For the detection of graphic errors, two cases were especially informative: errors at the beginning of words (e.g., "péléphone" instead of " téléphone" [telephone]) and errors created by the use of graphemes corresponding to similar phonemes (e.g., "falise" (instead of "valise" [suitcase]). An analysis of responses to "péléphone" and "falise"—because the two words have their error in the same place—sheds light on whether the detection of errors depends on the type of grapheme substitution that has been made. In fact, in "péléphone" the initial grapheme of the correct word has been replaced by a grapheme representing a distinctly different phoneme; but in "falise," the initial grapheme of the correct word has been replaced by a grapheme representing a phoneme only minimally different on the voicing feature (voiced /v/ and unvoiced /f/ phonemes). Poor readers did make more errors and fewer pertinent corrections in the latter case than in the former: 16 and 3 as opposed to 10 and 6, respectively.

The most plausible explanation for such a difference makes reference to phonetic similarity, because there is little similarity between the graphemes /f/ and /v/. The /f/–/v/ confusion indicates that poor readers who have not yet reached the CGP stage are not purely visual in their word processing. It is likely that in the early stages of reading acquisition process, such as the discrimination net phase, partial phonetic representations may be activated even for poor readers.

A Possible Typology of Poor Readers

Given the results presented so far, the responses of poor readers are quite homogeneous. They typically rely on their expectations given the context and only partially compare these expectations to the given written word. In certain cases it is only a global comparison that is made; in others, the subjects justify their acceptance or rejection of the written word according to the presence, or absence, of salient graphic clues. The behavior of this population is, thus, similar to the behavior of Harris and Coltheart's (1986) 5-to-6-year-olds (i.e., to subjects who have not yet begun reading in school): All our poor readers seem to be only at the sight-vocabulary phase and at the discrimination net phase.

However, some subgroups can be discerned in the poor reading subjects' more or less systematic use of contextual expectations. When the semantic

TABLE 13.3

Results for the Two Subgroups of Poor Readers

	Pseudononsense Words				Pseudosynonyms	
	CR	CJ	ISJ	SP	CR	CJ
Expecters	39%	8%	20%	13%	80%	24%
Prereaders	42%	33%	0%	3%	83%	83%
Good readers	97%	96%	0.6%	0.3%	79%	79%

Note: CR = correct responses; CJ = correct justifications;
ISJ = incorrect semantic justifications; SP = semantic paralexias.

errors (false justifications and paralexias) are studied carefully, it can be seen that not all poor readers made the same type of error. Table 13.3 shows how, beyond their similarities, poor readers may differ.

The results seem to divide the population into two types. The first type, "expecters," detect pseudononsense words only rarely. They also produce a high number of incorrect semantic justifications and semantic paralexias. Moreover, they provide few pertinent justifications for the rejection of a pseudononsense word or a pseudosynonym.

For these children, reading seems to be a guessing game. What Philippe said at the end of the test would seem to summarize their behavior: "There's no sense doing this; I don't know how to read. If I'm right, it's because I know the words by heart; the rest I guess." As Philippe clearly points out, the subjects of this subgroup mainly use contextual expectation. Some of them may also, occasionally, bring into play strategies of word analysis, but the effort such strategies demand is so great that they do not persevere with them.

The other group, "prereaders," produced results similar to that of good readers, with a difference more quantitative (number of responses) than qualitative (type of responses). Like good readers, these subjects can be characterized by their ability to correctly justify all their rejections, whether it be for PN's or PS's. Also, almost none of their errors can be explained by the rigid use of expectation strategies.

Furthermore, these children showed traces of subvocalization that did not seem to slow their ability to respond; in fact, these are the poor readers that responded the most quickly. This would seem to suggest that the CGP strategies of these children might be starting to become automatic.

However, poor readers on the whole, even those whose behavior is similar to that of good readers, do not seem to have reached the phase of automatic phonological recoding. And, according to Harris and Coltheart, this phase is extremely important in the process of learning to read and CGP strategies would dominate the reading of 8-year-olds. And it should be noted that the poor-reading subjects of this experiment were at least 9 years old.

CONCLUSION

If the procedures of word identification play a key role in reading, a description of the dominant procedures used both by good readers and those with learning difficulty is obviously important.

In the experiment summarized here, the responses of children having difficulty learning to read appear dominated by word identification procedures that, according to Harris and Coltheart (1986), are those used in the very first phases of familiarization with the written word. These are strategies of global recognition of words, sometimes dependent on a few localized graphic clues. Moreover, the responses of poor readers can be explained by these children's use of expectations brought about by the context of the picture. It seems that it is mainly this expectation that influences the "identification" of the written word. These strategies might be compensatory (cf. Stanovich, 1980) for these children's inability to bring into play pertinent and automatic word-identification procedures.

Moreover, in contrast to good readers, poor readers tend to be rigid in their attitude toward the task in two different ways: First, they do not progressively adapt their strategies to the task as good readers do, and, second, they seem unable to find various lexical alternatives. This rigidity, and particularly in the second case, might be explained by the fact that poor readers have an impoverished vocabulary, which in itself is one of the consequences of not learning to read. But this lack of flexibility might also be explained from the more general point of view of linguistic problems. Metalinguistic difficulties especially might play a critical role in the problems poor readers have in learning to read. It certainly would not be surprising to find that our poor readers have poor phonological abilities, for example.[2] Our comparison of good and poor readers on two tests of metalinguistic skills (one based on phonic awareness and the other on definitions of the terms *word* and *sentence*) may shed more light on these possibilities (cf. Sprenger-Charolles, 1988).

---

[2]In fact, a strong negative correlation has been found for the general population of poor readers between the production of incorrect semantic justifications in the first test and the responses given on a test of phonemic segmentation, (-0.72). Moreover, on this test of phonemic segmentation, the results of the subgroup of expecters (.01) is significantly inferior to those of prereaders.

ACKNOWLEDGMENTS

This chapter is based on a paper published by Delachaux and Niestlé (cf Sprenger-Charolles & Khomsi, 1989). It summarizes research supported by the French Medical Research Institute (INSERM, Center H. Rousselle and Unité Associée 1031 of the CNRS: "Acquisition and pathology of language in children").

REFERENCES

Berthoud-Papandropoulou, I. (1980). La réflexion métalinguistique chez l'enfant. Thèse, Université de Genève.
Bryant P., & Bradley, L. (1985). *Children's reading problems: Psychology and education*. Oxford: Basil Blackwell.
Catach, N. (1979). "Graphétique," "graphémique," "graphétique et graphémique française." In *Lexicon des langues romanes*. Berlin: Niemayer.
Coltheart, M. (1978). Lexical access in simple reading tasks. In G. Underwood (Ed.), *Strategies of information processing* (pp. 151–216). London: Academic Press.
Coltheart, M. (1987). Varieties of developmental dyslexia: A comment on Bryant and Impey. *Cognition, 27*, 97–101.
Doctor, E., & Coltheart, M. (1980). Phonological recoding in children's reading for meaning. *Memory and Cognition, 80*, 195–209.
Dubois, D., & Sprenger-Charolles, L. (1988). Perception/interprétation du langage écrit: Contexte et identification des mots au cours de la lecture. *Intellectica, 5*, 1, 113–146.
Goodman, K. S. (1976). Reading: A psychological guessing game. In H. Singer & R. B. Ruddell (Eds.), *Theoretical models and process in reading*. Newark, DE: International Reading Association.
Harris, M., & Coltheart, M. (1986). *Language processing in children and adults:* An introduction. London: Routledge & Kegan.
Holender, D. (1988). Représentations phonologiques dans la compréhension et dans la prononciation des mots éecrits. *Cahiers du Département des Langues et des Sciences du Langage (DLSL)*, Université de Lausanne, *6*, 31–84.
Karmiloff-Smith, A. (1979). *A functionnal approach to child language*. Cambridge: Cambridge University Press.
Khomsi, A. (1985). Stratégies métalinguistiques et traitement du mot écrit. In *Actes du colloque international de didactique et pédagogie du français*. Paris: INRP.
Kossanyi, P., Netchine, S., & Waiche, R. (1989). L'efficience et l'organisation intellectuelle d'enfants non lecteurs analysées à partir du WISC-R. *Revue de psychologie appliqué, 39*, 23–40.
Perfetti, C. A. (1985). *Reading ability*. New York: Oxford University Press.
Perfetti, C. A., Goldman, S. R., & Hogaboam, T. W. (1979). Reading skill and the identification of words in discourse context. *Memory and Cognition, 7*, 273–282.
Perfetti, C. A., & Roth, S. F. (1981). Some of the interactive processes in reading and their role in reading skill. In A. M. Lesgold & C. A. Perfetti (Eds.), *Interactive processes in reading* (pp. 269–297). Hillsdale NJ: Lawrence Erlbaum Associates.
Posner, M., & Snyder, C. R. (1975). Attention and cognitive control. In R. L. Solso (Ed.), *Information processing and cognition: The Loyola Symposium*. Hillsdale, NJ: Lawrence Erlbaum Associates.
Sprenger-Charolles, L. (1988). *L'apprentissage de la lecture et ses difficultés: Contribution*. Thèse de doctorat, Université de Paris V.
Sprenger-Charolles, L., & David, J. (Eds.) (1988). La lecture et son apprentissage. *Langue française, 80*.

Sprenger-Charolles, L. (1989). L'apprentissage de la lecture et ses difficultés: Synthèse de recherches. *Revue Française de Pédagogie, 87,* 77–106.

Sprenger-Charolles, L. (1989).: Processing of lexical ambiguities during reading. In *The resolution of discourse*. Hamburg: Buske Verlag (sous presse).

Sprenger-Charolles, L., & Khomsi, A. (1989). Les strategies d'identification de mots dans un contexte-image: Comparaisons entre "bons" et "mauvais" lecteurs. In L. Rieben & C. Perfetti (Eds.), *L'apprenti lecteur: recherches empiriques et implications pédagogiques.* Neuchatel and Paris: Delachaux & Niestle.

Stanovich, K. E. (1981). Attentional and automatic context effects in reading. In A. M. Lesgold & C. A. Perfetti (Eds.), *Interactive process in reading* (pp. 241–267). Hillsdale, NJ: Lawrence Erlbaum Associates.

Stanovich, K. E. (1980). Toward an interactive compensatory model of individual differences in the development of reading fluency. *Reading Research Quaterly, 16,* 32–71.

Stanovich, K. E. (1986). Mathew effects in reading: Some consequences of individual differences in the acquisition of literacy. *Reading Research Quaterly, 21,* 4, 360–406.

14 The Effects of Instructional Bias on Word Identification

Frank R. Vellutino
Donna M. Scanlon
Child Research and Study Center
State University of New York at Albany

INTRODUCTION

Facility in printed word identification is, without question, the most important prerequisite to the acquistion of skill in reading. A sizeable number of otherwise normal children encounter significant difficulty in acquiring skill in word identification, and this encumbers them in all other aspects of reading. Varied explanations have been offered to account for word identification problems in poor readers, but we are partial to the view that most of these children are basically impaired by language deficiencies that limit their ability to use linguistic representations to code information (Vellutino, 1979; Vellutino & Scanlon, 1982). Further, we believe that poor readers may be comprised of subgroups characterized by (a) deficiencies in semantic and syntactic development that limit their ability to use wholistic/meaning based strategies in learning to identify printed words; (b) deficiencies in phonological development that limit their ability to use analytic/synthetic or sound-based strategies for word identification; and (c) generalized language deficiencies that limit their ability to use both of these strategies for identification.

Word identification problems in these hypothesized subgroups could be the consequence of either constitutional (neurological and/or genetic) or experiential factors, but we suspect that the number of children with constitutionally derived deficits in word identification is a very small proportion of the total population of poor readers. We also suspect that most word identification problems stem from experiential deficits that impair the acquisition of linguistic competencies and language-based subskills.

This raises the question of the extent to which instructional biases account for such deficits. More specifically, we are inclined to believe that the philosophies, procedures, and techniques utilized by those responsible for teaching beginning or remedial reading may foster a "reading disability" by overemphasizing one or another strategy for processing and identifying printed words. For example, professionals who emphasize the use of whole-word, meaning-based strategies in teaching word identification skills encourage children to use the salient features and meanings of printed words to identify them, in addition to the semantic and syntactic constraints that may be provided by the sentences in which they appear (e.g., Goodman, 1970; Smith, 1971). Others emphasize analytic/synthetic strategies, fostering the use of grapheme–phoneme or letter–sound correspondence (phonetic) rules as the primary vehicle for identifying printed words (Gillingham & Stillman, 1960; Liberman & Shankweiler, 1979).

However, our own clinical observations suggest that the use of one of these approaches, to the exclusion of the other, would limit the child's ability to acquire skill in word identification. Conversely, we suspect that the complementary use of both would enhance his/her ability to acquire such skill. Because there was no firm evidence to support these speculations, we designed a laboratory study to evaluate them. In the sections that follow we discuss this study, highlighting the practical implications of certain of its central findings. A complete description of the study can be found in Vellutino and Scanlon (1987).

The experiment was both theoretically and practically motivated. This chapter focuses on aspects of the study dealing with whether different types of instruction can foster different processing strategies in word identification. In addressing this question, we sought to evaluate suggestions in the literature that whole-word/meaning-based methods and phonetic or "code-oriented" methods of instruction might have different utility at different stages of reading acquisition. In a comprehensive analysis of basal reading programs, Chall (1967) observed that children exposed to whole-word/meaning-based programs learned to identify an initial corpus of "sight" words more rapidly and made more initial progress in reading than did children exposed to code- oriented programs.

On the other hand, children exposed to code-oriented programs ultimately learned to identify new words with greater facility than did those exposed to whole-word/meaning-based programs. Brooks and Baron (reported in Brooks, 1977) obtained similar results in laboratory study of adults. We sought to assess the reliability of these findings in laboratory study of children. Moreover, these earlier investigations did not evaluate the possibility that whole-word and code-oriented methods of instruction, used as complements of one another, would be more effective in teaching word identification skills than would either of these methods alone. Procedures used in the present study were designed to test this hypothesis.

Subjects in this experiment were severely impaired and normally developing readers in second and sixth grade. All had an IQ of 90 or above on the Slosson Intelligence Test (Slosson, 1963), as well as normal vision and hearing, and none were encumbered by gross physical, emotional, or social disabilities. Poor readers were, on the average, below the 10th percentile on the Gilmore Oral Reading Test (Gilmore & Gilmore, 1968), whereas normal readers were at or above the 50th percentile on this test.

All subjects were also administered a test of phonemic segmentation ability. This test consisted of several subtests assessing explicit awareness of individual phonemes (sounds) in spoken words: for example, counting phonemes, vocalizing phonemes, detecting identities and differences in spoken words, and like items. Consistent with results obtained in previous studies (Bradley & Bryant, 1983, Fox & Routh, 1980; Liberman, Shankweiler, Fischer, & Carter, 1974), poor readers at both grade levels performed significantly below the normal readers on this test (for proportion correct, 2nd poor = 44%; 2nd normal = 58%; 6th poor = 60%; 6th normal = 74%).

Procedures

Subjects in each group were randomly assigned to one of *five* conditions. These groups were compared on experimental learning tasks that simulated the process of learning to read printed words that are alphabetically redundant, after receiving one of several treatments designed to promote different processing strategies.

In one condition—which we called *phonemic segmentation training* (PS)—subjects received 5 or 6 consecutive days of instruction (1/2 hour per day) in phoneme segmentation; that is, they were taught to segment words into their component sounds or phonemes. Our intent was to foster an analytic attitude in word processing. Thus, using both spoken and written words and pseudowords, subjects were given practice in counting phonemes, vocalizing phonemes, locating the positions of given phonemes, detecting identities and differences in given units, and detecting grapheme–phoneme or letter–sound correspondences. Because children were taught to detect letter–sound correspondences, we considered this approach to be comparable to a phonics approach.

However, we did *not* use a synthetic phonics approach, where students are taught each letter–sound association in isolation. Instead, instruction was designed to teach children to detect and abstract letter–sound correspondence in printed words presented as wholes. Children were expected to transfer this attitude to facilitate identification of a new set of words. We also hoped that this instruction would reduce the tendency to make the type of generalization errors illustrated in reading *was* as *saw*.

Phonemic segmentation training culminated in a practice word identification/code acquisition task (hereafter called code acquisition). This task simulated the process whereby children learn to read words containing invariant units such as *cat, fat, ran* and then generalize these units to the reading of new words, such as *can, fan* and *rat*.

Accordingly, the task consisted of an initial learning or *training component as well as a generalization learning or transfer* component. However, rather than reading *cat, fat,* and *ran,* our students learned to read pseudowords: *sij, duj, dif,* and *suf*. These stimuli were written using a novel alphabet, in which letter–sound associations were in one-to-one correspondence.

The procedure used for learning to identify the pseudowords presented on the training task was essentially a whole-word ("look say") format. Thus, on each trial, the examiner showed the child, one at a time, the four cards on which were printed the pseudowords used for initial learning and pronounced the verbal response (nonsense word) with which that pseudoword was paired. The cards were then (randomly) reordered and the child was asked to "read" each word as it was presented. Regardless of the response produced by the child, the examiner provided the correct response for a given pseudoword before presenting the next card.

The same procedure was repeated for 15 trials, but to foster an analytic attitude, the child was encouraged to search for letter–sound correspondences that were common to the pseudoword stimuli and to try to use these correspondences to "help in remembering the nonsense words and symbols that go together." She or he was also interrupted after the 5th and 10th trials and, in both instances, was asked questions that evaluated the extent to which she/he had begun to learn the sounds made by the letters in the pseudowords. For example, the examiner asked the child to name the sound made by each letter in the pseudowords, and all possible two-letter (consonant–vowel and vowel–consonant) combinations using these letters were presented to him/her. He or she was asked to vocalize each, and corrective feedback was given in each case.

On the following day, the child was administered the transfer component of the code acquisition task using permuted derivatives of those used on the training component (*jid, juf, sif, duj*). The administration format was identical to that used on the training task, except that there were no interruptions.

On the next school day, the same subjects were given a new code acquisition test that contained training and transfer subtests similar to those used during segmentation training. This test was the experimental task that was used to evaluate the effects of the different treatment conditions and differed from the practice code acquisition task in that (a) the pseudowords were written in different letter-like symbols and spoken nonsense words were not the same as those used during training (*gov, goz, vab, zab*); (b) the pseudowords used on the transfer subtest were reversed derivatives of those used on the training subtest (*vog, zog, baz, bav*); and (c) subjects were not prompted as to the strategy to employ on either subtest. It was similar to the practice task insofar as it used a "look say" presentation format. Each subtest consisted of 20 learning trials and was administered on 2 consecutive days.

In a second condition—which we called *whole-word training* (WW)—subjects were familiarized with the four nonsense words subsequently used as verbal responses on the code acquisition training subtest. Familiarization training consisted of two different tasks using the same nonsense words and simulated the process whereby one acquires new vocabulary words. It also allowed us to evaluate whether prior exposure to the words used on the code acquisition training subtest would affect performance on this subtest in the poor and normal reader groups. On the first task, each subject heard all four nonsense words randomly. To prevent rehearsal, the examiner then asked him/her to count (backwards) aloud for 6 seconds. Next, the subject was instructed to say all the nonsense words that she/he could remember (in any order) and was given 1 point for each one that was correct. This procedure was repeated for 20 trials.

After a 5-minute break, subjects were given the second task. This was a name-learning task on which the spoken nonsense syllables were paired with novel cartoon-like animal pictures. This task was designed to provide the nonsense syllables with concrete meanings. Children were told that they were learning the names of "funny looking animals" and were encouraged to remember "what they look like" as well as their names. The administration format used for the name-learning task was essentially the same as that for the practice word identification tasks (used in PS training), and the procedure was presented for 15 trials.

On 2 consecutive days following administration of the name-learning task, subjects in the whole-word condition were given the same code acquisition subtests given to subjects in the phonemic segmentation condition, using the same "look–say" presentation format.

In the third condition—*phonemic segmentation and whole-word training* (PSWW)—all subjects received both phonemic segmentation training and nonsense word familiarization training prior to presentation of the code acquisition subtests. Phonemic segmentation training preceded nonsense word familiarization training in all instances.

The fourth and fifth conditions were control conditions. In the Control-1 condition (C-1), subjects were given the training and transfer code acquisition subtests but were given no prior training. In the Control-2 condition (C-2), subjects received only the transfer subtest.

Other activities unrelated to the experiment were used where necessary to insure that the amount of time subjects spent with an examiner was the same for each child.

Salient Findings

Poor readers at both grade levels performed below the normal readers on both of the nonsense word familiarization tasks (data not shown), as well as on the training and transfer (code acquisition) subtests (see Fig. 14.1 and 14.2). Moreover, performance on the nonsense word familiarization tasks and on the phonemic segmentation tests were highly correlated with performance on the code acquisition subtests (data not shown). These findings support the suggestion that the poor reader's difficulties in word identification and code acquisition are caused by deficiencies in phonemic segmentation that may, themselves, be caused by more basic deficits in storing and retrieving the phonological (sound) attributes of spoken and written words (Bradley & Bryant, 1983; Gough & Hillinger, 1980; Liberman & Shankweiler, 1979). And considering that the experimental tasks evaluating these abilities controlled for previous learning, our data would seem to be consistent with our suggestion that reading disabilities may, in some cases, be caused by basic deficits in phonological development, that may be of constitutional origin.

More important, however, for present purposes, are the results generated by the different treatment conditions. As is evident from the graphs (Fig. 14.1 and 14.2 Panel A), both the phonemic segmentation training provided in the PS condition and the nonsense word familiarization training provided in the WW condition improved performance on the code acquisition subtests, for poor as well as for normal readers. However, these treatments had different effects depending on the stage of learning. Consistent with previous findings (Brooks, 1977; Chall, 1967), nonsense word familiarization—our analogue of whole-word meaning-based training—had a positive effect on the *initial* learning subtest of code acquisition, and especially on the first few trials of this subtest. More specifically, subjects who received practice in remembering the names and meanings of the printed pseudowords (WW) performed at a higher level at the outset than did subjects who received only phonemic segmentation training (PS) or no training (C-1) group. In fact, WW subjects maintained their advantage over PS and C-1 subjects for the first two to three trial blocks.

On the other hand, subjects who received only phonemic segmentation training (PS) *improved* their performance steadily across trial blocks. Ulti-

PANEL A: CODE ACQUISITION TRAINING

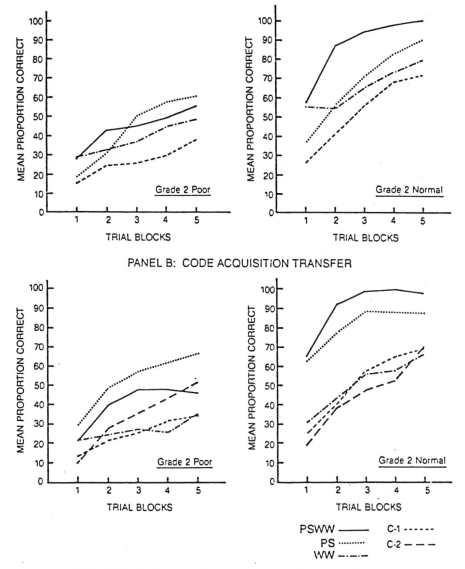

PANEL B: CODE ACQUISITION TRANSFER

PSWW ——— C-1 ------
PS ·········· C-2 — — —
WW —··—··—

FIG. 14.1 Performance by poor and normal readers in second grade. Adapted from Vellutino, F. R., & Scanlon, D. M. (1987). Phonological coding, phonological awareness, and reading ability: Evidence from a longitudinal and experimental study. *Merrill-Palmer Quarterly, 33,* 321–363.

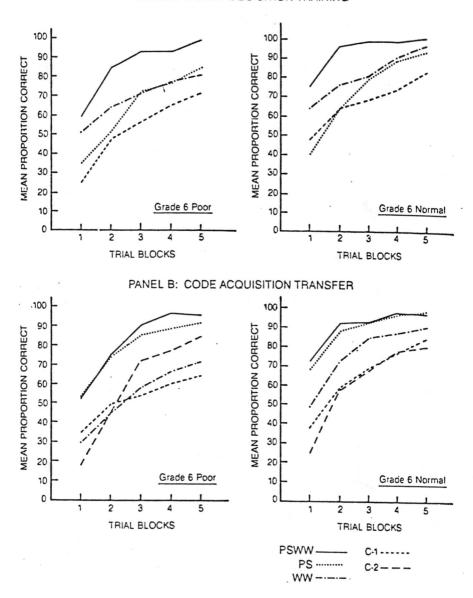

PANEL A: CODE ACQUISITION TRAINING

Grade 6 Poor

Grade 6 Normal

PANEL B: CODE ACQUISITION TRANSFER

Grade 6 Poor

Grade 6 Normal

PSWW ——— C-1 ······
PS ·········· C-2 — — —
WW —·—·—·

FIG. 14.2 Performance by poor and normal readers in sixth grade. Adapted from Vellutino, F. R., & Scanlon, D. M. (1987). Phonological Coding, phonological awareness, and reading ability: Evidence from a longitudinal and experimental study. *Merrill-Palmer Quarterly, 33,* 321–363.

mately, they performed as well as or better than subjects who received only nonsense word familiarization training (WW) and better than subjects in the control group (C-1). However, with one exception, subjects who received both nonsense word familiarization and phonemic segmentation training (PSWW) performed significantly better across *all* trials on the code acquisition training subtest than did subjects in all other groups. The one exception was the second-grade poor readers. For these subjects, phonemic segmentation training resulted in better performance on later trials of the code acquisition training subtest than did any of the other treatments. We suspect, however, that this was because these students had extraordinary difficulty in remembering the nonsense syllables used on the training subtest and therefore profited less from nonsense word familiarization training than did subjects who were the better readers.

A slightly different pattern of results emerged on the code acquisition transfer subtest (see Fig. 14.1 & 14.2, Panel B). What is most striking is that subjects who received only phonemic segmentation training (PS) performed considerably better than did subjects who received only nonsense word familiarization training (WW). The performance of those in the latter condition actually *declined* on the transfer subtest, most likely because the extra practice they received with the nonsense syllables used on the code acquisition training subtest interfered with their ability to learn the words used on the transfer subtest. This was not true for subjects receiving only phonemic segmentation training (PS), who actually improved on the transfer subtest. Moreover, in most instances, these subjects performed as well as subjects who received both phonemic segmentation and nonsense word familiarization training (PSWW), suggesting that successful performance on the transfer subtest was especially dependent on skill in phonemic analysis.

A reasonable explanation of these findings is that training in phoneme segmentation fostered detection and functional application of letter–sound units, as well as the type of fine-grained analysis that allows one to avoid generalization errors. This processing attitude did not appear to be employed by subjects who received no training in phonemic segmentation and who appeared to be reading the printed words rather globally. These subjects tended to make a large number of generalization errors, which appeared to be prompted by the visual similarities among the pseudowords.

One common example of the type of generalization error fostered by a global processing strategy is reversal errors. Recall that the pseudowords used on the transfer subtest were the reverse of those used on the training subtest (e.g., *goz/zog; gov/vog*), so reversal errors made on the transfer subtest were intrusions due to prior exposure to the pseudowords on the training subtest. The important thing to note is that the largest percentage of reversal errors was made by subjects who had *not* received training in phonemic segmentation. In contrast, the smallest percentage was made by subjects who *had* received such training. These treatment differences were evident in poor as well as in normal readers. Moreover, contrary to popular stereotypes, poor readers showed no greater tendency to make reversal errors than did normal readers. These results add substance to our suggestion that the different treatment conditions fostered different reading strategies; that is, instruction emphasizing phonemic analysis and detection of invariance apparently taught the children to approach reading analytically; instruction emphasizing meaning and name retrieval apparently encouraged subjects to adopt a global approach.

Additional support for this inference comes from another error analysis comparing whole-word and single-phoneme errors. Whole-word errors occurred if a subject incorrectly read one of the nonsense words on the code acquisition subtests as another (e.g., *vab* for *gov*). This type of error would seem to indicate whole-word processing. In contrast, a single-phoneme error occurred when the subject's response was a "near miss" that was incorrect only by one phoneme (e.g., *vib* for *vab*). We assume that this type of error signifies analytic processing.

We found that whole-word errors were much more common than single-phoneme errors in subjects who received only nonsense word familiarization training (WW) and in those in the control groups. However, the reverse pattern was evident in subjects who only received phonemic segmentation training (PS). Such different error patterns suggest that subjects in these respective groups used different reading strategies on the code acquisition subtests. But especially impressive is the fact that subjects who received both segmentation training and nonsense word familiarization training (PSWW) made more whole-word errors than single-phoneme errors on the training subtest, and more single-phoneme than whole-word errors on the transfer subtest. Evidently, these subjects shifted their processing attitude from a whole-word to an analytic strategy in accord with task demands.

Practical Implications

If the controlled procedures used in this experiment can be taken as reasonable approximations to initial instruction in teaching word-identification subskills—and we cautiously suggest that they *can* be viewed as such—then the practical implications of our results are clear cut. First and foremost, they provide strong support for our suggestion that the complementary use of both a whole-word/meaning-based and a code-oriented or phonics method of teaching word-identification subskills may be a more effective approach to initial instruction than the use of either one or the other of these methods exclusively. The data, in fact, suggest that each of these approaches has both positive and negative features as an instructional method and that combining them may capitalize on their strengths while compensating for their weaknesses.

The whole-word/meaning-based approach appears to facilitate rapid and integrated learning at the outset, quite likely because it capitalizes on the child's natural inclination to lean heavily on meaning in learning new relationships. In order to read a printed word with dispatch, one must have ready access to representations of that word's salient visual features as well as to representations of its name and meaning(s). Wholistic approaches to reading instruction presumably attune the learner to these attributes. In doing so, they allow him/her to use meaningful associates, in the form of vocabulary words and the concepts they represent, as connecting links to help integrate the letters representing given words into unified wholes.

The utililty of wholistic/meaning-based approaches is suggested in our finding that children who received nonsense word familiarization training performed better on the initial trials of the code acquisition training subtest than did children who did not receive this training. The importance of ready access to the names and meanings of printed words is suggested in the fact that *poor* readers who received nonsense word familiarization training had difficulty in learning the new "vocabulary words" presented during familiarization training. Further, they did not perform as well on the code acquisition training subtest as normal reading subjects who *also* received word familiarization training. Moreover, performance on the familiarization tasks was found to be highly correlated with performance on the code acquisition tasks in both reader groups. These findings, of course, imply that among the prerequisites to success in the use of a wholistic/meaning-based approach are adequate vocabulary development and facility in name retrieval.

A second implication, then, is that reading instruction may be usefully initiated with a whole-word/meaning-based approach. This conclusion can be buttressed with several other intuitively sound reasons for doing so, that, although not directly supported by our findings, are consistent with them. For one thing, it seems that an initial corpus of carefully chosen words (e.g., *the, cat, rat, dog, digs, ran, run, runs*, etc.) that the child learns to readily identify on sight would allow him/her at the outset to (a) grasp the concept of "reading"; (b) read connected text, if the words were combined to make sentences; (c) read for meaning; (d) make use of sentence context to correct errors; and (e) be initiated to the alphabetic principle by directing the child's attention to the letter–sound regularities in words such as *cat, rat, ran*, and *run*.

This latter point brings into focus the major negative feature of the whole-word/meaning-based approach to teaching word identification skills and, conversely, the utility of a code-oriented or phonics approach. If a teacher uses only the whole-word approach in teaching children to read in a writing system based on an alphabet, she/he risks fostering reading difficulties, given the orthographic redundancies and visual similarities that result because the same letters and letter patterns are used repeatedly. In addition, she/he greatly increases the load on the child's visual and verbal memory and, thereby, makes learning to read extraordinarily difficult. A wholistic approach, by definition, fosters the use of a global strategy, attuning one to salient features to access the names and meanings of printed words. Thus, if the child is equipped *only* with this strategy, she/he will not become sensitive to fine-grained differences in similar-appearing words and generalization errors will abound. Moreover, she/he may not become attuned to grapheme–phoneme (letter–sound) invariance as well as other types of orthographic redundancy and may not learn to make functional use of the alphabetic principle as a vehicle for "decoding" new words.

Our suggestion that the sole use of a wholistic approach may impede the acquisition of fluency in word identification is supported by the performance of subjects in the nonsense word familiarization (WW) training *and* control (C-1) conditions. These subjects made the largest number of generalization errors on the code acquisition transfer subtest. The likelihood that they were processing the printed words as wholes is suggested in the types of errors they made compared with those who received only segmentation training.

It should be clear that some form of phonetic analysis in teaching word-identification skills is important because it encourages the child to discriminate more carefully among printed words, facilitates detection of grapheme–phoneme invariance, and, ultimately, facilitates mastery of the alphabetic principle. Our data suggest that these are very important subskills in acquiring fluency in word identification. Support for our suggestion that training in phonemic analysis facilitates mastery of the alphabetic principal is provided by our finding that performance of subjects who received phonemic segmentation training rose sharply on the later trials of the code acquisition training subtest and did not decline on the transfer subtest. Moreover, these subjects maintained a higher level of performance on the transfer subtest than did subjects who had not received phonemic segmentation training. Evidently, those who received segmentation training became increasingly aware of the grapheme–phoneme units contained in the printed "words" they were learning to identify and began using these units in a rule-based or generative manner (as in generalizing the *at* in *cat* to *rat*). Further, training in phonemic analysis fostered fine-grained discrimination, as indicated in our observation that subjects who received phonemic segmentation training made the smallest number of reversal errors on the code acquisition transfer subtest.

However, we should again point out here that the approach to word analysis represented in our training program is unlike traditional synthetic phonics programs, which teach children individual letter sounds that they must "blend" or synthesize for recovery of a word's name. The intent of our training program was to teach children to search for letter–sound invariance in the printed pseudowords presented as wholes. Rather than teach individual letter sounds, we taught subjects to be strategically analytic and to pick up invariant units inductively. On the code acquisition tests, children had to detect letter–sound invariance on their own.

What we might call analytic phonics[1] avoids the difficulties some children have with blending, especially in blending words with stop consonants, where extraneous "schwa" sounds are produced. Fox example, with a synthetic phonics approach, the word *bag* becomes "buh a guh," which may be a source of confusion for many children. We therefore feel that the analytic approach holds promise both for beginning instruction and remediation. Our findings seem to support this possibility (see Vellutino & Scanlon, in preparation, for more detailed discussion of this point; see also Liberman, Shankweiler, Camp, Heifetz, & Werfelman, 1980, for some excellent practical suggestions in using a synthetic phonics approach). In fact, although our second-grade poor readers who received this instruction did not perform as well as their comparably instructed normal-reading peers, they performed as well as or better than normal-reading control subjects. Our training was brief; we suspect that more lengthy training of the type possible in the classroom setting would have even greater benefit for poor readers.

If our data provide strong support for the individual merits of the whole-word/meaning-based and the phonics methods in teaching word-identification skills, they provide even stronger support for the complementary use of both of these methods in teaching these skills. As we indicated earlier, those children who received both types of training generally performed better than those who received only one or the other and better than control subjects. The only exception was the second-grade poor readers who had extraordinary difficulty in learning the words used in code acquisition. But even for these subjects, there was a trend toward better performance among those who received both wholistic and analytic instruction.

Perhaps the real merit of using both approaches is that it facilitates the

---

[1]The term *analytic phonics* has traditionally been employed in reference to a method of teaching reading developed by Bloomfield (Bloomfield & Barnhart, 1961), which is based on the premise that the probability of learning letter sounds will be maximized if the child is presented with families of minimally contrasting, phonetically regular words, from which he/she can induce the alphabetic principle (e.g., *cat, rat, fat, fan, man*, etc.). It should be clear that our use of the term is intended to reflect our belief that the instructional program must not only facilitate a conceptual grasp of the alphabetic principle but must also foster an active search for letter–sound invariance. We think that this enterprise will require more direct instruction of a type similar to that used in our segmentation training program, where children were taught to segment both spoken and written "words" as a vehicle for discovering and making functional use of grapheme–phoneme invariance.

development and use of a variety of strategies for word identification. As was evident in the types of errors they made, children who received both nonsense word familiarization training and phonemic segmentation training appeared to be using a global processing strategy on initial learning trails but became increasingly analytic with more experience with the task.

We think that these findings are significant. The flexible use of several processing strategies would seem to be the most important goal of the instructional program, especially for the beginning reader, who must have alternative vehicles for word identification when the need arises. Indeed, flexibility in word processing is the mark of a mature reader, for it implies a comprehensive and functional knowledge of all the visual and linguistic information contained in a printed word, which,of course, must be cross-referenced and integrated if that word is to be readily identified (Vellutino & Shub, 1982). Conversely, inflexibility in processing is the mark of an immature or problem reader, for it implies significant knowledge gaps that encumber such a child in his/her attempts at word identification. This brings us full circle to our initial question.

We suggested that reading difficulties in many children are associated with instructional biases, advertant or inadvertent. Our data seem to support this suggestion. Subjects who were exposed to different treatments adopted different attitudes in processing the "words" they were learning to read. The word attributes to which they attended and the associations they learned were directly related to the training they received. Those children who received word familiarization training appeared to be processing the pseudowords wholistically. In contrast, those who received segmentation training were more analytic in processing these stimuli. At the same time, those who received both types of training appeared to be utilizing both strategies to a greater or lesser extent, depending on the stage of their learning. On the other hand, subjects in the control groups also adopted a wholistic processing attitude, as indicated in the similarities in their errors and those of subjects who received nonsense word familiarization training. This suggests that the beginning reader is naturally inclined toward wholistic processing and that structural analysis does not "come naturally" to the child but rather must be deliberately and directly taught.

We conclude from our results that the way in which a child approaches word identification and the word features to which she/he is attuned are largely determined by the instructional biases to which she/he is exposed. Thus, in many cases, the extent to which one either acquires fluency in word identification or fails to acquire such fluency may be directly related to the learning experiences provided by instruction. Some children, we suspect, may be equipped to compensate for instructional bias and become fluent readers. Others may not be so equipped and may well represent the largest proportion of those who have come to be called *disabled readers*.

REFERENCES

Bloomfield, L., & Barnhart,C. L. (1961). *Let's read*. Detroit: Wayne State University Press.

Bradley, L., & Bryant, P. E. (1983). Categorizing sounds and learning to read—A causal connection. *Nature, 303*, 419–421.

Brooks, L. (1977). Visual pattern in fluent word identification. In A. S. Reber & D. L. Scarborough (Eds.), *Toward a psychology of reading* (pp. 143–181). Hillsdale, NJ: Lawrence Erlbaum Associates.

Chall, J. S. (1967). *Learning to read—The great debate*. New York: McGraw-Hill.

Fox, B., & Routh, D. K. (1980). Phonemic analysis and severe reading disability in children. *Journal of Psycholinguistic Research, 9*, 115–119.

Gillingham, A., & Stillman, B. W. (1960). *Remedial training for children with specific disability in reading, spelling, and penmanship* (7th ed.). Cambridge, MA: Educators Publishing Service.

Gilmore, J. V., & Gilmore, E. C. (1968). *Gilmore Oral Reading Test*. New York: Harcourt, Brace, & World.

Goodman, K. S. (1970). Psycholinguistic universals in the reading process. *Journal of Typographic Research, 4*, 103–110.

Gough, P. B., & Hillinger, M. L. (1980). Learning to read: An unnatural act. *Bulletin of the Orton Society, 30*, 179–196.

Liberman, I. Y., & Shankweiler, D. (1979). Speech, the alphabet and teaching to read. In L. Resnick & P. Weaver (Eds.), *Theory and practice of early reading* (Vol. 2, pp. 109–132). Hillsdale, NJ: Lawrence Erlbaum, Associates.

Liberman, I. Y., Shankweiler, D., Camp, L., Heifetz, B., & Werfelman, M. (1980). Steps toward literacy. In P. J. Levinson & C. Sloan (Eds.), *Auditory processing and language: Clinical and research perspectives*. New York: Grune & Stratton.

Liberman, I. Y., Shankweiler, D., Fischer, F. W., & Carter, B. (1974). Explicit syllable and phoneme segmentation in the young child. *Journal of Experimental Child Psychology, 18*, 201–212.

Slosson, R. L. (1963). *Slosson Intelligence Test*. East Aurora, NJ: Slosson Educational Publishers.

Smith, F. (1971). *Understanding reading: A psycholinguistic analysis of reading and learning to read*. New York: Holt, Rinehart, & Winston.

Vellutino, F. R. (1979). *Dyslexia: Theory and research*. Cambridge, MA: The MIT Press.

Vellutino, F. R., & Scanlon, D. M. (1982). Verbal processing in poor and normal readers. In C. J. Brainerd & M. Pressley (Eds.), *Verbal processes in children* (pp. 189–264). New York: Springer-Verlag.

Vellutino, F. R., & Scanlon, D. M. (1987). Phonological coding, phonological awareness, and reading ability: Evidence from a longitudinal and experimental study. *Merrill–Palmer Quarterly, 33, 3*, 321–363.

Vellutino, F. R., & Scanlon, D. M. (in preparation). *Reading and coding ability: An experimental analysis*. New York: Cambridge University Press.

Vellutino, F. R., & Shub, M. J. (1982). Assessment of disorders in formal school language: Disorders in reading. *Topics in Language Disorders, 2*, 20–33.

Author Index

Rozin, P., 81, *84*, 143, *148*, 150, 156, 157, 158, *160*
Rubin, H., 111, *118*, 121
Rumelhart, D. E., 20, *30*, 34, *44*
Rutter, M., 164, 165, 166, *174*
Ruyter, L., 14, *17*

S

Sakamoto, T., 140, *148*
Samuels, S. J., 48, *56*, 57, 58, *72*
Santa, C. M., 153, *160*, 170, 171, *174*
Scanlon, D. M., 13, *17*, 23, *31*, 41, *44*, 108, 115, *119*, 189, 190, 195, 196, 201, *203*
Schneider, W., 20, *30*
Scott, J., 26, *28*
Seidenberg, M., 22, *30*, 68, 72, 106, *117*, 170, *174*
Sejnowski, T. J., 21, 26, *30*
Selkirk, E. O., 149, *160*
Seymour, P. H. K., 25, *30*, 80, 81, *84*, 135, 136, *148*
Shallice, T., 153, *160*
Shananhan, T., 87, *100*
Shankweiler, D., 5, 7, 8, 9, 10, 11, 13, *15*, *16*, *17*, 23, *29*, *44*, 61, *72*, 76, *84*, 105, 114, *118*, 121, 122, 123, 125, *132*, *133*, 139, *147*, 150, *159*, 190, 191, 194, 201, *203*
Share, D., 22, 23, 26, *29*, *30*, 60, 62, 72, 106, *118*, 131, *133*, 136, *147*, 165, *173*
Shub, D. M., 202, *203*
Siegel, L. S., 164, 166, 168, *174*
Simon, D. P., 140, *148*
Slingerland, B. H., *17*
Slosson, R. L., 191, *203*
Smith, F., 20, 21, *30*, 190, *203*
Smith, S. T., 10, *16*, *17*, 123, *132*
Smythe, P. C., 150, *159*
Snowling, M., 81, *84*
Snyder, C. R., 176, *186*
Sotsky, P., 143, *148*
Sprenger-Charolles, L., 185, *186*, *187*
Stanovich, K. E., 20, 22, *30*, 35, 39, 41, *44*, 54, *56*, 57, 58, 59, *73*, 106, 107, 108, 116, *118*, 121, 122, 124, 130, *133*, 151, 155, *160*, 164, 169, 172, *174*, 176, 185, *187*
Stein, C.L., 10, *17*
Stennett, R. G., 150, *159*
Stevenson, H. W., 140, *148*, 165, *174*
Stigler, J. W., 140, *148*, 165, *174*
Stillman, B. W., 190, *203*

Strawson, C., 88, *100*
Studdert-Kennedy, M., 5, 12, *16*
Sulzby, E., 48, *56*

T

Tanenhaus, M. K., 20, 21, 22, *30*, *31*, 68, 72, 170, *174*
Taylor, B. B., 27, *29*
Teale, W., 48, *56*
Teberosky, A., 86, *100*
Telleria Jauregui, B., 88, *100*
Tinzmann, M., 166, *173*
Tobin, P., 87, *100*, 122, *133*
Tola, G., 8, *15*
Torgesen, J. K., 9, *17*, 22, *31*, 39, *44*, 121, 127, *133*
Torneus, M., 23, *31*, 131, *133*
Treiman, R. A., 8, *17*, 23, 27, 28, *31*, 37, 39, 41, 43, *44*, 66, *73*, 76, 82, *84*, 88, *100*, 122, *133*, 150, 155, *160*
Tucker, G. W., 165, *174*
Tunmer, W. E., 19, 22, *29*, *31*, 47, 52, *56*, 61, *73*, 106, 107, 108, 109, 110, 112, 113, 115, 116, 117, *118*, *119*, 150, *160*
Turvey, M., 9, *16*

V

Van Orden, G. C., 34, *44*, 170, *174*
Vellutino, F. R., 8, 13, *17*, 19, 23, *31*, 41, *44*, 49, *56*, 108, 115, *119*, 163, 164, 169, *174*, 189, 190, 195, 196, 201, 202, *203*
Venezky, R., 23, 27, *29*, *31*, 58, *73*, 139, *147*, 155, *160*

W

Wagner, R. K., 9, *17*, 22, *31*, 39, *44*, *73*, 121, 127, *133*
Waiche, R., 178, *186*
Wall, S., *16*, 39, *44*, 131, 144, *147*, 156, *159*
Warrington, E. K., 153, *160*
Waters, G. S., 170, *174*
Weber, R., 57, *73*
Weintraub, S., 11, *15*
Welch, V., 58, 72, 87, *100*
Werfelman, M., 7, 9, *16*, 123, *132*, 201, *203*

Subject Index